Study Guide

to accompany

Coleman & Cressey

Social Problems

Seventh Edition

by

Laurence A. Basirico
Elon College

 LONGMAN

An Imprint of Addison Wesley Longman, Inc.

New York • Reading, Massachusetts • Menlo Park, California • Harlow, England
Don Mills, Ontario • Sydney • Mexico City • Madrid • Amsterdam

Study Guide to accompany Coleman & Cressey, *Social Problems*, **Seventh Edition.**

Copyright © 1999 by Addison Wesley Longman, Inc.

Please visit our website at http://longman.awl.com

ISBN: 0-321-04049-X

2345678910-DA-0100

CONTENTS

PREFACE

To the Student

This study guide is intended to accompany James William Coleman and Donald R. Cressey's *Social Problems*, 7th edition. It is not intended to, nor will it, serve as a substitute for Coleman and Cressey's text. Properly used in conjunction with Coleman and Cressey's text, this guide will help you understand the text material better and help prepare you for exams.

There are six parts to each chapter of this guide: a chapter outline, chapter learning objectives and essay questions, key points for review, key terms, a practice test, and projects. Below, you will find a description of each part and suggestions how to use them.

Chapter Outline
The chapter outline lists the major headings found in each chapter Coleman and Cressey's text. It is included here to help prepare you for what the chapter is about before you read it and to refresh your memory of what the chapter is about after you have read it. After reading Coleman and Cressey's text carefully, you should have a general idea as to what each of these sections in the outline is about. After you have read the complete chapter in the text, if there is something on the outline that you are not familiar with or do not remember, it would be a good idea to re-read that section in the text.

Chapter Learning Objectives and Essay Questions
The chapter learning objectives list the major ideas in each chapter that Coleman and Cressey are trying to get across. Read over the objectives before you begin reading the chapter in the text. These objectives should be used as a guide to help you focus your attention as you study the chapter. Read over the chapter objectives periodically as you are reading the chapter in order to help keep you focused on what you should be learning from the chapter. When you finish reading and studying the chapter in the text, use the chapter learning objectives as practice essay questions. Each of the objectives has been written in such a way as to act as an essay or discussion question.

Key Points for Review
The key points for review summarize some of the major ideas, theories, concepts, and research findings discussed in the respective chapters in the text. The key points have been designed to help you recall some of the major topics and to help refresh your memory about the material found in the chapter. They should not be used a substitute for reading and studying the text but, instead, as summary review of the material. You will not be able to answer satisfactorily the practice test, the learning objectives, or the projects without thoroughly reading the appropriate chapter in the text first.

Key Terms

The key terms are found in the respective chapter of Coleman and Cressey's textbook. In this study guide, each key term is listed followed by a page number in parentheses indicating where it is discussed in the textbook. Find each term, briefly define or explain it in the space provided, include an example that will help you remember it, and include any other comments from class or the text that may help you explain the term.

Practice Test

Each practice test consists of thirty multiple-choice questions. You should be able to answer these questions satisfactorily after studying the respective chapter in the text and after using the first four parts of the study guide material in each chapter. The answers to the practice questions are found at the end of the study guide. These questions have been written independently of the instructor's test manual, so simply memorizing the answers to them will not serve as adequate preparation for examinations that you take in class. You should use the practice tests and the answer key to help you study and review the key ideas found in the chapters. As you go through your results, make sure that you understand why each of the answers is correct or incorrect.

In addition to the multiple choice questions, you should use the chapter objectives as practice essay questions. Each objective has been formulated to be used as possible essay or discussion questions.

Projects

At the end of each chapter you will find one or more projects that deal with some aspects or themes found within the chapter. Most of the projects are divided into four sections: a field journal activity, an essay, a bibliography, and a research paper. Each project can be assigned in its entirety, or specific parts of the project can be assigned. The projects have been designed in such a way as to take you through various levels of thought or research about a topic in stages. Each project, in its entirety, is an example of how a research project can be carried out in stages that build upon each other. Each stage is described below.

The journal part of each project is usually an exercise in conducting some preliminary field research (for example, observation, interviews, web site explorations, and so on) and/or reflecting about a particular topic related to social problems. The field work journal is usually the beginning stage—and a very important part—of any social science research. The journal part of each project has been designed to give you direct, hands-on experience in conducting research and to give you the opportunity to reflect on important themes and issues regarding the study of social problems. The material you accumulate in your field work journal portion of the project will be used as the basis for the other parts of the project.

The essay option within each project usually asks you to discuss and analyze the material that you accumulated in the journal portion of the project. There are three purposes of the essay activities: 1) to have you apply some of the theories and concepts found within the related chapter in the text to the material that you collected in your field work journal; 2) to have you discuss, analyze, and summarize the material you collected in your journal, and to have you develop a first draft of the research paper, should you have it assigned to you.

The <u>bibliography</u> option usually requires that you develop a bibliography of articles and/or books written by social scientists about the theme or issue that you explored in the field work journal. The bibliography serves as a source of material that you can use should you be required to complete the research paper portion of the project.

The <u>research paper</u> option usually asks that you integrate material from your field work journal, your essay, and your bibliography to discuss a particular theme in depth. The purpose of this portion of the project is to have you integrate the ideas, theories, and conclusions of social scientists who have conducted research on the topic with the ideas and conclusions you have reached in your observations and analysis of the topic.

To the Instructor

Please read the above message to the students. It describes the parts to this study guide and the purposes of each part. A couple of items are particularly important and bear repeating to you.

First, the study guide is intended to be used as a supplement to the text and not a substitute. The students will neither obtain all of the material presented in the text nor a thorough discussion of the material that is included for discussion. However, if used appropriately, this study guide will serve as an invaluable source to help students understand and retain the text material.

Second, the learning objectives that are listed in each chapter have been designed to serve also as discussion or essay questions for examinations. Most can be used verbatim for examination questions.

Third, the projects at the end of each chapter of this study guide have been designed to have students complete research projects in stages or to have the students complete only one portion of the project. Any or all of the activities of a project can be assigned. Obviously, the projects are too extensive to require that students complete all the stages of more than a few of these. There are many ways in which to use the projects. Once you become familiar with the way in which they are organized you will probably develop your own methods of using them in your course. In the meantime, here are a few suggestions. I have used each of the following approaches in different classes that I teach using projects I designed for each course, and each works very well.

• Require students to complete one (or more) of each type of assignment (for example, one journal, one essay, one bibliography, and one research paper) on different topics that you choose.
• Require students to keep an overall journal for the semester and have them complete one journal activity from a project for each chapter of the text that you assign. If that is too much work for one semester, you might have them select a reasonable number to complete by the end of the semester.
• Require students to complete all of the options for one project—from field work journal to essay to bibliography to final research paper.

• Modify the projects to reflect a particular concern you might have or something you are emphasizing in class.
• Modify the requirements of the projects. The page length, number of bibliographic sources, observation time, and so on have been included as suggestions. Consider the needs of your course and the level of your students as you make your assignments.

On the following page I have included an example of an evaluation form that I generally use to provide feedback to students for different activities from the projects that they do in my classes.

This study guide has been written with the goal of making the study of social problems more understandable and accessible to students. I hope that you and your students find this study guide useful and are able to integrate it as a meaningful part of your course. I appreciate any comments or suggestions you may have for future editions. Please send them to me at the Department of Sociology, Elon College, Elon College, North Carolina 27244 or send them via e-mail to: basirico@numen.elon.edu.

—Laurence A. Basirico

Name_____

Project #_____

Type _____journal _____essay_____bibliography _____research paper

1. Was assignment turned in on time?
      Yes_____   No_____   Days late_____

2. Did student follow all instructions completely and correctly?

        1   2   3   4   5

Comment:

3. Was student conscientious in completing assignment? Did student put in sufficient time and thought relevant to the assignment?

        1   2   3   4   5

Comment:

4. Does the student correctly understand the social science ideas, perspectives, concepts, or theories on which the assignment is based?

        1   2   3   4   5

Comment:

5. Does the student follow a format appropriate to the assignment?

        1   2   3   4   5

Comment:

6. Is correct spelling and proper grammar used throughout the student's work?

        1   2   3   4   5

Comment:

7. Is the level of depth of analysis, exploration, or discussion appropriate to the assignment?

        1   2   3   4   5

Comment:

8. Is the length of the completed work appropriate for the assignment?

        1   2   3   4   5

Comment:

Grade:_____

Comment:

CHAPTER 1

SOCIOLOGY AND SOCIAL PROBLEMS

CHAPTER OUTLINE

What is a Social Problem?

Social Problems and Social Movements

Foundations of the Sociological Approach

Sociological Perspectives on Social Problems
    Perspectives on Society
        The Functionalist Perspective
        The Conflict Perspective
        The Feminist Perspective
        Interactionism
        Other Perspectives
        Applying the Sociological Perspective: An Example

Doing Sociological Research
    Public Records and Statistics
    The Case Study
    The Survey
    The Experiment

Interpreting Claims About Social Problems
    The Author
    The Support
    The Distribution
    The Content
        Does the Article or Speech Make Sense?
        Why Does the Speaker Use a Particular Style?
        Do an Author's Claims Fit in With What Others Say About the Subject?

CHAPTER LEARNING OBJECTIVES AND ESSAY QUESTIONS:

After studying this chapter, you should be able to:

• Discuss how sociology can provide a framework to comprehend and solve many American social problems.

• State and compare the three definitions of social problems and the shortcomings of each.

• Explain how social movements influence the public's thinking about social problems.

• State and use the basic concepts of sociology, including roles, norms, groups, social institutions, social classes, culture, society, and social structure.

• Outline, compare, and critique the different sociological perspectives on social problems and provide an example of how they can be applied.

• Describe four major sociological research methods that are used to study social problems and provide examples.

• Interpret and analyze the many claims made about the nature of social problems.

KEY POINTS FOR REVIEW

• The sociological study of social problems is founded on the belief that something can be done to solve social problems if we study our problems systematically and then act on our understanding. Sociology—the scientific study of societies and social groups—provides a systematic framework for making sense of our social problems.

• The common definition of a social problem is any condition that is harmful to society. Sociologists define social problems in two ways. The first is that a social problem exists when there is a sizable difference between the ideas of a society and its actual achievements. A second is that a social problem exists when a significant number of people believe that a certain condition is in fact a problem.

• The social issues that concern the public change from time to time. While these changes may be due to shifts in ideas and values, the solution of an old problem, or the creation of new ones, the most important forces affecting these changes are social movements—groups of people that have banned together to promote a particular cause. Social movements usually begin when a large number of people start complaining about something they feel is a problem. Shortly after, leaders emerge to help guide the movement. The factors that help a social movement gain public support and favorable government action include: the political power of the movement and its supporters, the strength of the movement's appeal to the people's values and prejudices, and the strength of the opposition to the movement.

• The basic concepts that provide the foundation upon which the sociological approach is built include role, norm, social institution, social class, culture, society, and social structure.

• There are two levels on which sociological perspectives operate. Macro theories—functionalism and conflict theory—try to make sense of the behavior of large groups of people and entire societies. Micro theories—the social psychological theories—try to make sense of the behavior of individuals and small groups.

• The functionalist perspective argues that society consists of interrelated institutions that have functions that they must perform in order to keep society healthy. If an institution does not carry out its essential social task it is said to be dysfunctional. Functionalism holds that a common set of norms and values bind groups, institutions, and societies together. From the functionalist position, social problems arise when society, or part of it, becomes disorganized. That is, social structure breaks down because the various parts no longer work together smoothly as they should. This may result from inadequate socialization of youth, lack of adequate social and economic opportunities, environmental destruction, or rapid social change. The major criticism of functionalism is that it sometimes blames social problems on individual deviance or temporary social disorganization while seeming to ignore the more basic deficiencies in the structure of society.

• The conflict perspective sees society as a diverse collection of social groups struggling for wealth, power, and prestige. From the conflict theorists' view, social order is maintained more by authority backed by the use of force than on shared values, attitudes and norms. There are a variety of approaches within conflict theory, each focusing on a different type of conflict. Karl Marx's version of conflict theory focuses primarily on class conflict. Another version of conflict theory focuses primarily on struggles between ethnic groups. The major criticism of conflict theory is that it may overemphasize the role of conflict as the source of social problems.

• Feminist theory is not a single theory but a group of theories that places primary importance on explaining women's situation in society and gender conflicts. It emphasizes the idea that women's lives are markedly different from men's because women are given the primary responsibility for child rearing and the care of the emotional and physical needs of others. Feminist theory also recognizes that the position of women has not just been different than that of men, but has been unequal as well. There are two major criticisms of feminist theory. One argument is that society, especially the family, does not oppress women but, rather, enriches them. The second criticism is that women may indeed be oppressed, but men are oppressed also due to the same kinds of impersonal gender stereotypes held within our culture.

• The social psychological perspectives are concerned with the behavior of individuals and small groups, and their relationships with society. The predominant social psychological perspective is known as Interactionism. Interactionist theory tries to look at the world from the eyes of the individuals involved, and see how they define themselves and their environment. To do this, George Herbert Mead argued that we have to understand how people communicate through symbols, how they are socialized, and how they develop self-concepts. Other social psychological perspectives include behaviorism—the view that all behavior is learned as the result of rewards and punishments—and personality theories—the view that people develop stable characteristics and traits that distinguish one person from another.

• Sociologists study social problems using methodology that involves a number of different techniques including the use of public records and statistics, case studies, personal interviews, participant observation, surveys, and experiments. Different social problems require different techniques to study them and each has its merits and drawbacks.

• Sometimes misleading messages about social problems are either intentionally or unintentionally conveyed. Therefore, whether or not you do research on social problems, it is often necessary to interpret claims made about them by politicians, journalists, sociologists, and the public. There area number of standards that can be used to measure the validity of a statement about a social problem. These include the author's qualifications and biases, how the study was funded, where an article is published or a speech is given, whether or not the article or speech makes sense, why a writer or speaker uses a particular style, and whether or not an author's claims fit in with what other say about the subject.

NOTES:

KEY TERMS

The following key terms are found in your textbook on the page number indicated in parentheses. In the space provided, write a brief definition of the key term **in your own words**. Then **provide an example** of the term, such as a culture in which the practice takes place, or people that you might know whose behavior illustrates the term, a current event that illustrates the term, how a term could be used to shed light on or help solve a particular social problem, and so on. You could include examples from the news, books, movies, or anything else that will illustrate the term and help you remember it. Include any comments from your class discussions or textbook that might help you remember and understand these key terms. Use additional paper if necessary, but keep it with your study guide to help you review for exams.

sociology (p. 2)

----

social problem (p. 2)

----

social movements (p. 4)

----

role (p. 6)

----

norm (p. 6)

_____

_____

_____

_____

deviants (p. 6)

_____

_____

_____

_____

social institutions (p.7)

_____

_____

_____

_____

social class (p. 7)

_____

_____

_____

_____

status (p. 7)

_____

_____

_____

_____

power (p. 7)

_____

_____

_____

_____

upper class (p. 7)

_____

_____

_____

_____

middle class (p. 7)

_____

_____

_____

_____

lower class (p. 7)

_____

_____

_____

_____

culture (p. 7)

_____

_____

_____

_____

subculture (p. 7)

_____

_____

_____

_____

society (p. 8)

_____

_____

_____

_____

social structure (p. 8)

_____

_____

_____

_____

macro theories (p. 9)

_____

_____

_____

_____

micro theories (p. 9)

_____

_____

_____

_____

functionalism (p. 9)

_____

_____

_____

_____

functions (p. 10)

_____

_____

_____

_____

dysfunctional (p. 10)

_____

_____

_____

_____

social disorganization (p. 10)

_____

_____

_____

_____

cultural lag (p. 10)

_____

_____

_____

_____

conflict theory (p. 11)

_____

_____

_____

_____

class conflict (p. 11)

_____

_____

_____

_____

bourgeoisie (p. 11)

_____

_____

_____

_____

proletariat (p. 11)

_____

_____

_____

_____

ethnic conflict (p. 12)

_____

_____

_____

_____

feminist theory (p. 13)

_____

_____

_____

_____

gender conflicts (p. 13)

_____

_____

_____

_____

patriarchy (p. 13)

_____

_____

_____

_____

liberal feminists (p. 13)

_____

_____

_____

_____

socialist feminists (p. 14)

_____

_____

_____

_____

radical feminists (p. 14)

_____

_____

_____

_____

sexism (p. 14)

_____

_____

_____

_____

social psychology (p. 9)

_____

_____

_____

_____

interactionism (p. 14)

_____

_____

_____

_____

definition of the situation (p. 14)

_____

_____

_____

_____

symbols (p. 15)

_____

_____

_____

_____

socialization (p. 15)

_____

_____

_____

_____

self-concept (p. 15)

_____

_____

_____

_____

generalized other (p. 15)

_____

_____

_____

_____

behaviorism (p. 15)

_____

_____

_____

_____

personality theories (p. 16)

----

personality (p. 16)

----

biosocial perspective (p. 16)

----

methodology (p. 18)

----

case studies (p. 20)

----

personal interviews (p. 20)

----

participant observation (p. 20)

----

survey (p. 20)

----

sample (p. 20)

----

experiment (p. 21)

PRACTICE TEST

Multiple Choice

1. The sociological definition of social problems that goes beyond the value judgments of sociologists emphasizes:
   a) a condition that is harmful to society
   b) a significant number of people who believe a social problem exists
   c) the gap between the ideals of a society and its achievements
   d) the gaps between various income groups, minority groups, and gender groups

2. One criticism of the definition of social problems that emphasizes the gap between the ideals of a society and its actual achievements is that this definition:
   a) depends too much on what average people believe
   b) depends too much on the judgment of sociologists about the ideals of a society
   c) focuses too much on social movements
   d) relies on what is considered harmful to society

3. One problem with defining social problems as conditions that are harmful to society is that this definition:
   a) over-emphasizes the ideals of society
   b) depends on the beliefs of persons rather than objective conditions
   c) fails to clarify the meaning of harmful and society
   d) cannot explain all of American society's harmful conditions

4. Sociology is an important way to study social problems because it:
   a) offers a framework to sort and evaluate the facts
   b) contains the kinds of biases that help persons who are victimized by social problems
   c) is a better discipline than psychology
   d) has studied social problems longer than other fields

5. The most important force affecting changes in public opinions about social problems is:
   a) statistics
   b) cultural ideals
   c) social movements
   d) social changes

6. Sociologists would argue that the denial of civil rights to black and other Americans became a social problem only when:
   a) the first civil rights laws were passed
   b) the social movement for civil rights began
   c) the government recognized the problem of civil rights
   d) religious groups emphasized the idea of civil rights for all

7. Concepts like role, group, and social institution are valuable for the study of social problems because they:
   a) clearly identify the causes of social problems
   b) provide part of a framework to make sense of social problems
   c) make up the social psychological perspective on social problems
   d) most clearly identify solutions to social problems

8. Political power and appeal to a people's values are two factors that:
   a) doom a social movement to failure
   b) create the most opposition to social movements
   c) rarely influence the outcome of a social movement
   d) help a social movement gain public support

9. One reason why governments often cannot solve a social problem is that government programs:
   a) do not use valid sociological research to guide their efforts
   b) do not understand the conflict between cultural ideals and how people really live
   c) often have conflicting rules
   d) often have no real power to change society

10. A set of behaviors and expectations associated with a social position is called a:
    a) status
    b) norm
    c) role
    d) group

11. The most important social rules that tell us what behavior is acceptable are called:
    a) groups
    b) roles
    c) folkways
    d) mores

12. Stable patterns of thoughts and actions centered on performance of important social tasks are called social:
    a) groups
    b) institutions
    c) roles
    d) norms

13. If individuals have an organized and recurrent relationship with one another they make up
    a) social class
    b) culture
    c) society
    d) group

14. When a group has its own ideas and beliefs, yet is influenced by the larger culture, it is called a:
    a) social group
    b) culture
    c) subculture
    d) institution

15. Categories of persons who share common life chances are called a:
    a) group
    b) culture
    c) social class
    d) society

16. Theories that are concerned primarily with the behavior of individuals and small groups are called:
    a) micro theories
    b) macro theories
    c) social psychological theories
    d) sociobiological theories

17. Which of the following sociological perspectives contends that social problems arise from the breakdown of social structure?
    a) the functionalist perspective
    b) the conflict perspective
    c) the biosocial perspective
    d) personality theory

18. According to the _____ perspective, social problems arise from disagreements over power or values.
    a) functionalist
    b) social psychological
    c) interactionist
    d) conflict

19. Although feminist theory is really a group of theories, rather than a single theory, its primary concern is similar to the viewpoint found within which sociological perspective?:
    a) functionalist
    b) conflict
    c) social psychological
    d) interactionist

20. The interactionist theory of sociology emphasizes:
    a) the id, ego, and superego
    b) observable behavior
    c) subcultures and countercultures
    d) participation in the symbolic universe of culture

21. If you believe the body has needs that influence social behavior and can create social problems you are following _____ theories.
    a) Freudian
    b) biosocial
    c) personality
    d) interactionist

22. According to functionalist theory, when an action interferes with the effort to carry out essential social tasks, it is said to be:
    a) functional
    b) interactional
    c) conflict-creating
    d) dysfunctional

23. Behaviorism is an approach to human behavior that emphasizes:
    a) instinctual drives, particularly sex
    b) reinforcements received for certain behavior
    c) the crucial role of class conflict
    d) the definition of the situation

24. One of the problems in using public records and statistics for research on social problems is that:
    a) politics influences the gathering of statistics
    b) researchers face many ethical constraints
    c) data is not actually gathered from normal people
    d) gathering the data is too expensive

25. The virtue of the experimental approach is its:
    a) use of participant observers
    b) careful control of variables
    c) inexpensive research procedures
    d) relevance to real social situations

26. Jane is doing research on the American military and listened to a speech televised on numerous networks about cutting the defense budget. Which of the following would it be most worthwhile for Jane to investigate in order to evaluate the speech's claims?
    a) the numbers of persons who listened to the speech
    b) whether the speaker had good public speaking skills
    c) whether other experts agreed with the speaker's conclusions
    d) who owned the various television stations that broadcast the speech

27. The biggest advantage of the case study method of studying social problems is:
    a) the relevancy of the method
    b) the freedom from ethical constraints
    c) direct contact with those under study
    d) the wide number of cases the researcher can study

28. We need to evaluate and interpret claims about social problems because:
    a) the available data is so complicated
    b) many claims are false
    c) all claims contain ethical issues
    d) we need to distribute claims fairly

29. John wants to study college students' attitudes and behaviors regarding drug use. The most appropriate research method to choose would be:
    a) the survey
    b) the case study
    c) the experiment
    d) collections of official statistics

30. Funders and supporters of social problems research:
    a) are generally committed to objective social research
    b) frequently sponsor research that will produce findings contrary to their interests
    c) usually insist upon a particular writing style
    d) usually sponsor research that will support their personal and economic interests

19

PROJECTS

PROJECT 1.1 Identifying and Defining Social Problems

There are various ways to determine whether or not a condition is a social problem. Commonly defined, a social problem is any condition that is harmful to society. Sociologists define social problems in two ways. First, a social problem exists when there is a sizable difference between the ideas of a society and its actual achievements. Second, a social problem exists when a significant number of people believe that a certain condition is in fact a problem.

Journal instructions:
1. Re-read the sections of the chapter in which the various definitions of social problems are discussed. List the important characteristics of each definition in your journal.

2. Look through back editions of newspapers and newsmagazines (such as *The New York Times, Los Angeles Times, Washington Post, Time Magazine, Newsweek,* and so on) for the past six months and identify seven to ten conditions which appear to be social problems. Look at the news stories, essays, editorials, opinion polls, letters to the editor and so on.

3. Identify and examine a web site pertaining to each of the social problems you identified above.

3. Discuss how each of the definitions of social problems applies or does not apply to each of the conditions that you identified. Be sure to be thorough in your discussion. To help you with your discussion, address the following questions:
 a) Does the majority of the public define the condition as a problem?
 b) Which segments of the population are most likely to define the condition as a problem?
 c) Would sociologists define the condition as a problem? If so, why? If not, why not?

4. After you identify and discuss the conditions you selected as social problems, evaluate the various definitions of social problems. Based on your research and analysis which one(s) do think are the most useful for defining social problems? Which are the least useful? Why?

Option: essay
Using the information that you compiled in your journal, write an essay (around three to four pages, typed) in which you discuss the relevance of the definitions of social problems. That is, discuss and illustrate how the various definitions apply or do not apply, when they are most useful, the disadvantages of each, the advantages of each, and so on. The information that you gathered and analysis you did in the above journal exercise plus other theories, ideas, and concepts found in chapter 1 should provide you with enough information to write your essay.

Option: bibliography
Select one of the social problems you identified above. Using your library's indexes and/or computerized indexes, develop a bibliography of ten to fifteen articles from the popular literature (newspapers, news magazines, magazines, and so on) and from the sociological literature (sociology journals) about the social problem you selected. Be sure to have a good balance between sociology journals and popular articles.

INSTRUCTIONS FOR THIS PROJECT ARE CONTINUED ON THE NEXT PAGE.

Additionally, identify at least one web site that contains sociological views and one that contains popular views about the problem. Type your bibliography using the bibliographic style found in the sociology journals.

Option: research paper
Complete the above journal and bibliographic instructions if you have not already done so. Write a paper (around five to seven pages, typed) in which you:

1. Introduce the condition you selected as a social problem and discuss it in terms of the various definitions of social problems.

2. Integrate material from your bibliography (both popular and sociological literature) that you have found that support your contention that the condition is actually a social problem from the point of view of the various definitions of social problems.

3. Provide proper documentation of your references throughout the paper and include a reference page.

PROJECT 1.2 Identifying and Analyzing a Social Movement

The most important forces affecting changes in public opinion regarding social problems are social movements. Social movements are groups of people that have banned together to promote a particular cause. Social movements tend to follow a typical pattern. In this project, you will explore the way in which social movements develop and affect public opinion.

Journal instructions:
1. Look through back issues of the newspapers from a year ago or more. Identify a social movement that is associated with a particular social problem.

2. Obtain a variety of articles, editorials, letters to the editors, essays, web sites, and so forth about the social movement.

3. Trace the pattern of social movement.
        a) What are/were the goals of the movement?
        b) What social problem is the focus of the movement?
        c) Who are/were the leader(s) of the movement?
        d) What types of political tactics did the movement use to obtain its goals?
        e) What values and prejudices did the movement appeal to?
        f) Identify any opposition to the movement.
        g) How successful was the movement in achieving its goals?

Option: essay
Use the information that you collected in your journal (above) and discussions from your text to write an essay (three to five pages, typed) about a particular social movement. Be sure to integrate your census findings, interviews, news editorials, and ideas from your text in your discussion. Is their more than one interpretation of the data? How might the data be interpreted differently? Discuss and support your views.

Option: bibliography
Use your library's and/or computerized indexes (for example, *Social Science Index, Sociological Abstracts, First Search,* or others) to develop a bibliography of ten to fifteen sociology articles (that is, articles from sociology journals) that discuss a social movement similar to the one you analyzed in your journal. Additionally, identify at least one sociological web site that discusses the social movement. Type your bibliography using the bibliographic style found in your textbook or in the sociology articles.

Option: research paper
If you have not done so already, complete the above journal, essay and bibliography instructions. Write a paper (around seven pages, typed) in which you discuss the development and outcomes of the social movement you selected. In your paper, be sure to:

1. Identify the social movement and the social problem to which it is related.

2. Explain how the social problem fits one or more sociological definitions of a social problem.

3. Discuss the development of the social movement you selected by using material from the text and material from at least five of the articles from the bibliography you developed. At least two of the articles must be from social science journals. Provide proper documentation and include a reference page.

PROJECT 1.3 Using Sociological Concepts and Methods to Analyze a Social Problem

As your book points out, the sociological approach utilizes concepts that enable us to explore social problems thoroughly. Some of these concepts include: norms, roles, socialization, groups, social classes, culture, subculture, deviants, social institutions, and many others. Additionally, the sociological approach uses a methodology that helps to discover data about social problems The objective of this project is to have you gain some practice in using sociological concepts and methods to explore social problems.

Journal instructions:
1. Choose a social problem that you are interested in studying or one discussed at some point in the text.

2. Find five to ten articles about the issue from newspapers or magazines and identify three web sites pertaining to the social problem you selected.

3. Briefly discuss how each of the following concepts could be used to help describe or analyze the social problem you selected: norms, deviants, roles, socialization, groups, social classes, culture, subculture, and social institutions. Wherever possible, use examples from the news items you found to help illustrate how the concepts could be used.

4. Briefly discuss which sociological research methods—public records and statistics, case studies, personal interviews, participant observation, surveys, and experiments—could be used to find out further information about the social problem and about sociological concepts that are related to the problem.

Option: essay
Use your journal notes to write an essay (around three to five pages, typed) in which you use as many of the above sociological concepts as possible (use a minimum of five) to discuss the social problem you selected from a sociological approach. In addition, discuss how various sociological methods could be used to help obtain further information. Be very specific in your discussion.

Option: bibliography
Through library research and/or computerized indexes, compile a bibliography of ten to fifteen sociology articles (that is, articles from sociology journals) and/or books (excluding textbooks) about the social problem you selected above. Additionally, identify at least one sociological web sites pertaining to the social problem. Type your bibliography following the format used in your textbook or found in the sociology articles.

Option: research paper
If you have not already done so, complete the above journal and bibliography activities. Write a paper (around five to seven pages, typed) in which you use at least five sociological concepts and four or five articles from your bibliography to discuss the social problem you selected. As a conclusion to your paper, include a discussion of how specific research methods could be used to conduct further research about this social problem. In your paper, include a discussion of why and how this knowledge is useful within different occupations. Provide proper documentation of your references throughout the paper and include a reference page.

PROJECT 1.4 Applying Sociological Perspectives to Social Problems

Sociologists use a number of different perspectives to understand social problems. The text discusses a few of these: the functionalist perspective, the conflict perspective, social psychological perspectives (including interactionism, behaviorism, and personality theories), and the biosocial perspective. The objective of this project is to have you learn how each of these perspectives can help you to understand social problems from different points of view.

Journal instructions:
1. Reread the section in chapter one about the various sociological perspectives listed above. Briefly summarize in your own words how each of the perspectives views social problems (around a paragraph each).

2. Identify a social problem that currently exists. Briefly discuss how each of the sociological perspectives might view the social problem you selected.

3. Locate and read ten articles or essays found in the news and/or web sites about the problem you selected. As you read each article, write down things that support the main argument of any or all of the sociological perspectives or things that illustrate any or all of the sociological perspectives.

4. After you have completed the above steps, answer the following questions:
   a) Which sociological perspectives did you find the most support for and/or illustrations of in the news articles you read?
   b) Which perspectives did you find the least support and/or illustrations for?
   c) Which perspective do you think offers the most accurate and useful approach to understanding the social problem you selected?

Option: essay
Using the information and ideas you developed as part of you above journal project, write an essay (around three to five pages, typed) in which you compare how the various sociological perspectives can be applied to understanding the particular social problem that you selected.

Option: bibliography
Through library research and/or computerized indexes, compile a bibliography of ten to fifteen sociology articles and/or books (excluding textbooks) about the social problem you selected above. Additionally, identify at least one sociological web site pertaining to the social problem. Type your bibliography following the format used in one of the sociology articles.

Option: research paper
If you have not already done so, complete the above journal and bibliography activities. Write a paper (around five to seven pages, typed) in which you use material from at least four articles from your bibliography to discuss how one or more sociological perspectives can be used to analyze the social problem you selected. Use information that you already developed in your journal work (above) to help you with your discussion. Provide proper documentation of your references throughout the paper and include a reference page.

PROJECT 1.5 Interpreting Claims About Social Problems

As discussed in your book, it is often important to be able to evaluate whether claims about social problems are in fact true. The text examines a number of ways to help you examine the validity of such claims. The objective of this project is to have you gain some experience in interpreting claims about social problems.

Journal instructions:
1. Reread the section in chapter one that discusses how to interpret claims about social problems. Briefly list each of these in your journal and summarize what each is about.

2. Read a news article, view a television shown and examine a web site about a controversial social problem.

3. Examine the claims made by the article's author, the television spokesperson, and the web site using the ways of interpreting claims presented in chapter one of the text. That is, who is the author? What was the content? Who supported the research about the problem? Where were the views read about or seen (that is, the news source or television program)? Does the article, speech, or position taken by the web site make sense? Why does the writer or speaker use a particular style? Do the author's or spokesperson's claims fit in with what others say about the topic?

Option: Essay
Using the material that you developed in the above journal activity, write an essay (around three to five pages, typed) in which you analyze the claims made about the social problem you selected.

Option: Bibliography
Using the library and/or computerized indexes, develop a bibliography of ten to fifteen articles from sociology journals about the above condition that has been claimed to be a social problem. Additionally, identify one sociological web site relevant to the problem you selected. Type the bibliography format found in one of the sociology journals.

Option: Research Paper
Write a paper (around five to seven pages, typed) in which you evaluate the claims made about a social problem that appear in a news article or a television show. Compare the claims about the problem that appear in the news article or television show with the claims about the problem that appear in the sociology articles. Do the claims that appear in the popular media about the social problem appear to be as valid as the claims that appear in the articles found in sociology journals? Explain. Use at least five of the articles from the bibliography you developed. Be sure to provide proper bibliographic documentation throughout your paper and a works cited page.

CHAPTER 2

PROBLEMS OF THE FAMILY

CHAPTER OUTLINE

Families Around the World

Understanding Family Diversity
        Changing Family Patterns
        Class and Ethnic Differences

Family Problems
        Divorce
                Who Gets Divorced?
                Why the Upward Trend?
                Is Divorce a Social Problem?
                Blended Families
        Births Outside of Marriage
        Violence
                Violence Between Husband and Wife
                Child Abuse
        Child Rearing
        Work and Family Inequality

Solving the Problems of the Family
        Better Preparation
        Reducing Family Conflicts
        Changing Social Expectations
        Helping Parents

Sociological Perspectives on Problems of the Family
        The Functionalist Perspective
        The Conflict Perspective
        The Feminist Perspective
        The Interactionist Perspective

CHAPTER LEARNING OBJECTIVES AND ESSAY QUESTIONS

After studying this chapter, you should be able to:

• Discuss the extent to which the modern family is or is in decline.

• Describe the social nature of the families around the world.

• State and discuss how the modern family is changing.

• Analyze a variety of family problems, including divorce, blended families, births outside of marriage, and violence.

• Discuss some ways of solving problems of the family.

• Contrast and compare the functionalist, conflict, feminist, and interactionist perspectives on family problems.

KEY POINTS FOR REVIEW

• The definition of "the family" is a matter of debate. The interactionist perspective offers a flexible definition of family as simply any group of people who define themselves as a family.

• While the family is universal to all human societies, its structures and traditions vary enormously from one place to another. For example, families in different societies differ in how many spouses there are in one family (monogamy or polygamy) and how separate the parents and children are from a wider range of relatives (nuclear or extended families). Whatever form the family takes, it always makes sense within the context of a particular society.

• The family in modern times has been changing rapidly. Some see the changes as a sign of the impending collapse of the family system, while others see the family as resilient. Previously, before the industrial revolution, the family was the basic unit of economic production and it was very hard to survive outside of family bonds. The industrial revolution transformed family life as individuals gained more economic independence. Now there is no one "normal" type of family but a diversity of types.

• Family patterns have changed widely especially since the end of World War II. For example, people are staying single longer and there are more one-person households—the average age at marriage has increased by three years between 1970 and 1988. Married couples have fewer children than in the past—since 1970 the percentage of families with three or more children has dropped by fifty percent. There has been rapid growth in the number of single-parent families—almost one in four The economic role of the wife has increased—the typical family is now a dual-earner family. There has been a growing recognition of gay and lesbian couples.

• Families also differ enormously along class and ethnic lines. Primarily because of economic reasons, people from the poverty and working classes generally marry younger, have more children, have a higher divorce rate, have more single mother, and more extensive extended kinship networks than those from higher classes. African American women are more likely to be the head of single-parent homes, have a much higher birth rate, and are less likely to marry than other Americans. There are two reasons for this. First, blacks are much more likely to be poor than people from other ethnic groups. Second, the prejudice and discrimination that have been aimed at African Americans has produced a lack of desirable male marriage partners for black women.

• Five important family issues are divorce, births outside of marriage, violence, child rearing, and the inequalities of family life. The United States has the highest divorce rate—almost one out of two marriages—of any industrialized nation. Divorce is now most common among lower income people, younger people, and in the first few years of marriage. While some consider divorce a result of personal failure, sociologists account for the increase in divorce as a result of social forces including the declining stigma associated with divorce, the passing of "no-fault" divorce laws, the norm of marrying primarily for romantic reasons, and, concomitantly, the fact that the basic economic unit is no longer the family.

• There are numerous problems associated with divorce. It is likely to cause a considerable amount of personal suffering. It is usually more difficult for the wife because her standard of living typically goes down, while the husband's goes up, and she is most likely to assume the burden of childrearing. The greatest concern about divorce centers around children. Many children of divorce show high levels of fear, grief, sadness, and anger. Additionally they are more likely to drop out of school, be arrested for a crime, become pregnant as teenagers, and are more likely to become divorced themselves than children whose parents are not divorced. However, it is unclear if these problems are a result of the divorce itself or began during a conflict-ridden marriage.

• Since the vast majority of people who divorce eventually remarry, there has been an increase in the creation of blended families. The likelihood of blended families will encounter difficulties largely depends on whether or not either or both of the spouses have children and the ages of the children at the time the blended family is created. Families that blend when the children are younger tend to face fewer difficulties than when the children are older.

• More than a quarter of all births are now to single women. Some of the causes are the rise in sexual activity among teenagers combined with failure to use contraceptive techniques, and the growing unwillingness of young couples to marry simply because the woman becomes pregnant. The greatest problem of unmarried mothers comes from the fact that many of them are not ready for the responsibilities of parenthood. Additionally, teenagers who become pregnant are more likely to drop out of school, work at low-paying jobs or be unemployed, have a higher rate of infant mortality and more serious health problems than other mothers.

• There are a variety of types of violence that are common events in many families. One of the most common forms is violence between husband and wife. Studies suggest that a "cycle of violence" may be passed down from one generation to the next. Another form of violence is child abuse. Child abuse is more likely to occur in single parent homes, large families, and lower social classes.

• Another problem related to the family is child rearing. Today's parents are much more responsible for the support and upbringing of their children than in the past. Single-parent families are especially burdened with financial problems and problems of supervision and guidance. While the effect of working mothers on children is negligible, dual-earner families

28

have some special problems in childrearing, the biggest being lack of accessible high-quality child care. Problems of jealousy and discipline have also been found in many blended families, especially if the parents remarry when the children are in the rebellious years of adolescence.

• A final family problem that Coleman and Cressey discuss is the couple's conceptions of their work and family roles. Traditionally, it was assumed that the husband would have most decision-making power within the family and the wife's role was to be a homemaker and raise the children. However, the increase of wage-earning women has led to significant changes in the degree of equality and in the types of roles the couple performs. This lack of clearly defined roles is often problematic for married couples.

• There have been of suggested solutions to the problems of the family. One is to better prepare people for marriage. This can be done by discouraging early marriage, marriage educational programs in high schools and colleges, more effective sex education programs in the schools, and greater access to birth control services for teenagers who need them. A second approach to helping families solve problems is to recognize the changing social expectations about families. Families need not be defined by traditional patterns and families could benefit by recognizing that a variety of family patterns work well. A third approach to helping families solve problems is to help them reduce conflict. Whereas open disagreements and arguments can be a normal and excellent way of managing family conflict, sometimes differences become so great as to require help from counselors regarding changing gender roles, sexual behavior, and the division of labor. A third suggested approach is the creation of government-supported preschool and day-care programs in order to help parents.

• According to the functionalist perspective, the family is the most basic social institution, with its most vital functions being reproduction, the socialization of children, support and protection of children, and status ascription. Functionalists see the historical roots of our family problems in the social disorganization caused by industrialization. With the declining importance of farming, the family lost its role as the basic unit of economic production and the extended family underwent significant changes. The present family system is in trouble, from this view, because it has not had enough time to adapt to the social and economic changes brought about by industrialization.

• From the conflict perspective, the problems of the family arise from fundamental struggles between dominant and subordinate groups. Conflicts center around the struggle between male dominance and female liberation and around struggles between the lower and higher social classes. The inability for men in lower class families to obtain adequate employment may lead to a sense of failure and in turn lead to other problems related to family break-up. Conflict theorists recommend that the government undertake various programs to eliminate occupational discrimination against women and minorities, support proposals for government-sponsored day-care centers, and advocate government efforts to combat sexism.

• From the feminist perspective, the traditional family is problematic because it is an exploitive institution organized for the benefit of the husband at the expense of his wife. The husband has the power, prestige, and independence, while the wife has to do the dirty work and carry out the subordinate role. Feminists disagree about how to solve this problem. Some reject the concept of family as an outdated carry over from patriarchal times, while others envision a new kind of family structure based on complete equality between the sexes and a division of labor based upon spouses individual skills rather than gender stereotypes.

29

• The interactionist perspective on the family focuses primarily on the family's role in the socialization of children and interaction between family members. Some solutions proposed by interactionist theorists include de-emphasizing the ideal of romantic love, which can lead to significant disillusionment and unhappiness in marriage, and developing larger support networks to share the emotional and practical burdens of family life.

NOTES:

KEY TERMS

The following key terms are found in your textbook on the page number indicated in parentheses. In the space provided, write a brief definition of the key term **in your own words**. Then **provide an example** of the term, such as a culture in which the practice takes place, or people that you might know whose behavior illustrates the term, a current event that illustrates the term, how a term could be used to shed light on or help solve a particular social problem, and so on. You could include examples from the news, books, movies, or anything else that will illustrate the term and help you remember it. Include any comments from your class discussions or textbook that might help you remember and understand these key terms. Use additional paper if necessary, but keep it with your study guide to help you review for exams.

family (p. 33)

_____

_____

_____

_____

monogamy (p. 33)

_____

_____

_____

_____

polygamy (p. 33)

_____

_____

_____

_____

nuclear family (p. 33)

_____

_____

_____

31

extended family (p. 33)

_____

_____

_____

_____

romantic love (p. 34)

_____

_____

_____

_____

patriarchal system (p. 34

_____

_____

_____

_____

single-parent family (p. 35)

_____

_____

_____

_____

dual-earner families (p. 36)

_____

_____

_____

_____

blended families (p. 42)

_____

_____

_____

_____

runaways (p.49)

_____

_____

_____

_____

pushouts (p. 49)

_____

_____

_____

_____

NOTES:

PRACTICE TEST

Multiple Choice

1. Anthropologist George Murdock discovered that over 70 percent of the societies he studied:
   a) prohibited incest
   b) promoted monogamy
   c) allowed polygamy
   d) had failing family systems

2. A married couple and their children make up a(n) _____ family.
   a) ideal
   b) blended
   c) extended
   d) nuclear

3. The typical family in most agricultural countries around the world is the _____ family.
   a) nuclear
   b) monogamous
   c) extended
   d) blended

4. Which of the following is most typical of modern nuclear families?
   a) dependency on the extended family
   b) an emphasis on romantic love
   c) an emphasis on family obligations
   d) a requirement of economic sharing

5. During the last two centuries, other social institutions have taken over many of the family's traditional functions. This change occurred because:
   a) the extended family created by industrialization was too large to allow progress to continue
   b) more children were needed
   c) the nuclear family created by industrialization was smaller and less stable
   d) other social institutions wanted more control over the citizens

6. The industrial revolution transformed family life in all of the following ways, EXCEPT for:
   a) strengthening the extended form of the family
   b) forcing young persons to leave home to make a living
   c) spurring other institutions to take over other responsibilities
   d) weakening the family's economic base

7. Which of the following would be part of an egalitarian marriage?
   a) a male provider and woman homemaker
   b) shared decision-making between the husband and the wife
   c) the woman earning an income and the man helping in the house
   d) men, women, and children working outside the home

8. The typical American family today is a(n) _____ family.
   a) single parent
   b) one wage earner
   c) dual-earner
   d) blended family

9. All of the following are reasons why families are getting smaller, EXCEPT for:
   a) staying single longer
   b) having fewer children
   c) a decline in sexuality
   d) growth of single parent families

10. Which of the following groups has the highest divorce rate?
    a) the highly educated
    b) the middle class
    c) the poor
    d) the wealthy

11. The new stereotype of the single person:
    a) invokes pity from married persons
    b) emphasizes affluence and a carefree lifestyle
    c) emphasizes poverty and a restricted life
    d) is the lonely bachelor or the neglected spinster

12. The American public consistently rates _____ as their single most important goal.
    a) good sex
    b) stability
    c) a good family life
    d) wealth and fame

13. Coleman and Cressey, and most other sociologists, conclude that the family today:
    a) is declining in importance to most people
    b) is largely disappearing
    c) involves little contact with kin
    d) remains as important as in the past

14. The American teenage unwed birth rate is far higher than other countries because American teenagers are:
    a) more sexually active
    b) less likely to use birth control
    c) more inclined to want to become mothers
    d) more economically insecure

15. All of the following are reasons for increased divorce rates, EXCEPT for:
    a) an increased emphasis on the importance of romantic love as a basis for marriage
    b) changes in women's roles
    c) pressures from kin
    d) changes in attitudes toward divorce

16. According to sociologist William Julius Wilson, one reason why many African American families are headed by women is because of:
    a) an accelerating labor market for young black women
    b) a deteriorating labor market for young black males
    c) the growth of gangs and other criminal activities in the ghetto
    d) a preference of black women to live alone

17. Sociologists tend to agree that the vitality and survival of a society depends on:
    a) how children are raised
    b) establishing strong religious institutions
    c) strengthening educational systems more so than family systems
    d) reestablishing the extended family

18. All of the following are characteristics of children most likely to be abused, EXCEPT for:
    a) living in broken homes
    b) living in poor, low status homes
    c) suffering abuse from their mothers
    d) suffering abuse from their fathers

19. When violence is passed down from one generation to the next it is called:
    a) the cycle of violence
    b) process of generational relationships
    c) parental abuse cycle
    d) frustration and aggression

20. Some technological advances such as the automobile have:
    a) actually created more work for parents
    b) eliminated the need for having a parent in the home at all times
    c) increased the divorce rate
    d) led to a decline of the extended family

21. In traditional families, women's subordination tends to lead to:
    a) poverty
    b) breakup of the family
    c) happier family relationships
    d) frustration and anger

22. Children who are forced to fend for themselves because their families no longer want them are called _____ children.
    a) pushout
    b) runaway
    c) abused
    d) neglected

23. Which of the following is NOT true about experiences of single-parent families?
    a) They represent a decline in attention the school and other social institutions give to children.
    b) The majority of children in single-parent families live in poverty.
    c) Children suffer from lack of parental supervision and guidance.
    d) The percent of children living with one parent has decreased recently.

36

24. All of the following are ways to help parents better raise children, EXCEPT for:
    a) income tax benefits
    b) guaranteeing family leaves from work
    c) providing family allowances
    d) establishing a network of government-supported preschools and day care programs

25. The easiest way to achieve the goal of strengthening the family is by:
    a) sponsoring after school programs
    b) discouraging early marriage
    c) providing funds for the couple
    d) requiring higher licensing fees

26. All of the following are ways to deal with family conflicts, EXCEPT for:
    a) counseling programs
    b) federal family mediation services
    c) new family forms based on equality
    d) an airing of disagreements

27. Which of the following is a program which only America and a few other countries fail to provide for families?
    a) family counseling
    b) birth control devices
    c) welfare payments
    d) family or child allowances

28. Which sociological perspective is most likely to view the problems of the family as due to faulty socialization?
    a) conflict
    b) functionalist
    c) social psychological
    d) anthropological

29. The conflict perspective is most likely to view family problems as the result of:
    a) struggles between male dominance and female liberation
    b) struggles between female dominance and male liberation
    c) struggles between the reproductive and status ascription functions of the family
    d) struggles over the socialization of the children

30. All of the following are considered to be functions of the family, EXCEPT for:
    a) providing for reproduction
    b) providing for formal education
    c) serving as a mechanism for status ascription
    d) supporting and protecting children

PROJECTS

PROJECT 2.1 Using Sociological Perspectives to Examine Family Systems

The major sociological perspectives—functionalist, conflict, feminist, and interactionist—provide very different approaches to analyzing the family, identifying family problems, and proposing solutions. The objective of this project is to have you gain some practice in using each of these perspectives to explore family problems.

Journal instructions:
1. Reread the section in chapter 2 about sociological perspectives on family systems. In addition, read the chapter about family systems in any current introduction to sociology textbook and the chapter on sociological perspectives (or sociological theories) in any current textbook on the sociology of the family. In your journal, write a brief summary of the view that functionalist, conflict, feminist, and interactionist perspectives take toward the family, what they see as the source of family problems, and the solutions they propose.

2. For _each_ of the four perspectives, develop a list of five or six questions that _each_ would lead you to ask about families or family problems. For example, from the functionalist perspective you might ask: What are the major functions that the family provides? How do families accomplish the functions of socialization, status ascription, sexual regulation, and so on? How are the roles of family members interdependent? For conflict theory, you might ask: What are the scarce resources that are the source of conflict for family members? Who are the dominant and subordinate ones? What are the power struggles about? For the feminist perspective, you might ask questions regarding the types of inequality that exists between men and women, or about the ways in which women are exploited in the family. For interactionist theory, you might ask: How do parents socialize children? What are the outcomes of different types of socialization? Remember, these are only a few questions. Come with five or six for each perspective and write them down in your journal.

3. Examine your own family using the questions you developed for each of the sociological perspectives. For **each** of the perspectives, spend about two hours observing and thinking about relationships within your own family. Use the questions you formulated to help guide you in your observations. Record your observations in your journal.

Option: essay
Using the information you gathered in your field work journal (above) write an essay (around four to five pages, typed) in which you examine your family and any related problems using each of the sociological perspectives. Remember to step outside of your own familiar perspective of your family and to discuss it **from the point of view of each of the sociological perspectives.** Answer each of the questions you posed. Explain the way it operates and is organized. Identify problems and the source of the problems. Compare the three perspectives. Which one do you think offers the most accurate explanation of your experience of your family?

PROJECT INSTRUCTIONS ARE CONTINUED ON THE FOLLOWING PAGE.

Option: bibliography
Select a problem that has existed within your family (based on your analysis of it, above). Develop a bibliography of ten to fifteen articles from sociology journals and/or sociology books about the problem you selected. Type your bibliography following the format found in one of the sociology journals.

Option: research paper
Write a paper (around seven pages, typed) in which you use material from your journal entries (above), your essay, and at least four items from your bibliography to explore a family problem that your family has experienced. Make sure your integrate material from at least four items in your bibliography and use at least one sociological perspective to explore the problem. There are a number of different ways from which you can approach your paper. Some possibilities: Use examples from your family experience to illustrate the findings found in the bibliographic material. Use material from the bibliography to explain similar situations found within your family. Use both the bibliographic material and your own family experiences to support a particular sociological perspective on a family problem. There are other possible angles. These are just a few. Be sure to document all of your sources throughout your paper and include a reference page.

PROJECT 2.2 Work and Family Inequality: Increasing or Decreasing?

Family problems often exist because of the changing roles between husbands and wives. The redefinition of roles has placed considerable stress on the family. With the changing roles comes a change in the degree of equality between husbands and wives. Even though women are making gains in the workplace, an area which is particularly prone to role confusion is that of household labor. Social scientists disagree as to the amount of equality in the division of household labor that exists between husbands and wives. The following are a few typical situations in which parents in almost every family with children often find themselves: a pediatrician's office, a dentist's office, a PTA meeting, a school bus stop, a drop-off and pick-up area outside an elementary or middle school for children whose parents drive them, a child-care center early in the morning when children are being dropped off and at pick-up time, a grocery store, a playground, an afternoon elementary school program, an afternoon or evening children's sporting event, and many others. The objective of this project is to have you compare your conclusions about the division of household labor with the findings of social scientists.

Journal instructions:
1. Observe six or seven of the above situations (or others that you can think of) for around thirty minutes to an hour <u>each</u> and note how many men and home many women are caring for their children, or performing household or childrearing duties. Record your observations in your journal.

2. Think about the types of duties and responsibilities that have to be fulfilled by husbands and wives, for example, buying the food, preparing meals, washing the dishes, earning income, paying bills, fixing things round the house, and many others. Make a list of these items in your journal. (Ask your parents for some suggestions as to what to include on this list.) Then compare the way in which these responsibilities are, have been, and will be met in three generations of your family. How will they likely be carried out in your family when you get married (or, if you are already married, how are they fulfilled now), the family you were raised in, and the family in which your parents were raised (that is, your grandparents). If possible, discuss this with your parents and grandparents. In your journal, discuss why the duties and responsibilities in these families are/were distributed between the males and females.

3. Ask your parents, grandparents, friends, and others who may be married to explain why the household responsibilities are divided the way they are in their homes and record their answers in your journal.

Option: essay
Using your journal observations and interviews about household labor, write an essay (around five pages, typed) in which you discuss which household and child rearing responsibilities are being fulfilled by males and females, and whether or not these responsibilities are shifting, and discuss the types of problems that can and do arise between husbands and wives that are related to these responsibilities.

PROJECT INSTRUCTIONS ARE CONTINUED ON THE NEXT PAGE

Option: bibliography
Using your library's periodical and book indexes, develop a bibliography of fifteen to twenty articles from sociology journals and/or sociology books about gender equality (or inequality) with regard to household labor. Additionally, find at least one sociologically oriented web site that deals with the issue of gender equality. Type your bibliography in proper bibliographic form, using the reference page in the social science journals or your textbook as an example.

Option: research paper
Write a paper (around seven to nine pages) in which you integrate ideas and findings from five of the sources in your bibliography with the information you wrote about in your journal to discuss the division of household labor in the family and the extent to which family inequality is a problem. Use information such as statistics on current trends, sociological perspectives, examples from your journal and so on in your paper. Be sure to document your references throughout the paper and include a reference (works cited) page.

PROJECT 2.3 Family Violence and Child Abuse

Family violence and violence in intimate relationships—including battered women, battered men, child abuse, child molestation, elder abuse, and sibling abuse—are widespread social problems. The objectives of this project are to sensitize you to the extent to which family abuse occurs and to compare how family abuse/violence is discussed in social science journals and in news reports.

Journal instructions:
1. Use your library's indexes and/or computerized searches to locate around twenty newspaper and news magazine articles and web sites that have reported about various forms of family abuse and violence either nationally and/or in the area where you live for the past year.

2. For each article and web site:
> a) Indicate the type of abuse or violence that each article describes (battered women, battered men, child abuse, elder abuse, sibling abuse, or child molestation).
> b) Make a list of the factors associated with the abuse or violence in each situation (for example, who was abused, age, income level, number of parents within household, and so on).

3. Use the information in each article to explain as best you can the reasons for the abuse/violence. If possible, use sociological perspectives to explain reasons for the abuse.

4. Summarize the factors associated with the abuse or violence that you read about in the articles and web sites. For example, what percentage of situations involved alcohol and/or other drugs? What percentage of cases involved a person who grew up in a violent family? And so on.

5. Summarize your conclusions about the explanations for family violence that you were able to find evidence for from the articles and web sites.

Option: essay
Using the information and analysis from your observations (above) write an essay (around five pages, typed) in which you discuss factors associated with domestic violence and explanations for family violence in the area and during the time period about which you conducted your research.

Option: bibliography
Develop a bibliography of fifteen articles from sociology journals and/or sociology books about family abuse and/or violence. Additionally, find at least one sociological web site that deals with family abuse and/or violence. Type your bibliography using proper bibliographic style.

Option: research paper
Write a paper (around seven to nine pages, typed) in which you use material from four or five articles from you bibliography to discuss the results of your analysis of news reports of family abuse/violence. Some things to include in your discussion may be:
> a) Compare how sociological studies and news reports discuss violence and abuse;
> b) Apply some of the ideas found in the sociology journals, sociology books, and sociological web sites to the results of your analysis. For example, are there any sociological theories, explanations, or conclusions that you can use to explain the cases that you observed in the news reports?
> c) Use examples or conclusions from your observations of news reports to illustrate the ideas or conclusions found in the sociological sources

PROJECT 2.4 Who Gets Divorced?

While the divorce rate is very high today, not everyone is at the same risk of divorce. Clearly, there are social variables related to the level of risk—age at marriage, education, presence of children, premarital birth, socioeconomic status, parents' marital history, and race. The objectives of this project are to have you gain some experience in conducting a survey and to have you gain a better understanding of what leads to divorce.

Journal instructions:
1. This survey can be conducted alone or with a group of students. Locate a sample of around one hundred students from your school that you can use to complete the survey found on the following pages of this study guide. For the purposes of this project it might be easiest to use a "convenience sample" consisting of one or more classes at your college. Obtain permission from the appropriate professors before distributing the questionnaires to the classes.

2. If you do this survey with other members of your class, place the completed questionnaires in a location that you will each have access to.

3. Your objective is to determine what variables (factors) help to explain whether or not people are likely to get divorced. If you are analyzing your results by computer, cross-tabulate question #1 with each of the other questions. If you are doing your analysis by hand, proceed as follows:

a) Separate the questionnaires into two piles based on question #1: divorced parents and not divorced parents.
b) For each pile, determine the number of responses given to each possible response for each question. For example, for question #2 indicate how many people said 0 - 1 year, how many people said 2 - 4 years, and so on.
c) Summarize your results for divorced and not divorced parents on two blank questionnaire forms. That is, use a questionnaire form to summarize the answers of people with divorced parents and another form to summarize the answers of people whose parents are not divorced.

Note: If you know how to perform computerized statistical analysis you can do so instead of performing the above analysis by hand. If you do a computerized analysis, obtain a frequency distribution of the questionnaire responses and then cross-tabulate question #1 with each of the other questions.

4. In your journal, discuss whether or not there are obvious differences in the responses related to divorced and not divorced parents.

5. In your journal, discuss which items on the questionnaire might be used if you were to explain divorce with the functionalist perspective, the conflict perspective, and the social psychological perspectives.

Option: essay
Using the results of the above survey, write an essay (around five pages, typed) in which you discuss risk factors associated with divorce. In your essay, try to incorporate responses from the open-ended question #14 into your discussion of risk factors.

PROJECT INSTRUCTIONS ARE CONTINUED ON THE FOLLOWING PAGE.

Use responses to this question as examples or as explanations of some of the risk factors. Do the results of your survey lend themselves to any particular sociological perspective? If so, discuss as part of your essay.

Option: bibliography
Develop a bibliography of ten articles from popular periodicals (newspapers, magazines, self-help books, and so on) and ten articles from sociology journals and/or sociology books within the past few years that contain discussions about the causes of divorce. Additionally, locate two web sites that deal with divorce. Type your bibliography using the format found in one of the sociology journals.

Option: research paper
Use material from four or five articles from your bibliography (at least two should be from sociology journals and/or sociology books) and your observations (above) to write a paper (around seven pages, typed) in which you discuss factors associated with the risk of divorce. If you have already completed the above essay, you can use that as a first draft of your paper. Integrate your bibliographic sources into your essay. You can use them to help explain factors associated with risk, or you can use your survey results to help illustrate ideas found within the articles. Provide proper documentation of your references throughout your paper and include a reference page.

DIVORCE SURVEY IS FOUND ON THE NEXT PAGE. FEEL FREE TO MAKE COPIES WITHOUT PERMISSION FROM THE PUBLISHER.

Divorce Survey

INSTRUCTIONS:
This survey is being conducted for a class in social problems. The purpose of the survey is to identify some of the factors that might increase or decrease the risk of separation and/or divorce.

Please answer the following questions about your parents as best as you can. The questions refer to your biological or adopted parents, <u>not your stepparents.</u> All questions refer to the most current time when your parents were married to each other. For example, age at marriage means age at marriage to **each other**. Highest education means highest education they had obtained **prior to or during their marriage to each other**, not after being separated or divorced. Education refers to the highest education they had obtained **as of the time they were married to each other** (not the highest level achieved after their separation). Income refers to most current level of income **while married to each other**. And so on.

1. Are your parents separated/divorced from each other?   Yes_____   No_____

2. How long have your parents been married or were married to each other?

   Check one:
0 - 1 years	_____
2 - 4 years	_____
5 - 7 years	_____
8 - 10 years	_____
11 - 15 years	_____
more than 15 years	_____

3. Age at marriage?

   Check one for each parent:

	mother	father
below 17	_____	_____
18 - 21	_____	_____
22 - 25	_____	_____
26 - 30	_____	_____
31 or above	_____	_____

4. Highest education **completed**

   Check one for each parent:

	mother	father
elementary school	_____	_____
high school	_____	_____
college	_____	_____
post-college education	_____	_____
(graduate school, law school, medical school, etc)	_____	_____

5. Number of children_____

6. Did they have a premarital child?   Yes_____   No_____   Don't know_____

7. Occupation

        mother_____

        father_____

8. Income level (combined)
    Check one:
        under 15,000   _____
        15,000 - 25,000   _____
        26,000 - 50,000   _____
        51,000-100,000   _____
        above 100,000   _____

9. Were either of your parents' parents divorced?
        mother   Yes_____   No_____   Don't know_____
        father   Yes_____   No_____   Don't know_____

10. Have either of your parents been divorced before marrying each other?
        mother   Yes_____   No_____   Don't know_____
        father   Yes_____   No_____   Don't know_____

11. Race

        mother_____

        father_____

12. Religion

        mother_____

        father_____

12. Did they cohabit with each other before being married? Yes_____   No_____

    If yes, how long?_____

14. If your parents are separated or divorced, what do **you** think led your parents to separate or divorce? Describe as best you can in your own words.

46

CHAPTER 3

PROBLEMS OF EDUCATION

CHAPTER OUTLINE

Equal Educational Opportunity for All?
    Social Class and Achievement
        Family Background
        The Schools
    Minority Education
    Gender Bias

The Quality of Education
    Authority and Rebellion
    Declining Achievement?

Solving the Problems of Education
    Toward Equal Educational Opportunity
        Effective Integration
        Compensatory Education
        Fighting Gender Inequality
        Reforming School Finance
    Improving the Schools
        Requiring More Work
        Restructuring the Schools
        Better Teachers

Sociological Perspectives on the Problems of Education
    The Functionalist Perspective
    The Conflict Perspective
    The Feminist Perspective
    The Interactionist Perspective

CHAPTER LEARNING OBJECTIVES AND ESSAY QUESTIONS

After studying this chapter, you should be able to:

• Explain why education is so important for Americans.

• Discuss the extent to which education creates opportunities for a variety of American groups, including social class, minority groups, and gender.

• Compare, discuss, and critique several three theories about who runs the government.

• Explore and discuss the tension created by the democratic principles taught in school and the reality of school authoritarianism.

• Explain the controversy over the quality of American education.

• Discuss why American students score so poorly on standardized achievement tests.

• Outline and discuss the ways in which America can address the problems of education and improve the educational system.

• Discuss how the different sociological perspectives look at education and the problems of education.

KEY POINTS FOR REVIEW

• Most Americans believe that education is essential for success in life. American universities are the best in the world and U.S. citizens are more educated than any other people in the world. Yet, there is some question as to whether or not the American education system provides adequate opportunities for the poor and minorities, whether or not it serves the needs of middle class people, and whether or not it provides adequate training for a competitive work force.

• Numerous studies have found social class to be the single most effective predictor of achievement in school. Children from higher social classes come from home environments that emphasize and value the importance of knowledge and achievement. Additionally, schools are organized in ways that often ignore the educational needs of the poor.

• The education system favors the middle and upper class in a number of ways. First, the way schools are financed affects educational opportunities. There are significant differences among school districts on how much tax is levied and spent toward education. School districts in which there are expensive homes are able to collect more property taxes for education. Second, children from lower class families cannot afford to attend the high quality private and prep schools that many children from higher class families attend. Third, children from poor families cannot afford as much education and cannot take advantage of as many educational opportunities at the college level as children from the higher social classes. Fourth, teachers tend to have lower expectations of lower class children and there is much evidence that this affects

their achievement. Fifth, lower class children are less likely than higher social class children to

48

be put in the "gifted" tracks in schools.

• Minorities have a long history of unequal treatment in the American educational system. During the slavery era, African Americans were seldom given any education. Until 40 years ago, African Americans in the South were forced to attend segregated schools. Even though intentional legal segregation was ended (de jure segregation), actual segregation (de facto segregation) lingers. Busing students from various school districts has been one attempt to overcome de facto segregation, but is now only marginally successful. There is much debate among social scientists and mixed findings about the effectiveness of integrated schooling on academic achievement.

• In the past, the American educational system openly discriminated against females in much the same way it discriminated against racial and ethnic minorities. Today, important progress toward gender equality has been made, and more females than males actually graduate from high school and college. Yet, subtle sexism still remains in the form of attitudes and behaviors of teachers that reflect gender stereotypes. For example, females are discouraged from pursuing subjects like science and math, are less likely to be in the technologically oriented majors that often lead to the highest paying jobs, tend to receive less attention than males, and are not expected as much as males to be as active, adventurous, and inventive.

• There are a number of issues in the debate about the quality and goals of America's educational system. One issue concerns the degree to which schools should emphasize discipline. A stated goal of education in America is to teach children democratic principles and the ability to think as individuals. Yet, the bureaucratic structure of America's school system both reflects and requires authoritarianism. Conflict theorists feel that there is a hidden curriculum in the schools to teach conformity and obedience to authority. Others feel that a lack of discipline is the biggest problem in schools today.

• A second issue concerning educational quality deals with declining achievement. More than three million Americans are functionally illiterate and are unable to meet the demand for a more educated work force. Even though there is an increase in the rate of high school graduation and in the number of years the average person spends in school, American students perform very poorly on standardized tests for academic achievement when compare with other industrialized nations.

• There are three common explanations for these educational problems. The first attacks the tests themselves arguing that test scores don't accurately reflect how much students are actually learning. The second explanation blames the schools overemphasis on non-academic subjects and the softening of standards. The third explanation is that the home environment is less conducive to educational achievement than it was in the past. Excessive television viewing, lack of reading, and less time given to the educational needs of children because of changes in family structure may contribute to declining achievement.

• There are three broad proposals for improving the existing educational system in America . The first is to provide more equal educational opportunities for everyone. Four specific ways have been suggested. First, develop effective means achieving racial and ethnic integration through, for example, merging suburban school districts with inner-city schools, creating magnet schools with unique educational programs that can attract students from various ethnic groups, and encouraging the integration of residential areas so that neighborhood schools would automatically be integrated. Second, provide special programs and assistance to the poor and minorities, such as Head Start. Third, provide males and females with equal academic and extra-

49

curricular programs. Fourth, reform the system of school finance in individual states through greater federal funding. Each of these suggestions has its advantages and its pitfalls.

• The second broad proposal for improving the educational system is to improve the quality of education itself. There are three suggestions to accomplish this. First, raise the schools' requirements and make students work harder. Second, restructure the schools so that they become more efficient and more competitive. Attempts at this include the voucher system in which federal support is withdrawn from public schools and parents are given a voucher to be spent at any school (public or private), open enrollment that would allow students to attend any school they want, decentralization programs that give control of local schools to boards elected in each neighborhood, privatization of public schools in order to cut administrative overhead and staff, and "back to basic" programs that focus on basic skills of reading, writing, and mathematics. The third suggestion for improving educational quality is to recruit and keep better teachers. This might be accomplished through higher salaries and less bureaucracy within education.

• A third proposal for improving education in America is to develop programs and policies that would create cultural changes about the value of education. Americans tend not to value education as much as people in many European countries (such as Germany, France, and many third world nations) do. Many Americans feel that there is a contradiction between being an intellectual and being involved in "the real world." Besides giving benefits to athletes, it would be beneficial for the American system of education to develop more programs that reward the intellectual life.

• From the functionalist perspective, education has become expected to serve a variety of conflicting tasks that it cannot adequately fulfill—such as teaching students a body of skills and knowledge, evaluating them on these skills and knowledge, providing opportunities for upward social mobility, transmitting cultural values and attitudes, reducing unemployment by keeping young people out of the labor market, providing socialization of children that has resulted from the changing traditional family. Some functionalists argue that in order to make the schools more effective some new programs need to be eliminated and schools must be reorganized and coordinated with other social institutions.

• From the conflict perspective, providing equal educational and upward mobility opportunities for the poor have never been goals of America's educational system and that schools are organized to do the opposite: prevent members of subordinate groups from competing with members of more privileged classes. Conflict theorists argue that the best and perhaps only way to improve the educational system is to reshape the educational system so that it provides everyone with equal opportunity.

• The feminist perspective is concerned about the role of the schools in perpetuating gender stereotypes and their lack of equal emphasis on high academic achievement for females. Further, feminists argue that the seven-hour-a-day, nine-month-a-year standard may have worked well to fit in with the rhythms of the farm family, but this system is out of tune with the family of today.

• The interactionist perspective is concerned primarily with the ways in which students' views of reality are shaped within the educational experience. Some interactionist theorists have suggested that authoritarianism, common in schools, impedes learning and encourages undemocratic behavior later in life. Others feel that the competition and fear of failure present in schools creates anxiety and insecurity. Yet other theorists do not feel that the social

50

relationships in traditional schools are harmful. Thus, from the interactionist perspective, it seems logical to provide the greatest possible range of educational alternatives so that the needs of each student can be met.

NOTES:

KEY TERMS

The following key terms are found in your textbook on the page number indicated in parentheses. In the space provided, write a brief definition of the key term **in your own words**. Then **provide an example** of the term, such as a culture in which the practice takes place, or people that you might know whose behavior illustrates the term, a current event that illustrates the term, how a term could be used to shed light on or help solve a particular social problem, and so on. You could include examples from the news, books, movies, or anything else that will illustrate the term and help you remember it. Include any comments from your class discussions or textbook that might help you remember and understand these key terms. Use additional paper if necessary, but keep it with your study guide to help you review for exams.

de jure segregation (p. 71)

_____

_____

_____

_____

de facto segregation (p. 71)

_____

_____

_____

_____

sexism (p. 73)

_____

_____

_____

_____

hidden curriculum (p. 75)

_____

_____

_____

functionally illiterate (p. 76)

_____

_____

_____

_____

grade inflation (p. 78)

_____

_____

_____

_____

compensatory education (p. 81)

_____

_____

_____

_____

magnet schools (p. 81)

_____

_____

_____

_____

affirmative action (p. 82)

_____

_____

_____

_____

voucher system (p. 86)

_____

_____

_____

_____

home schooling (p. 87)

_____

_____

_____

_____

NOTES:

PRACTICE TEST

Multiple Choice

1. One reason why we consider American education a failure is because we:
    a) no longer need education as much as before
    b) so few students graduate from high school
    c) we set very high educational goals
    d) education should only be for a chosen few

2. In small, traditional societies, most education took place in the:
    a) church
    b) workplace
    c) home
    d) one-room school house

3. WHICH statement about education today is true?
    a) Virtually every American receives some formal education.
    b) A high school education is now the exception, not the rule.
    c) The total number of teachers in the United States is less than two million.
    d) Education today differs little from education in small, traditional societies.

4. Family financing has an important effect on educational achievement because:
    a) wealthier families qualify for less financial support
    b) poorer families qualify for much financial support
    c) poorer families cannot afford as much education as wealthier families
    d) almost all education is financed by families

5. Studies have consistently shown that:
    a) social class is closely related achievement in school
    b) schools largely provide equal education for all
    c) compensatory education has actually helped poor children to do better than many middle class students
    d) social class has no impact on education

6. Many studies have found that teachers' expectations influence students' performance. This is probably due to:
    a) the students' lack of self esteem
    b) the negative role of teachers in school
    c) the lack of educational standards
    d) the self-fulfilling prophecy

7. All of the following are reasons why higher status students do better in school, EXCEPT for:
    a) family background of students
    b) language background of students
    c) the organization of the school
    d) sponsorship of the school

8. In 1954, the Supreme Court outlawed de jure segregation, but _____ segregation is still a major problem.
   a) legal
   b) de facto
   c) unconstitutional
   d) de lego

9. Which of the following is still part of the hidden curriculum of the school?
   a) reading
   b) critical thinking
   c) lack of discipline
   d) conformity

10. James Coleman's famous report on the impact of integration on disadvantaged students discovered that:
    a) disadvantaged students did better when in the same classes as middle class students
    b) middle class students did better when in the same classes as disadvantaged students
    c) integration had little impact on overall school performance
    d) educational achievement was impossible to measure

11. Many Hispanic students do less well in school than others for all of the following reasons, EXCEPT for:
    a) language problems
    b) poverty
    c) lower I.Q.
    d) recent immigration

12. Performance on standardized achievement tests for high school students:
    a) has been steadily increasing in recent years
    b) is not really a way to measure educational achievement
    c) are not given any more
    d) declined significantly since their peak in the 1960s

13. On reason why Americans are concerned about increasing illiteracy is that:
    a) teachers, who are already overworked, can do no more
    b) the country needs a more educated work force
    c) fewer jobs require as much education as the schools now provide
    d) schools care less about illiteracy

14. When schools lower standards and give students high grades for poor performance, it is called:
    a) grade deflation
    b) grade inflation
    c) remedial grading
    d) non structured grading

15. Which of the following is NOT a factor in the decline of scores on standardized achievement tests?
    a) students' individual motivation
    b) the change in the nature of the schools
    c) the nature of the tests
    d) the students' social environment

16. One consequence of promoting school integration through massive bussing was:
    a) damage to the environment
    b) opposition to approaches like magnet schools
    c) restless student behavior on busses
    d) whites placing their children in private schools

17. Structural changes in the family have led to all of the following problems, EXCEPT for:
    a) having less time and energy to give to their children
    b) having less time to assist their children with their studies
    c) placing less value on educational activity
    d) not being able to attend parent-teacher meetings

18. Probably the most appealing way to integrate the schools is to:
    a) purchase new busses
    b) develop more magnet schools
    c) legally force integration
    d) integrate residential areas

19. Providing the poor and minorities with special programs and assistance is called:
    a) compensatory education
    b) effective integration
    c) residential integration
    d) affirmative action

20. The only real solution to the problem of unequal school financing is:
    a) urging wealthy school districts to help fund poor districts
    b) a greater federal role in financing education
    c) the federal government paying for primary but not for secondary education
    d) greater state involvement in educational testing

21. Schools help reduce unemployment by keeping many young people out of the labor market. This is a _____ of education.
    a) social function
    b) manifest function
    c) latent function
    d) dysfunction

22. The concept of _____ tries to attract students from all ethnic backgrounds to one special place.
    a) compensatory education
    b) Head Start
    c) the talent search
    d) the magnet schools

23. Research on Head Start and Title I programs concluded that these programs:
    a) have little impact on children
    b) greatly help middle class but not underprivileged students
    c) significantly improve the performance of underprivileged students
    d) promote equality but not educational achievement

24. Which of the following is NOT a way to improve education?
    a) require more work of students
    b) easing overall grading standards
    c) restructuring the organization of schools
    d) employing better teachers

25. Special admissions programs for graduate and professional schools is called:
    a) affirmative action
    b) compensatory education
    c) preferential treatment
    d) minority

26. The bureaucratic structure of the school:
    a) reflects democratic ideals
    b) reflects and requires authoritarianism
    c) helps schools run smoothly
    d) has largely disappeared since 1900

27. Which of the following is part of many students' home environment that is often blamed for a decline in school achievement?
    a) teachers' attitudes
    b) television
    c) parent involvement in the school
    d) student attendance at school

28. Jane was a sociologist studying education in the classroom. She noted that the teachers and materials used in the classroom perpetuated sexist attitudes through the encouragement of stereotypes. Which perspective on education was she using?
    a) functionalist
    b) conflict
    c) social psychological
    d) anthropological

29. If parents are given a financial credit for their child's education that they can spend at their school of choice, it is called:
    a) magnet schools
    b) Head Start
    c) the decentralization approach
    d) the voucher system

30. The main focus of the social psychological perspective on education is:
    a) how school children learn
    b) the functions of education for society
    c) how education denies opportunities to the poor
    d) psychological readiness of teachers

PROJECTS

PROJECT 3.1 Using Sociological Perspectives to Examine Educational Systems

The educational system can be examined from a number of different sociological perspectives. It can be examined in terms of the functions it fulfills for societies and students, in terms of how it fulfills the needs of the dominant groups in society, or in terms of how it affects students developmentally. The objective of this project is to have you use the functionalist, conflict, and social psychological perspectives to examine education today.

Journal instructions:
1. In your journal, briefly outline how each of the sociological perspectives explains and describes the educational system in America.

2. Develop a list of questions about your own educational experiences that you could ask using each of the sociological perspectives For example, what were some of the specific manifest and latent functions of your educational experience and how were they met? What values and norms that justified inequality were taught through a hidden curriculum? How was inequality fostered through education? How was your thinking and development affected by your education? And so on. Carefully construct around nine or ten questions and write them down in your journal.

3. Using the questions you developed, reflect upon your own education from elementary school through the present. In your journal, briefly discuss experiences that you can remember that fit the explanations of the three sociological perspectives on education. Write about as many experiences and examples as you can remember.

4. Spend around two to three hours observing in an elementary school and two to three hours observing in a high school in your area. Use your time observing to try to answer the questions that you developed. Record your observations in your journal.

5. Using your reflections and observations, identify three problems related to education in America today. Be sure to identify problems based upon your reflections and observations

Option: essay
Using your reflections from your journal on your own education and your observations of the schools, write an essay (around four to five pages, typed) in which you use the three sociological perspectives to discuss problems in education. Be sure to use and integrate your reflections and observations into your discussion.

Option: bibliography
Develop a bibliography of ten to fifteen articles from sociology journals and/or books written by sociologists about some aspect of education in America that you addressed in your essay and/or journal (above). Type your bibliography following the format found in one of the sociology journals.

PROJECT INSTRUCTIONS ARE CONTINUED ON THE NEXT PAGE.

Option: research paper
Write a paper (around seven pages, typed) about some aspect of American education that you addressed in your essay and/or journal (above) that you think is problematic in the educational system today. Integrate material from at least four of the items in your bibliography, material from your journal, and ideas from at least one of the sociological perspectives on education. Be sure to document your sources throughout your paper and include a reference page.

NOTES:

PROJECT 3.2 Educational Policies and Issues

Coleman and Cressey discuss a number of suggested policies for trying to improve educational quality and achieve educational equality in American. The objective of this project is to have you identify and examine some of these policies that are relevant and being tried today.

Journal instruction:
1. Look through national and local newspapers, and news magazines, for the past year (using periodicals indexes) to identify three national and local issues and policy debates about education (for example, vouchers, bussing, magnet schools, decentralization, privatization, and so on). Find two to three articles on each issue you select and, in your journal, briefly summarize what the articles say about the issue. Additionally, locate two web sites that deal with educational policies and issues and summarize their findings.

2. Conduct interviews with at least three of the following: a superintendent for your local school system, a principal of a high school or elementary school, a college administrator (president, vice president, provost, dean, and so on), a local politician (city manager, county commissioner, city council person, and so on), a state politician, and a federal politician. Ask each person whom you interview to identify what they think the major issues, problems, and policy debates are regarding education today, what the issues, problems, or debates are about, and what their position is regarding the issue, problem, or debate in question. Record their responses in your journal.

Option: essay
Using the information you obtained and developed in your journal, material from chapter four in Coleman and Cressey's text, and material from the chapter on education from any current introduction to sociology text, write an essay (around four to five pages, typed) describing issues, problems, and debates in education today. Some things you might discuss are: What are the major issues, problems, and debates? Do local, state, and national politicians have different views on the matter? How do school administrators view the problem? How does the material in chapter four of the text and in the introduction to sociology text help you to interpret the issues from a sociological perspective? Be sure to use material that you collected for your journal (above).

Option: bibliography
Select one of the issues, problems, or debates about education that you identified above. Develop a bibliography consisting of five to ten articles from sociology journals and/ or sociology books, and five to ten articles that appear in the popular press (newspapers, news magazines, commentary magazines, and so on). Additionally, find two web sites (at least one should have a sociological orientation) about educational issues. Type your bibliography following the format found in one of the sociology journals.

Option: research paper
Write a paper (around seven pages, typed) in which you discuss the issue, problem, or debate for which you developed your bibliography (above). Use at least five items from your bibliography and be sure that at least three items are articles from sociology journals or sociology books. Some things that you might discuss are: What are ways of dealing with the problem or issue? What are the different sides of the debate? What sociological perspectives could be used, and how, to provide insight about the issue, problem, or debate? What does the sociological approach have to offer about the issue, problem, or debate? Be sure to provide proper documentation throughout your paper and include a reference page.

61

PROJECT 3.3 Education and Social Stratification

Like other social systems, the educational system reflects and can perpetuate social inequality. This is not necessarily the result of the curriculum itself or the quality of the teachers in the schools—although it may be—but may be the result of other opportunities and life chances that are related to educational systems, such as the student's family background, social class, and so on. This was illustrated well in two movies about two different types of education systems: *Dead Poets' Society* and *Stand and Deliver*. The objective of this project is to have you use these two movies to explore ways in which social class can affect one's educational experience.

Journal instructions:
1. Reread the sections in chapter four about unequal opportunities in education. It would also be a good idea to go to a current introduction to sociology text and review the chapters on social stratification, socialization, and minority groups. Most introductory texts will have chapters on these topics.

2. View the above movies and, in your journal, answer (or discuss) the following questions about each:

    a) Describe the social characteristics of the students who attend each school (for example, social class, previous education, ethnicity, race, gender, family's education, and anything else that seems important).

    b) What stereotypes and prejudices toward the students are held by teachers, administrators, parents, members of the community, and so on?

    c) Discuss the result of these stereotypes and prejudices in terms of theories of socialization and identity such as Charles Horton Cooley's "looking glass self", "the self-fulfilling prophecy," George Herbert Mead's "role taking," or any others that you may have read or learned about in this course or other sociology courses you have taken.

    d) What is taught in each school (curriculum, types of courses, values, hidden-curriculum, and so on)?

    e) What opportunities or contacts for college and jobs are available to students in each school?

    f) How much time, energy, and value is given to the students' education in the students' families?

    g) What happens to students in each school when they get into trouble?

    h) What happens to students in each school if they fail?

    i) What are the problems of education within each school?

    j) Use the functionalist, conflict, feminist, and interactionist perspectives on education to discuss education in each of these movies.

Option: essay
Pretend you are a sociologist-turned-movie critic. Write an essay (around four to five pages, typed) in which you use your sociological insights about education and inequality that you developed in your journal (above) to review and compare the movies.

Option: bibliography
Develop a bibliography of ten to fifteen articles from sociology journals, sociology books, and popular periodicals (newspapers, magazines, and so on) about inequality and education. Additionally, include two web sites that deal with educational issues. Be sure that at least eight of your articles are from sociology journals, sociology books, or sociologically oriented web sites.

PROJECT INSTRUCTIONS ARE CONTINUED ON THE NEXT PAGE.

Option: research paper
Write a paper (around seven pages, typed) in which you use information from your journal (above), your textbook, and at least five items from your bibliography to analyze the above movies. Be sure that at least three of the items from your bibliography are articles from sociology journals and/or sociology books. You might use the movies to illustrate one or more sociological ideas regarding inequality and education, or you might use sociological ideas from your journal and bibliography to analyze the movies, or a combination of both. Be sure to provide proper documentation throughout your paper and include a reference page.

NOTES:

PROJECT 3.4 Bilingual Education

One of problems of education that Coleman and Cressey mention stems from the inability of some minorities to speak English. There has been a long-standing debate about the advantages and disadvantages of bilingual education in American society. The objective of this project is to have you examine the sides of the debate and to use a sociological perspective to help you determine for your self what your views are regarding bilingual education. You will be able to do this activity only if there is a school in your area with bilingual programs. Call your local Board of Education to see if there is one in your area.

Journal instructions:
1. Spend three to four hours observing in an elementary school with bilingual programs and three to four hours observing in an elementary school without bilingual programs. Obtain the permission of the school principals before you begin your observations. Obtain as much of the following information as possible and record it in your journal:

> a) classroom structure (for example, seating arrangements, decorations, material on bulletin boards and walls, and so on);
> b) racial and ethnic composition of the student body;
> c) racial and ethnic composition of the faculty;
> d) social class of the students (estimate as best as possible from indicators such as clothing, or ask the teacher);
> e) the curriculum;
> f) books;
> g) non-academic activities (lunch, recreation, clubs, and so on);
> h) interaction among peers;
> i) amount of class participation by English-speaking and limited-English speaking students;
> j) classroom problems.

2. Interview an administrator (for example, principal or assistant principal), a guidance counselor, and a teacher from each of the two schools. Ask them the following questions and record their answers in your journal:

> a) How successful do you think the overall academic program at the school is?
> b) Are the needs of all students being met?
> c) How do you feel about bilingual education?
> d) What are the views of the members of the community and parents about bilingual education?
> e) How does the faculty feel about bilingual education?
> f) Do you think the school should continue or (if it does not have) establish bilingual educational programs?
> g) What do you feel are the advantages, disadvantages, and problems of bilingual education?

3. Obtain information about the **Sapir-Whorf Hypothesis** (sometimes known as "the linguistic relativity hypothesis.") You should be able to find out about this hypothesis (developed by anthropologists Edward Sapir and Benjamin Whorf) in almost any introduction to sociology text book. Briefly summarize in your journal about how language influences the way people perceive the world around them. Considering this, write a few comments in your journal about why bilingual education is such a controversial topic.

PROJECT INSTRUCTIONS ARE CONTINUED ON THE NEXT PAGE.

Option: essay
Based upon your observations, interviews, and ideas developed in your journal (above), write an essay (around four to five pages, typed) in which you discuss the advantages, disadvantages, problems, and prospects of bilingual education for the education system in America. Make sure that you base your essay on information and ideas you developed from your field work (above) and not any predetermined ideas you have about bilingual education.

Option: bibliography
Develop a bibliography of fifteen to twenty articles from sociology journals, sociology books, and popular periodicals (newspapers, magazines, and so on) about advantages and problems associated with bilingual education. Additionally, identify two or three web sites that deal with issues of bilingual education. Some excellent discussions are found in the following:

Bernstein, Richard. 1990 "In U.S. Schools: A War of Words." *New York Times Magazine.* (October, 14): 34.

Eshleman, J. Ross, Barbara G. Cashion, and Laurence A. Basirico. 1993. *Sociology: An Introduction.* 4th edition. New York: HarperCollins Publishers.

Hakuta, Kenji. 1986. *Mirror of Language: The Debate on Bilingualism.* New York: Basic Books.

Haugen, Einar. 1987. *Blessings of Babel: Bilingualism and Language Planning..* Berlin: Mouton de Gruyter.

Henry, William. 1990. "Beyond the Melting Pot." *Time.* (April 9): 28.

Romaine, Suzanne. 1989. *Bilingualism.* Oxford: Basil Blackwell.

Stoller, P. "The Language Planning Activities of the U.S. Office of bilingual Education." *International Journal of the Sociology of Language*, 11: 45-60.

There are many others, but these should offer you a good start. Type your bibliography following the format found in one of the sociology journals.

Option: research paper
Based upon your observations and interviews from your journal (above) and at least five items from your bibliography, write a paper (around seven pages, typed) in which you compare similarities, differences, advantages, disadvantages, issues, and problems of bilingual and English-only educational programs. Be sure to provide proper documentation throughout your paper and include a reference page.

CHAPTER 4

PROBLEMS OF THE ECONOMY

CHAPTER OUTLINE

The World Economy

Understanding Our Economic System
      The Corporations
            Who Runs the Corporations?
            The Multinationals
            Corporate Crimes
      The Government
      Small Business
      The Workers
            The Work Force
            Worker Alienation
            Death on the Job
            Labor Unions

The New Economic Realities
      Three Economic Eras?
      Measuring the Changes
      The Causes

Solving the Problems of the Economy
      The Role of the Government: Bystander or Planner?
      Investing in the Future
      Restructuring the Workplace
      Adjusting to Economic Change
      Building a Sustainable Economy

Sociological Perspectives on Problems of the Economy
      The Functionalist Perspective
      The Conflict Perspective
      The Feminist Perspective
      The Interactionist Perspective

CHAPTER LEARNING OBJECTIVES AND ESSAY QUESTIONS:

After studying this chapter, you should be able to:

• Describe the American economic system and the roles of the world economy, the corporations, government, small business, and workers in the current economic crisis.

• Analyze the nature of today's economic realities, explore how they have changed, and why.

• Outline two ways America could solve the current economic crisis.

• Describe and compare the different sociological perspectives on problems of the economy.

KEY POINTS FOR REVIEW

• Faith in the American dream seems to be fading for most Americans, yet those at the top seem to be obtaining more than their fair share of the economic resources. The American economic system is undergoing fundamental changes that are calling the assumption of prosperity for all into question.

• In order to fully understand the economic problems of a single country the world economy must be examined. While all countries are part of the world economy, not all countries play an equal part in it. There is a significant distinction between the wealthy industrialized nations and the poor or Third World nations.

• There are a number of different economic systems practiced nations in the world economy. In communist nations the government exercises direct control over a nation's economic systems. The economies are planned by the government and there is little competition. Capitalist systems are characterized by private property, market control of the production and distribution of commodities, and privately owned businesses competing with each other for profit. Capitalism tends to be practiced in one of two ways. Individualistic capitalism stresses the importance of the individual profit rather than the welfare of the group and little government intervention. Communitarian capitalism stresses the interests of the larger society and government regulated competition so that the needs of group do not lose out to individuals that may profit.

• The four most important aspects in the contemporary economy are corporations, government, small businesses, and workers. Corporations control the vast majority of the business assets and wealth in the United States and have enormous power to influence the government and shape people's lives. Because of their massive amount of power, the federal government has passed anti-trust laws to try to prevent collusion between large corporations and to try to insure open competition. However, these laws are not completely enforced.

• While corporations are owned by many different stockholders, most stock is owned by a small group of wealthy individuals that control the corporations. High-level corporate managers are a distinct social class that act to promote their own self-interest.

• Most large corporations have become multinational, having expanded across national

67

boundaries in their sales, manufacturing, distribution, and financial operations. While the expansion of powerful multinational corporations may be a first step toward world unity, it has also created many problems. These include problems of international control and regulation, and the exploitation of Third World countries.

• A social problem related to corporations is corporate crime. Fraud underlies much corporate crime. Making false claims about a product and price fixing are among the most common types of fraud.

• While it is often underestimated, the government plays an important part in the economic life of countries that practice individualist capitalism. The governments of industrialized nations are major employers of millions of people and regulate the economic activities of the private sector. There is much debate about whether government regulation of what corporations can and cannot do actually benefits or damages the economy. Governments can also influence the economy by controlling the budget deficit and through tax policies.

• Small business plays a key role in the economy. The share of the work force that is self employed has grown dramatically over the past two decades. However, small businesses face a variety of problems that corporations do not. They are less able to restrict competition among themselves, have less political power, receive fewer government benefits, and have fewer economic resources to develop and market new products than large corporations.

• The heart of the economic system— the workforce—has changed radically in this century in three significant ways. First, farm workers, owners, and managers—once the largest job category—have steadily declined. Second, because of increasing competition from foreign products and automation, there has been a shift of workers away from manufacturing and other blue-collar occupations into white-collar and service occupations. These changes have brought hardships especially to the working class. The third, and perhaps most important, change involves the role of women in the work force. Married women have entered the work force in unprecedented numbers, with over 61 percent of them now holding jobs outside of the home.

• Some social problems associated with the workforce include unemployment, underemployment, the increasing use of part-time workers, worker alienation, and accidental death on the job. While labor unions originally were created to help support the interests of employees in overcoming some of these problems, unions currently are in a serious decline.

• With record low unemployment, low inflation, and a soaring stock market, it seems that these are the best of economic times in America. yet, many people feel insecure about their jobs. The wages of most workers have been going down when inflation is accounted for. What happens in any one particular year is not as important as long term trends. Since the end of World War II, the US has undergone two economic eras and is now beginning a third. The nation experienced record high economic growth from the end of World War II through 1973. The oil crisis of 1973 marked the beginning of an unsettled era in the American economy. And now, it appears that we are entering an era of high growth again

• While it seems that the US is enjoying a prosperous economy, today's gains have been won at the cost of the workers and much of the middle class. The average American still faces economic hardships even though the economy appears to be booming. From 1973 through 1997 hourly wage of workers in private industry declined 13 percent. While the average man's wages dropped by over $2.00 an hour (when adjusted for inflation), the average woman's pay increased by $.34 an hour. However, women still earn only about three fourths per hour as men. The wages of lowest paid workers have dropped, but the top ten percent of workers have seen pay increases. In short, income inequality has been increasing as evidenced by a decline in real wages, a sharp drop in leisure time and high level of personal stress , and an increase between the "haves" and the "have nots."

• One of the major causes of America's current economic reality is the changing world economy. Practices by corporations in the United States in the post-World War II era have contributed to the economic problems. The use of cheap labor in poor nations has increased unemployment in the U.S. Additionally, the U.S. has lost much of its competitive edge against foreign companies. This is due to the continued use of aging and inefficient factories built before World War II, less reinvestment than foreign counties in new plants and equipment, less investment in research and development, a disproportionate amount of investment on military projects, and being oriented to the interests of a corporation's stockholders rather the long-term good of the corporation. Finally, the exploitation of the vast stores of natural resources found within the environment of the U.S. and the drain placed upon them by the rapid growth of population have hurt the economic climate.

• Proposals for dealing with our economic problems can be grouped into two broad categories: ways to improve the economy and ways to improve the quality of life by adjusting to the new economic environment. These responses are not mutually exclusive.

• While some strategies to revitalize the economy—such as reducing the federal deficit or improving the educational system—are agreed upon by liberals and conservatives, they disagree about most of the proposed solutions. The conservative approach advocates a cut back on the size of the government in order to free more money for private investment. This includes a sharp reduction in taxes with the ultimate goal of promoting more investment by the wealthy, an idea known as supply-side economics. By contrast, the liberal approach is form more government sponsored economic planning with major corporations, unions, and environment groups to develop a comprehensive economic plan to improve the economic environment.

• Another proposal to improve the economy is to restructure the workplace in order to improve our productivity. One proposal is to model the decision-making process after an approach that has been successful in Japanese corporations. Economic democracy would give workers more power over the decisions of top corporate officials.

• Some believe that there is nothing we can do that will create a new economic boom and that we must take measures to adjust to slower growth and longer periods of recession. This could include such measures as creating large-scale programs of job retraining and government-sponsored "make-work" programs in which jobs are created for people who are unable to find any other work. Environmentalists have responded to the economic crisis by arguing that the economy should be made as diversified and as environmentally sustainable as possible. Finally, other proposals argue that quality of life does not necessarily have to be measured in terms of average income or standard of living. Thus, other suggestions for improving quality of live include making a safer workplace, improving the lives of the elderly and poor, cleaning the environment, and upgrading the educational system.

• From the functionalist perspective, the economic system is like a machine that produces and distributes the commodities a society needs. Problems arise when the system fails to provide the society what it needs. Functionalists blame contemporary economic problems on the rapid changes that have thrown the traditional economic system out of balance.

69

• Conflict theorists view the economic system as benefiting certain groups at the expense of others. From this perspective, most economic problems arise because one group, or a coalition of groups, seizes economic power and acts in ways that advance its own interest at the expense of the rest of society. Changes in the economic system reflect competition among different groups. According to conflict theory the underlying cause of most economic problems is the exploitation of workers by their employers and other members of powerful elites.

• The feminist perspective points to the role women have played in recent economic developments. First, feminists argue that women have been extremely flexible in adapting to historic changes in their economic roles, shifting from an earlier economic contribution of caring for the home and children to their current economic role of working outside of the home to help make ends meet for the family. A second focus of feminists is on the continued economic exploitation of women in the work place, with women still being paid at a significantly lesser wage rate than men.

• The interactionist perspective focuses more on the impact of economic systems on individuals and small groups rather than on explaining large-scale economic problems.

KEY TERMS

The following key terms are found in your textbook on the page number indicated in parentheses. In the space provided, write a brief definition of the key term **in your own words**. Then **provide an example** of the term, such as a culture in which the practice takes place, or people that you might know whose behavior illustrates the term, a current event that illustrates the term, how a term could be used to shed light on or help solve a particular social problem, and so on. You could include examples from the news, books, movies, or anything else that will illustrate the term and help you remember it. Include any comments from your class discussions or textbook that might help you remember and understand these key terms. Use additional paper if necessary, but keep it with your study guide to help you review for exams.

world economy (p. 99)

_____

_____

_____

_____

Third World (p. 100)

_____

_____

_____

_____

communist nations (p. 100)

_____

_____

_____

_____

capitalism (p. 100)

_____

_____

_____

individualistic capitalism (p. 101)

_____

_____

_____

_____

communitarian communism (p. 101)

_____

_____

_____

_____

monopolies (p. 102)

_____

_____

_____

_____

oligopoly (p. 102)

_____

_____

_____

_____

multinational corporations (p. 104)

_____

_____

_____

_____

fraud (p. 105)

_____

_____

_____

_____

price fixing (p. 106)

_____

_____

_____

_____

laissez faire capitalism (p. 101)

_____

_____

_____

_____

budget deficit (p. 107)

_____

_____

_____

_____

inflation (p. 107)

_____

_____

_____

_____

deregulation (p. 107)

_____

_____

_____

_____

discouraged workers (p. 110)

_____

_____

_____

_____

worker alienation (p. 111)

_____

_____

_____

_____

blue-collar occupations (p. 114)

_____

_____

_____

_____

white-collar occupations (p. 114)

_____

_____

_____

_____

worker alienation (p.111)

_____

_____

_____

_____

service occupations (p. 109)

_____

_____

_____

_____

underemployment (p. 110)

_____

_____

_____

_____

inflation (p. 107)

_____

_____

_____

_____

business cycle (p. 115)

_____

_____

_____

_____

productivity (p. 115)

_____

_____

_____

_____

real wages (p. 115)

_____

_____

_____

_____

sustainable society (p. 126)

_____

_____

_____

_____

economic democracy (p. 124)

_____

_____

_____

_____

lean production (p. 123)

_____

_____

_____

_____

PRACTICE TEST

Multiple Choice

1. Which of the following statements about the American economy is true?
   a) The American economy contains few significant problems.
   b) Economists can only understand the American economy as a separate unit.
   c) Economists can only understand the American economy as part of the world economy.
   d) America has the only remaining pure capitalist economy.

2. When an industry is dominated by a few large companies it is called a(n):
   a) monopoly
   b) interlocking directorate
   c) oligopoly
   d) corporation

3. The corporate technostructure refers to:
   a) the power elite
   b) managers who make important decisions
   c) banks and family members who make up a corporate interest group
   d) a small group of interlocking directorships

4. One of the worst abuses of multinational corporations in the Third World is:
   a) the loss of economic and political independence of Third World countries
   b) the immigration of workers to Third World countries
   c) their indecision about profits produced by multinational corporations
   d) bringing new technology to poor nations

5. One reason for the success of the Japanese economy in the past thirty years is their companies' ability to:
   a) pay higher wages
   b) involve workers in the decision-making process
   c) restrict corporate fraud
   d) share profits with their workers

6. Manufacturing and industry are examples of _____ occupations.
   a) white collar
   b) blue collar
   c) government protected
   d) political

7. Which of the following statements about the dangers of working today is true?
   a) Some employers do not care about the deaths and injuries they cause workers.
   b) The government has effectively promoted workers' safety.
   c) Fewer than 10,000 deaths a year can be related to occupational diseases.
   d) Few industrial deaths are actually preventable.

8. The major cause of America's faltering productivity is:
   a) failure to reinvest in new factories
   b) too high wages to workers
   c) uneducated workers
   d) unfair practices by foreign competitors

9. American labor unions tend to be concentrated in the _____ sector of the economy.
   a) agricultural
   b) management
   c) manufacturing
   d) service

10. Which of the following is NOT a way the government plays a key role in the economy?
    a) The government provides jobs and paychecks for millions of people.
    b) The government regulates the economic activities of the private sector.
    c) The government manipulate the amount of money in circulation.
    d) The government prohibits former government employees from working for corporations once they leave office.

11. Which of the following changes has brought great hardship to many members of the working class?
    a) a decline in smokestack industries
    b) an increase in the number of jobs in high tech industries
    c) a decline in the number of jobs in agricultural industries
    d) a decline in the number of women in the workplace

12. Which of the following is a consequence of changes taking place in the economy?
    a) more sharing of the country's wealth
    b) an increasing gap between the haves and the have-nots
    c) fewer women in the workforce
    d) more opportunity for young people at the beginning of their careers

13. Which of the following is TRUE of women in the workplace today?
    a) their wage increases have finally begun to outpace that of men's
    b) they have achieved equality of wages
    c) the average woman still makes only 75% of the average man' wages
    d) women have not made any significant gains in the workplace

14. The principle dividing line in the modern world is between wealth industrialized nations and the poor agricultural nations referred to as the:
    a) Modern World
    b) Third World
    c) Preindustrial World
    d) Capitalist World

15. When workers take over troubled companies and loosen the big corporations domination of the economy, it is called:
    a) rational planning
    b) economic rebuilding
    c) economic dysfunctions
    d) economic democracy

16. According to the classic business cycle, when unemployment goes up:
    a) inflation increases
    b) inflation declines
    c) immigration increases
    d) government debt decreases

17. If a single corporation is able to take complete control of the market it has created a(n):
    a) oligarchy
    b) conglomerate
    c) monopoly
    d) competitive industry

18. The "price leader" in an industry is usually:
    a) regulated by the government
    b) the largest corporation
    c) a small, adventurous corporation
    d) a monopoly

19. Making false claims for a product is called:
    a) price fixing
    b) fraud
    c) industrial espionage
    d) power conflicts

20. One reason why American products are less competitive with those of other countries is:
    a) faltering productivity
    b)excessive taxes
    c) increased productivity
    d) too much reinvestment

21. Small businesses cannot safeguard their profitability as successfully as large corporations because they:
    a) are so few in number
    b) cannot restrict competition among themselves
    c) cannot create new or innovative ideas
    d) must pay high wages to their employees

22. The three broad categories for dealing with the economic crisis are restructuring the economy, adjusting to economic change and:
    a) developing quality circles
    b) removing governmental interference
    c) building a sustainable economy
    d) strong economic planning

23. All of the following are ways America could adjust to economic change, EXCEPT for:
    a) the institution of large-scale economic planning
    b) spreading the work around
    c) government-created job programs
    d) environmental and other programs to improve the quality of life

24. If you feel that education and training for the unemployed and better law enforcement to deter corporate crime are the ways to solve economic problems you probably agree with the _____ perspective.
    a) functionalist
    b) conflict
    c) interactionist
    d) feminist

25. According to the interactionist perspective, an economic problem that affects the employed sector of the population is/are :
    a) that rapid changes that have thrown the traditional system out of balance
    b) the exploitation of workers by their employers
    c) feelings of boredom and uselessness
    d) a strong achievement orientation that often leads to dissatisfaction and anxiety

26. An increase in the unemployment rate generally:
    a) increases the level of intimacy and cohesiveness of families
    b) has little impact on psychological health
    c) leads to an increase in the rate of child abuse
    d) is functional for American society

27. According to the _____ perspective on the economy, the underlying cause of most economic programs is the exploitation of workers by their employers and other elites.
    a) functionalist
    b) interactionist
    c) capitalist
    d) conflict

28. C. Wright Mills felt that high level corporate managers usually make decisions:
    a) that promote their own self-interests
    b) that benefit the majority of the stockholders in the corporation
    c) that promote the long-term health of the corporation
    d) that insure that consumers will receive high-quality products

29. In which of the following types of economic systems is there the most government planning?
    a) capitalism
    b) individualistic capitalism
    c) communitarian capitalism
    d) communism

30. Labor unions originally developed:
    a) as a means for management to exercise greater control over the employees
    b) as a means for employees to improve their working conditions and increase their bargaining power with their employers
    c) as a means for government to exercise greater control over corporations
    d) as means for government to exercise greater control over managers

PROJECTS

PROJECT 4.1 Examining Multinational Corporations

A multinational corporation owns companies in one or more foreign nations where they employ workers and produce and sell their products. for better or worse, the existence of multinational corporations has an enormous impact on the state of the American economy and on the lives of American people.

Journal instructions:
1. Identify three multinational corporations that you would like to learn about or that have appeared in the news lately. There are many from which to choose. Some examples include General Motors, Ford, Chrysler, Volkswagen, Toyota, International Telephone and Telegraph Corporation, Beatrice, General Electric, Pepsico, Coca Cola, Shell, and many others. Select corporations that manufacture different products. For example, do not select all automobile manufacturers or food manufacturers.

2. Find ten to twenty articles about the multinational corporations that you selected that have appeared during the past few years in financial newspapers and magazines (such as *The New York Times, The Wall Street Journal, Forbes, Business Week,* etc.). Additionally, find a few homepages on the internet for some multinational corporations. Use these articles and web sites to answer the following questions in your journal;
   a) What types of national and international issues and policies (such as trade agreements, tariffs, foreign policy, and many others affect the policies, operation, or success of the corporation?
   b) What types of issues and policies (related to areas such as family, health care, employment, income, environment, and others) that affect people in the U.S. and other countries does the corporations policies create?

Option: essay
Reread the section in the text about sociological perspectives on the economy. Using your answers to the above questions (and other information provided in the articles you read), write an essay (around five pages, typed) in which you discuss the issues, problems, and policies that appear to be common to multinational corporations from the point of view of each of the sociological perspectives. Be sure to use specific examples from the articles you read to illustrate your ideas.

Option: bibliography
Develop a bibliography of ten to twelve articles from sociology journals, and two or three sociological web sites, that deal with issues related to multinational corporations. Type your bibliography using the format found in one of the sociology journals.

Option: research paper
Complete the above journal and bibliographic instructions if you have not already done so. Write a paper (around five to seven pages, typed) in which you discuss one of the issues related to multinational corporations that you identified in your field work journal. Be sure to integrate material from five of the sociology journals in your bibliography. Provide proper documentation of your references throughout the paper and include a reference page.

PROJECT 4.2 Taking a Cross-cultural Look at Economic Systems

Chapter 4 in the text describes a few different types of economic systems that exist within the world economy: communism, capitalism, individualistic capitalism, and communitarian capitalism. While it is easy for us to take an ethnocentric view and say that our economic system is the best, it is important to take a culturally relativist approach to examining the various economic systems within the world economy. Is capitalism as it is practiced in the United States the best form of economy for the U.S. and for other societies? Are there some societies that benefit more from communist or communitarian capitalist systems? How does a society's system affect other institutions in that society? How does understanding a society's economic system help us to understand the economic problems a society may face? The objective of this project is to have you systematically examine some of these questions.

Journal instructions:
1. Reread the section in your text that describes the types of economic systems in the world economy. In addition, read the relevant sections about economic systems in an introduction to sociology text book. In your journal, summarize what the various types of systems are and identify at least one country in which each economic system is practiced.

2. Identify someone that you know that is from a country that has an economic system that is somewhat different than the individualistic capitalist economic system that is practiced in the United States (for example, an international exchange student, a student that has studied abroad for a semester, a professor, an administrator at your college, a friend or neighbor, a businessperson, and so on).

3. Conduct an in-depth interview with that person about what it is like to live under an economic system different than the United States. Discuss the following items with that person and keep detailed notes in your journal:

   a) Economic system. What type of economic system exists in the country of the person you are interviewing?

   b) Employment. What are the rates of unemployment (approximate) in that country? Do people have the option of seeking any type of employment they wish? How difficult (or easy) is it to obtain employment? What types of jobs are available? Is there a minimum wage? What are the wages like for different occupations? Do most people seem to be satisfied with their jobs and their working conditions?

   c) Health care. How is the health care system organized? Do people have guaranteed health coverage? Do they have to pay for their own health insurance? What happens if people do not have health insurance? What is the quality of health care like? Does everyone receive the same quality of health care?

   d) Family policies. What type of non-parental child care exists? What types of family policies exist at work (for example, maternity leave, family leave, sick leave, pension plans, and so on.)

   e) Education. Is there both both private and public education? How is the quality of each?

   f) Consumerism. Is there a wide variety of products—food,clothing,automobiles, and so on—available for purchase? How does the cost of the products compare with similar products in the U.S.? How does the quality of products compare?

PROJECT INSTRUCTIONS ARE CONTINUED ON THE FOLLOWING PAGE.

g) Housing. Is there a problem with homelessness? Are housing costs controlled by the government? How difficult is it to find a satisfactory place to live? Is the cost of homes similar to comparable homes in the U.S.?

h) Issues and problems. What are some of the most important economic issues and problems in that country? Would the country benefit from having a different type of economic system?

Option: essay
Using the information you gathered in your journal (above), write an essay (around three to five pages, typed) in which you compare the economic system you explored with that of the United States. As part of your comparison, discuss the functions, dysfunctions, advantages and disadvantages of an economic system different than that practiced in the United States. Be sure to use specific examples from your journal notes to illustrate your main points.

Option: bibliography
Develop a bibliography of ten articles from sociology journals, and two or three sociological web sites, that discuss one or more issues related to the form of economic system that you examined in your journal and essay (above). For example, you might find articles about how health care or education exists in a country that practices communitarian capitalism, communism, or socialism. Type your bibliography in the format found in one of the sociology journals.

Option: research paper
Write a paper (around five to seven pages, typed) in which you compare the United States and a country that has a different form of economic system about some aspect of life that is directly related to the type of economic system practiced (for example, health care, education, day care, and so on). Be sure to integrate material from at least four articles from sociology journals, your own journal notes (above), and material from the text book. Provide proper documentation throughout your paper and include a reference page.

PROJECT 4.3 Exploring the Debate About Free World Trade

Coleman and Cressey present a debate about whether or not policies should be enacted that provide for free and open trade between countries within the global economy. A number of issues within recent years have called attention to this debate: the North American Free Trade Agreement (NAFTA), the General Agreement on Tariffs and Trade, U.S. imposed tariffs on Japanese luxury automobiles, and others. Clearly, this is a controversial debate that will continue to exist for some time. The objective of this project is to have you explore one of these free trade issues in depth and to weigh the pros and cons of free trade.

Journal instructions:
1. Locate and read ten to fifteen articles from newspapers, news magazines, business magazines, or commentary magazines that address one important free trade issue or policy that has occurred within the last five years. Additionally, locate two web sites that deal with this issue. Be sure to find articles that support the issue in question and articles that oppose it.

2. In your journal, list the title, author, date, and magazine for each article and web site. Summarize the main points and the position taken by the author of each article.

3. Reread the section in chapter 1 of the text that discusses how to interpret the claims made by an author. Then, in your journal, briefly evaluate the claims made by each of the articles that you summarized.

4. Summarize and list the advantages and disadvantages of the policy or issue presented within the articles.

5. Briefly discuss how each of the three sociological perspectives discussed in chapter 2—functionalism, conflict theory, and the social psychological perspectives—might explain the consequences of enacting the policy in question.

Option: essay
Using the information and ideas you developed in your journal (above), write an essay (around five pages, typed) in which you weigh the advantages and disadvantages of enacting the policy you explored. Be sure to use as many sociological ideas as possible and try to objectively evaluate each side of the debate. In your conclusion, present your position, using as much objective information and as many sociological ideas as possible.

Option: bibliography
Develop a bibliography of ten to fifteen articles from sociology journals, sociology books, and sociologically-based web sites that are relevant to the debate about free trade, free trade issues, or free trade policies. Type your bibliography using the format found in one of the sociology journals.

Option: research paper
Write a paper (around seven pages, typed) in which you integrate material from at least five articles from sociological sources (sociology journals or books written by sociologists) and the material you developed in your journal and/or essay (above) to discuss the advantages and disadvantages of free trade. Your discussion can be about free trade in general, but you should focus your examples and main points about the issue you explored above. Be sure to provide proper documentation throughout your paper and include a reference page.

PROJECT 4.4 Labor Unions

Labor unions have existed for a long time in many countries . However, they are currently being met with a great deal of resistance in capitalist countries and are declining both in their numbers and in their power. The objective of this activity is to have you examine the advantages and disadvantages of labor unions for employees, businesses, and for society.

Journal instructions:
1. Identify a person that you know that is a member of a labor union. Discuss with him or her—and record in your journal—the types of issues that the union deals with, how helpful the union is in his/her job, and the advantages and disadvantages of having a labor union.

2. Ask your friend to take you to a local meeting of the labor union. Observe, and record in your journal, the types of issues that the union discusses, how the meeting is organized, how problems are resolved, and so on.

3. Interview a labor union leader and ask him/her to explain to you the purpose of having a union, whether or not unions are effective, why they are currently declining, and why many companies do not permit their employees to be in unions. In addition, ask the union leader to give you an example of an important dispute in which the union had been involved in within the last few years.

4. Interview an administrator or manager at a company that has a labor union and one at a company that does not allow labor unions. Ask the administrator or manager what the advantages and disadvantages of labor unions are and why there is or is not a union present to represent the employees at that company.

Option: essay
Write an essay (around three to five pages, typed) using information compiled in your journal (above) about the current state of unions in the United States and the advantages and disadvantages of unions for employees and for companies.

Option: bibliography
Develop a bibliography of five to ten articles from popular periodicals (newspapers, magazines, and so on) about a labor union issue that has occurred within the last few years and five to ten articles from sociology journals about issues related to labor unions. Type your bibliography using the format found in one of the sociology journals.

Option: research paper
Using information you developed in your journal and at least six articles from the bibliography your developed (at least three from sociology journals), write a paper (around five to seven pages, typed) in which you discuss an issue involving labor unions within the last few years. Address the following items in your paper:
     a) What was the issue about?
     b) What are the pros and cons of the positions taken by the union and the pros and cons of the positions taken by those who opposed the union?
     b) What was the outcome of the dispute?
     c) How would functionalism, conflict theory, and the social psychological perspectives approach the dispute? That is, how do you think each would explain why the dispute was occurring and the outcome of the dispute?

CHAPTER 5

PROBLEMS OF GOVERNMENT

CHAPTER OUTLINE

The Growth of Government

Who Runs the Government?
      Three Theoretical Approaches
            The Elitists
            The Pluralists
            The Structuralists
      The Political Process: Citizens and Special Interests
            An Appraisal

The Problems of Government
      Scandals and Corruption
      Growing Public Cynicism
      The Military Dilemma
      Freedom or Oppression?
      Burdens and Benefits

Solving the Problems of Government
      Reforming Campaign Finance
      Restructuring Government
      Limiting Government Secrecy
      Getting Politically Involved

Sociological Perspectives on Problems of Government
      The Functionalist Perspective
      The Conflict Perspective
      The Feminist Perspective
      The Interactionist Perspective
      Other Perspectives

CHAPTER LEARNING OBJECTIVES AND ESSAY QUESTIONS

After studying this chapter, you should be able to:

• Explain the importance of power and politics in everyday life.

• Discuss the characteristics and consequences of bureaucracy.

• Compare, discuss, and critique several three theories about who runs the government.

• Identify and discuss various dilemmas of government.

• Explain why the military poses problems for democratic societies.

• Analyze the costs and benefits of government programs.

• Discuss four ways to solve the problems of government.

• State and compare how the different sociological perspectives explain the problems of government.

KEY POINTS FOR REVIEW

• Government policies affect nearly every aspect of our lives including marriage, families, personal relationships, business practices, religious practices, environmental practices, leisure time activities, and much more. Government has become the principal institution for dealing with our social problems. Society's failure to deal with a problem effectively are likely the result of political failures.

• Governments throughout the world have been growing rapidly since the beginning of this century. The total workforce employed by the government has risen from 6.5 to 15.8 percent since 1929. The influence of government on the daily lives of citizens has grown as well, being less tightly bound by custom and tradition than before. This is largely because it has become necessary for government to accommodate for the loss of functions previously performed by other institutions as other institutions have changed.

• Along with the growth of government and big business has come the growth of bureaucracies—formal organization with a hierarchy and a set of formal rules in which members perform specialized tasks. Over 90 percent of all Americans are employed in some form of bureaucratic organization. The strength of bureaucracies is that they are stable and efficient. Their weaknesses include an over-reliance on regulations and red tape. As a result, the organization's goals often become displaced. The sociologists Max Weber was concerned about the depersonalizing effects of bureaucratization.

• There are three major explanations as to who runs the government: elitist, pluralist, and structuralist. The elitist view is that government policy is shaped by a small and relatively unified "power elite" who are in the highest ranks of the economy, the government, and the military. The pluralist view is that government decisions are determined by the competition among many different interest groups or "veto groups" and that no single group predominates. The structuralist view is that the structure of capitalist societies requires that the government protect the interests of the upper class in order to keep the system from collapsing.

• Social scientists do not believe that an ideal democracy exists in the United States. One of the major problems is citizen-apathy. This results from a lack of wealth and education and distrust of the government. Second, it is difficult to decide where particular politicians stand on the issues. Voters seldom get a chance to talk directly with candidates and have to rely on the mass media which is largely controlled by large corporations. Citizens do sometimes influence legislation through social movements and the lobbying of special-interest groups. However, one of the primary sources of funding for special interest groups is the political action committees (PACs) set up by people with a particular interest in a specific policy, such as large corporations.

• There are a few basic conclusions about the way the political process operates. First, numerous competing interest groups participate in the struggle to shape government policy. Second, these groups are not equals and the decision-making process tends to be dominated by the elite groups. Third, average citizens can be and have been successful in influencing legislation when they ban together and form social movements. There are concrete limits as to what the government can do.

• Most of the problems of government revolve around how well it represents the will of the people. Scandals and corruption are two things that limit the government's ability to accomplish this task. Sometimes corruption occurs in ways that are legal. The system of campaign finance creates a conflict of interest among politicians who often pay off their campaign debts by supporting particular policies or providing government jobs in exchange for campaign contributions. Corruption also occurs illegally in the form of bribery. Scandals involving government are heavily played upon by the media that has a thirst for such matters, sometimes creating problems about issues that are irrelevant to political policies.

• A related problem is the rise in public cynicism and a decreasing lack of American's confidence in their government. Many Americans look at their government as unresponsive, bureaucratic, and inefficient, riddled with self serving and corrupt employees. However, there is really no reason to believe that the government has gotten less democratic or more corrupt than in the past, but that the rise in cynicism is due to new methods of investigative reporting by the media.

• Another problem that governments often face stems from the need for a military. While a military is essential, it can pose a problem in democratic societies. In some countries, the military has taken over the government. Additionally, because the military requires such enormous economic expenditures, military spending can provide a boost to a lagging economy. This economic fact can lead to an interdependence between the military, giant corporations, and government, thus having a major impact on government policies and decision-making.

• The most significant problem confronting modern government is how to protect personal freedom while still maintaining social order. The expression of one's person's rights may interfere with the rights of another and the needs of society. Maintaining the delicate balance between freedom and control can be problematic for governments.

• Government is supposed to be concerned with social justice and to create programs that insure freedom and equality for all. However, these programs cost money and someone must pay for them. Taxation is one of the most difficult issues political leaders face. How much taxes should people pay and who should pay are the biggest questions. The United States has the lowest overall tax rate of any industrialized nation. Concurrently, it also has the lowest level of social services.

• There have been a number of responses to the challenge of creating a more democratic government. One response is the attempt to reform the laws regarding political campaign funding in order to provide all candidates with equal time to express their views. A second solution may be to restructure government in such a way that its power be decentralized, giving more power to local governments. Third is the attempt to create stronger laws to limit government secrecy and protect the right of free political expression. Fourth is the attempt to involve more citizens in political organizations.

• The functionalist perspective examines government in terms the functions it serves for society. These include the enforcing society's norms, acting as the final arbiter of disputes arising between individuals and/or groups, directing society and coordinating other social institutions, dealing the social needs that are left unmet by other social institutions, and handling international relations. According to the functionalist perspective, the problems of government have come about because of the rapid social and technological changes that have made it very difficult for mangy governments to perform these functions effectively. Functionalists say that in order to deal with this problem government must be reshaped.

• From the conflict perspective, the government is a source of tremendous political power that is used to advance the interests of those who control it, namely, the upper class. Conflict theorists feel that government works to repress conflict rather than to resolve it and that the solution to this problem is to give a stronger voice to the "common" man and woman.

• The feminist perspective focuses on the underrepresentation of women at all levels of government. Feminists view this underrepresentation as a real tragedy because it not only deprives women around the world of their basic human rights, but it deprives the decision making process of the wisdom and common sense the world's women have to offer.

• The interactionist perspective holds that the political system is guided by the ideas, definitions, and beliefs we hold about it. Thus, interactionists are very concerned about the everyday cynicism that has crept into our view of the government. Additionally, interactionists are concerned about the way in which people learn their political values and perspectives.

• Personality theorists focus on the relationships between political systems and individual personality. How a nation's people affects its political system and how political systems affect personality are two areas of concern from the social psychological perspectives.

NOTES:

KEY TERMS

The following key terms are found in your textbook on the page number indicated in parentheses. In the space provided, write a brief definition of the key term **in your own words**. Then **provide an example** of the term, such as a culture in which the practice takes place, or people that you might know whose behavior illustrates the term, a current event that illustrates the term, how a term could be used to shed light on or help solve a particular social problem, and so on. You could include examples from the news, books, movies, or anything else that will illustrate the term and help you remember it. Include any comments from your class discussions or textbook that might help you remember and understand these key terms. Use additional paper if necessary, but keep it with your study guide to help you review for exams.

bureaucracy (p. 136)

_____

_____

_____

_____

goal displacement (p. 137)

_____

_____

_____

_____

elitists (p. 137)

_____

_____

_____

_____

pluralists (p. 137)

_____

_____

_____

structuralists (p. 138)

_____

_____

_____

_____

special-interest groups (p. 142)

_____

_____

_____

_____

lobbying (p. 142)

_____

_____

_____

_____

conflict of interest (p. 145)

_____

_____

_____

_____

spoils system (p. 145)

_____

_____

_____

_____

bribery (p. 145)

_____

_____

_____

_____

military industrial complex (p. 149)

_____

_____

_____

_____

defense conversion (p. 145)

_____

_____

_____

_____

term limitations (p. 155)

_____

_____

_____

_____

covert socialization (p. 157)

_____

_____

_____

_____

political socialization (p. 161)

_____

_____

_____

_____

authoritarian personality (p. 161)

_____

_____

_____

_____

NOTES:

PRACTICE TEST

Multiple Choice

1. If one can determine what is a criminal act and start or avoid wars, he or she has:
   a) influence
   b) power
   c) technique
   d) control of government

2. In modern societies, the principal institution for dealing with social problems is:
   a) the economy
   b) separate corporations
   c) the government
   d) individuals

3. The central concern of any democratic government is:
   a) the need to reflect fairly the will of the people
   b) the fear of the misuse of power
   c) protecting the rights of established interests
   d) a lack of relevancy in modern society

4. When employees in a bureaucracy care more about their jobs and continue to play it safe, the bureaucracy might experience a(n):
   a) overwhelming problem of red tape
   b) depersonalization
   c) displacement of goals
   d) bureaucratic breakdown

5. One reason why government has grown so much is because:
   a) growth in the power of local areas
   b) the need to uphold the nation's important customs
   c) its response to problems in other social institutions
   d) the need to balance the power of local areas

6. Which of the following statements about the growth of government is NOT true?
   a) The percentage of the labor force employed by government since 1980 has significantly declined.
   b) The influence of government on the life of citizens has grown.
   c) Government has taken over some of the functions once performed by families.
   d) Government influence over the economy has dramatically increased.

7. Organizations that are characterized by a hierarchy of authority and impersonal enforcement of rules are called:
   a) bureaucracies
   b) governments
   c) labyrinths
   d) special interest groups

8. Special interest groups' principal activity is:
    a) voting
    b) lobbying
    c) investing
    d) research

9. In an ideal democracy, political power is:
    a) almost nonexistent
    b) placed in the hands of a few
    c) shared by all citizens
    d) held by religious institutions

10. Which of the following statements about lobbyists and special interest groups is true?
    a) The poor and workers are well represented by lobbyists.
    b) Lobbyists provide a channel of communication between citizens and their government.
    c) Special interest groups actually have little impact on government.
    d) Lobbyists are effectively regulated by government.

11. If you believe that a small unified ruling class exists, then you follow the _____ theory of who has power in American society.
    a) elitist
    b) pluralist
    c) PAC
    d) structuralist

12. Which of the following statements reflects a pluralist view of American politics?
    a) Political decision are made by a single "power elite."
    b) Powerful groups share many common interests together.
    c) The structure of capitalist societies insures an equal voice to all members of society.
    d) Political decisions are decided in a contest among many competing groups.

13. The structuralist explanation of who has the power in American society contends that:
    a) the structure of capitalist societies forces the government to protect the interests of the upper class
    b) the structure of capitalist societies creates a system in which most citizens have an opportunity to be heard
    c) the government contains structures that the tenets of ideal democracy are carried out
    d) even though there is a class system in America, it is structured in such a way that the number of people in a social class is proportionate to the amount of power that class holds

14. One reason why many American voters are apathetic is because of:
    a) personal laziness
    b) support of special interest groups
    c) a feeling of powerlessness
    d) a large trust in government

15. Special-interest groups are:
    a) groups that are formed by the government to insure that take an interest in seeing to it that the voice of all citizens, especially the lower classes, are heard
    d) citizen groups that are formed to make sure that government attends to programs that are essential to the overall well-being of society
    c) any groups that promote legislation in which they have a particular stake
    d) groups that tend promote social programs even at the risk of losing personal financial profits

16. Extensive military spending creates long-range damage to the economy for all of the following reasons EXCEPT:
    a) military research and development takes scientific talent away from more productive civilian research
    b) military spending generally weakens an economy that may already be sagging
    c) military products have no practical use in the economy
    d) excessive military spending can lead a nation to become less competitive in other economic areas with other nations

17. One way the military exercises influence in American society is its:
    a) shining record of achievement
    b) strict control of waste and corruption
    c) use of powerful lobbyists
    d) opposition to communist countries

18. As a former military General, and as a republican President of United States, Dwight Eisenhower:
    a) warned of the dangers of letting the military-industrial complex wield too much influence in U.S. society and politics
    b) warned of the dangers of not recognizing the need for the development of the military-industrial complex
    c) enjoined Columbia University, where he was president, to be a major player in the military-industrial complex
    d) recognized the importance of promoting a strong military-industrial complex to countless local economics

19. The military-industrial complex that former President Eisenhower spoke of refers to:
    a) a feeling of inferiority among Americans about the strength of America's military and economic institutions in relation to other industrialized countries
    b) the perception by other industrialized countries that American society is weakening both militarily and economically
    c) the interconnection of American institutions—such as military, economic, educational, governmental, and so on—that have an interest in weapons and defense spending
    d) 24 million acres of land that the Department of Defense retains for its own use, including the manufacture of weapons and the training of military personnel

20. Which of the following is NOT an example of a violation of civil liberties?
    a) Watergate
    b) corporate use of polygraphs
    c) the hunt for communist agents
    d) FBI use of wiretaps and burglaries

21. One reason why upholding rights is difficult to do in practice is that:
    a) democratic countries have no real rights in theory
    b) most Americans do not believe in rights
    c) no one is quite sure what important rights are
    d) expression of one person's rights may interfere with the rights of another

22. How did the federal government take the easy way out in 1981 when the taxpayers were demanding lower taxes, yet the cost of running the government and the demand for services were increasing?
    a) It ran an ever-larger deficit.
    b) It printed more money.
    c) It increased taxes.
    d) It took over several corporations in order to raise the extra revenue needed.

23. Which of the following groups carries the greatest tax burden in America?
    a) the wealthy
    b) the working and middle class
    c) the upper middle class
    d) persons on welfare

24. Which modern industrial country has the lowest overall tax rate?
    a) France
    b) the United States
    c) Great Britain
    d) Japan

25. Which of the following is probably the most important way to make the United States more democratic?
    a) extending the vote to more persons
    b) prohibiting incumbency
    c) regulating campaign financing
    d) banning the media from political campaigns

26. If you see the government as a source of tremendous political power used to advance the interests of those who control it, you are likely to agree with the _____ perspective.
    a) feminist
    b) interactionist
    c) functional
    d) conflict

27. The ways in which people learn political values and perspectives is through:
    a) democratic dramas
    b) functional government
    c) political socialization
    d) history books

28. Which of the following is NOT of the functions of government?
    a) enforcing society's norms when other methods fail
    b) arbitrating disputes between individuals and/or groups
    c) overall planning and direction of society
    d) controlling persons who might want to change society

29. Government secrecy can be problematic to a democracy because it can:
    a) cover up government mistakes, scandals, and corruption
    b) interfere with the actions of speculators
    c) limit the amount of information the government has
    d) violate civil liberties

30. Which of the following is NOT an obstacle to getting citizens more involved in the process of government?
    a) dependency on the media
    b) increase in the total population
    c) anonymity of the modern city
    d) the decline in the importance of the vote

NOTES:

PROJECTS

PROJECT 5.1 Identifying Problems of Government

Coleman and Cressey feel somewhat gloomy about the future of American government. Is their view overly pessimistic, or is it a realistic picture of American government? The objective of this activity is to have you examine the extent to which problems of government exist today and what types of problems they are.

Journal instructions:
1. Search the back issues of national and local newspapers and news magazines for the past year for articles regarding problems of government discussed by Coleman and Cressey in chapter 5. As a sample, use one week per month (the same week) throughout the year. Since most national newspapers and news magazines can be found on microfiche, microfilm, or computer files, this will not take as long as it sounds that it might. In your journal, keep a detailed record of any government-related problems that are mentioned. Be sure to also record the bibliographic information so that you can return to these articles later on if necessary.

2. From your research of the news, summarize the types and extent to which government problems exist. What can you conclude from your research? Do you think that Coleman and Cressey are correct? What do you think is the biggest problem faced by government during the past year?

Option: essay
Write an essay (around three to four pages, typed) in which you use material you compiled in your journal (above) to discuss problems in government over the past year. Here are some possible ideas to explore in your essay. What types of problems exist? How often did they occur? Does this seem to be any different than in previous years? Are the problems as serious as Coleman and Cressey suggest that they are? Why are they problems? How can the functionalist, conflict, and social psychological perspectives provide insight into understanding why the problems exist and how they might be solved? In your essay, be sure to use relevant news articles from your journal as illustrations and evidence of your ideas. Be sure to document them properly throughout the paper and cite them on a reference page.

Option: bibliography
Develop a bibliography of ten to fifteen articles from sociology journals and/or books written by sociologists about one or more of the types of government problems that you found in your journal (above). Additionally, identify 2 sociological web sites that address the issue of government problems. Type your bibliography using the format found in one of the sociology journals.

Option: research paper
Using material and ideas from your journal and essay (above) and at least five articles from your bibliography of sociology journals and/or sociology books, write a paper (around five to seven pages, typed) in which you discuss the extent and nature of problems of government in the United States today. Be sure to provide proper documentation for any articles and books (including the newspaper articles) throughout your paper and include a reference page.

PROJECT 5.2 Whose Interests are Served by Interest Groups?

As Coleman and Cressey mention in the text, there are many special interest groups that try to influence government legislation. Whose interests do the special interest groups represent? Are all Americans served equally by interest groups? What problems might they pose for a democratic society? The objective of this project is to have you examine the extent to which interest groups exist, how they operate, and whose interests they serve.

Journal instructions:
1. Review the sections in chapter 5 about interest groups and about theories of who controls the government.

2. Look through past issues of national and local newspapers or magazines to identify five different interest groups that have tried to influence legislation about specific issues or policies during the past six months. (Or you might want to use periodical indexes in your library or on-line—for example, *Reader's Guide to Periodical Literature, Newsbank*, and others.) Additionally, identify one or two web sites that pertain to groups attempting to influence legislation. Make a record of these issues in your journal.

3. Locate, read, and note in your journal two or three news reports (from newspapers, news magazines, commentary magazines, web sites, and so on) about EACH of the five interest groups and what they were trying to accomplish. Then, for EACH interest group you identified, use the news reports to briefly answer the following questions:
    a) Identify the group or organization that the interest group represents.
    b) What did they try to accomplish?
    c) What methods did they use to try to influence legislators?
    d) Who specifically did they try to influence?
    e) Estimate the possible cost of their attempts to influence government decisions.
    f) Do you think the interest group represents common social values or the interests of a particular group?
    g) Do you think that the type of influence used by the interest group was legitimate? Do you think that it was fair to all groups who may have had different positions on the issue or policy in question? Why or why not?
    h) How successful do you think the interest group was (or might be) in influencing government legislation?

Option: essay
1. Interview two local, state, or national politicians (one Republican and one Democrat) about the role of interest groups in influencing legislation. Make a list of interview questions based on the items in question three above. (For example: "What are some examples of issues or policies with which you are familiar that interest groups have tried to exert influence over?" "Who did the interest groups represent?" "How did they try to persuade you or other legislators?" And so on.)

2. Based upon what you have compiled in your journal (above) and from your interviews, write an essay (around five pages, typed) in which you use the functionalist and conflict perspectives on government to discuss interest groups.

PROJECT INSTRUCTIONS ARE CONTINUED ON THE FOLLOWING PAGE.

Option: bibliography
Develop a bibliography of ten to fifteen articles from sociology journals, sociology books, commentary magazines, news papers or magazines, and so on about one of the interest groups that you identified in your field journal (above). The *CQ Researcher* (formerly *Congressional Quarterly's Editorial Research Reports*) is an excellent source of articles that contain summaries of research and bibliographies on a wide range of social issues. Make sure that at least five items in your bibliography are from sociology journals. The articles from sociology journals do not necessarily have to be specifically about the interest group you selected. The may deal with issues that pertain to interest groups in general and that you might be able to use to discuss the interest group you selected. Additionally, identify two sociological web sites that pertain to interest groups. Type your bibliography following the format found in one of the sociology journals.

Option: research paper
1. Using the bibliography and information that you obtained from doing your journal and essay for this project (above), find out as much of the following information as you can about the interest group on which you developed your bibliography:
   a) the history of the interest group
   b) how the interest group is organized
   c) who the group's leaders are
   d) some of the issues and policies in which the interest group has been involved
   e) the specific groups or organization that the interest group represents
   f) how the interest group finances its activities
   g) the methods that the interest group uses to exert influence
   h) how successful the interest group has been
   i) the size of the interest group's membership
   j) the interest group's ideology

2. To help you obtain the above information, observe at least one of the following: a rally or meeting sponsored by the interest group you are studying, an office out of which the interest group operates, a PAC office sponsored by the interest group. You can probably find about your local PACs or interest groups through your local government office or Chamber of Commerce.

3. Obtain some specific examples—petitions, media advertising, pamphlets, video tapes, and so on—of how the interest group has tried to exert influence.

4. Write a paper (around seven pages, typed) in which you use the functionalist and conflict perspectives on government to discuss the interest group about which you conducted your research. Be sure to provide proper documentation throughout your paper and include a reference page.

PROJECT 5.3 Who Rules America?

Coleman and Cressey discuss three views about how major decisions are made in America: the elitist view, the pluralist view, and the structuralist view. The objective of this project is to have you examine each of these views and to try to determine which is the most appropriate explanation of who rules America.

Journal instructions:
1. Carefully reread the sections in chapter 5 of your text that discusses each of the views of who runs the government. Summarize these in your journal.

2. Look through past issues of newspapers, news magazines, or commentary magazines in order to identify a political decision that you think illustrates the elitist view, one that illustrates the pluralist view, and one that illustrates the structuralist view. For example, do you think a particular Supreme Court appointment illustrates elitism, pluralism, or structuralism? Do you think a decision to become involved in a war illustrates elitism, pluralism, or structuralism? Do you think that enacting a particular tax policy illustrates elitism, pluralism, or structuralism? Remember, find one issue or policy that illustrates each view.

Option: essay
Using the information you compiled in your journal (above), write an essay (around three to five pages, typed) in which you compare the extent to which each of the three views of who runs the government is an accurate depiction of the United States.

Option: bibliography
Conduct further library research about each of the political decisions that you discussed in the journal part of this activity. Develop a bibliography of ten to fifteen items using a wide variety of sources: articles in sociology journals, news magazines, commentary magazines, reviews of government proceedings (such as the *Congressional Digest, CQ Researcher*, and so on). Look for articles that contain information about how the decisions were made, who made them, whose political, economic, or social interests the decision benefited, and so on. You will probably need to find around four or five references for each decision you are addressing in order to obtain the information you need. Type the bibliography following in the format found in one of the sociology journals.

Option: research paper
Write a paper (around five to seven pages, typed) in which you discuss an answer to the question, "Who rules America?" As part of your discussion, use the material you compiled in your journal, essay, and bibliography to critique each of the theories of who runs the government, provide evidence to support or refute one or more of the theories, apply functionalist and conflict theories of government to the examples you found, and so on. Be sure to use a minimum of five items from your bibliography in your discussion. Provide proper documentation throughout your paper and include a reference page.

PROJECT 5.4 Political Socialization

Political socialization refers to the ways in which people are encouraged to adopt particular political perspectives, attitudes, values, and beliefs. Political socialization occurs in much the same way as any other socialization, beginning at a very young age and continuing throughout the life cycle. The objective of this project is to have you examine your own political socialization.

Journal instructions:
1. Go to an introduction to sociology textbook and read the chapter on socialization. In your journal, outline and summarize the theories of socialization and the agents of socialization.

2. In your journal, briefly describe your current political views and affiliation. Include descriptions of such things as:
> a) your overall political philosophy (conservative, liberal, moderate, and so on)
> b) your party preference
> c) your degree of political activism (For example, are you a member of any political clubs such as the Young Democrats? How often do you participate in political rallies? Do you write to your congressperson? Do you vote regularly? Do you actively campaign for any candidates? And so on).
> d) your political views on particular issues (such as abortion, gun control, taxes, capital punishment, and so on)
> e) anything else that describes your political views and affiliation

3. After you have completed the description of your political self, think about the ways in which you have come to have these particular perspectives and behaviors. Think about and discuss in your journal the ways you have been socialized through various agents of socialization during your childhood, adolescence, and adult life so far. For example:
> a) Did members of your family have any particular political preferences? Were they politically active? Were they involved in any occupation that tended to favor particular political attitudes?
> b) Were you politically socialized in school n any way? Did you begin each day with the Pledge of Allegiance? How politically active were the parents of the students who attended the school and what were their views?
> c) Did you receive any form of political socialization from your religious affiliations? Did religious leaders make their political views explicitly known and encourage the congregation to vote in particular ways about particular issues?
> d) What types of political views and behaviors did your friends have? Were they conservative, liberal, Democrat, Republican? Were they very active politically?
> e) What was the overall political climate when you were growing up? Who was president? Who were your state and local politicians?

4. While much of our political perspective is shaped through early socialization experiences, it continues to be shaped throughout our adult life. For one week, keep a record in your journal of your observations of how political socialization occurs in your daily life. Carefully observe and consider how family, religion, peers, school, the media, reference groups, in-groups, politicians, and other agents of socialization influence your political attitudes and behaviors.

PROJECT INSTRUCTIONS ARE CONTINUED ON THE FOLLOWING PAGE

Option: essay
Using the material you developed in your journal (above), write an essay (around five pages, typed) in which you present an autobiographical account of your past and present political socialization, and your predictions about your future political attitudes and behaviors. When making predictions about your future political attitudes and behaviors, be sure to base it upon what your political socialization has been and what it may be like in the future.

Option: bibliography
Conduct library research to develop a bibliography of around ten to fifteen articles from sociology or political science journals, sociology books, or political science books that discuss political socialization. Identify at least one sociological web site that deals with political socialization. Type your bibliography following the format found in one of the sociology journals.

Option: research paper
Write a paper (around five to seven pages, typed) in which you use information from at least five items in your bibliography to discuss your own political socialization and your observations of political socialization in everyday life that you wrote about in your journal (above). Use bibliographic material to explain what you have observed, or use your observations as illustrations of what the articles discuss, or both. Be sure to provide proper documentation throughout your paper and include a reference page.

CHAPTER 6

HEALTH AND ILLNESS

CHAPTER OUTLINE

What is Good Health?

Physical Illness
      Unhealthy Lifestyles
      Physical Injuries: Suicide, Accidents, and Violent Crime
      Environmental Hazards
      Contagious Disease
      Poverty

Mental Disorders
      What Are Mental Disorders?
            Personal Maladjustment
            Social Deviance
      Classifying Mental Disorders
      The Distribution of Mental Disorders
      The Causes of Mental Disorder
            Biology
            Developmental Theories
            Traumas and Social Stress
            Labeling Theory
            Environment

Health Care in the United States
      Doctors and Nurses
            The Hospitals
            Paying the Cost
      The Crisis in American Health Care
            Failing the Patients: Unequal Access
            Runaway Costs

National Health Care: Canada and Britain
      Great Britain
      Canada

Ethical Dilemmas

Solving the Problems of the Health Care System
    Preventive Medicine
    Medical Personnel
    Restructuring the Health Care System
    Community Mental Health Treatment

Sociological Perspectives on Problems of Health and Illness
    The Functionalist Perspective
    The Conflict Perspective
    The Feminist Perspective
    The Interactionist Perspective

CHAPTER LEARNING OBJECTIVES AND ESSAY QUESTIONS

After studying this chapter, you should be able to:

• Explain why ill health is a condition many persons fear.

• Define the meaning of good health.

• Explain how unhealthy life styles, environmental hazards, and contagious diseases promote illnesses.

• Outline and discuss the concept of mental health and the types of mental disorders.

• Trace the history and structure of health care in the U.S.

• Discuss recent changes in health care in the US and the problems associated with these changes.

• Summarize the national health care plans underway in Canada and Britain.

• Describe the several ethical issues facing American health care.

• Outline and discuss several ways to solve the problems of the sick and improve the health care system.

• State and explain the different sociological perspectives on health and illness.

KEY POINTS FOR REVIEW

• Society has a profound influence on our health, especially the way we interpret our physical and mental conditions and the way we define good health. Additionally, social factors can affect how healthy we are.

107

• Health involves social and psychological conditions as well as biological ones. The way good health is defined varies among different nations and even different classes within the same nations. Overall, the world's population today is healthier and will live longer than those of any other generation in history. This is largely due to a great improvement in living conditions in the twentieth century. However, changes in our lifestyle have also led to many contemporary health problems.

• A number of factors contribute to health problems today. First is unhealthy lifestyles, including lack of physical activity, poor diet, smoking, and stress. A second factor is physical injuries such as suicide, accidents, and violent crime. Accidents account for more deaths than suicides and homicides combined, yet, the death rates from intentional violence has been increasing in recent years. Sociologists focus more on social reasons for suicide, such as lack of supportive social groups, whereas psychologists focus more on individual characteristics, such as depression. A third factor is environmental hazards such as pollution, found to be related to bronchitis, heart disease, emphysema, and various types of cancer. A fourth factor is contagious diseases that affect our daily lives. A fifth factor is poverty. Poor people have more health problems—such as lower life expectancies, higher rates of infant death, more contagious disease, heart ailments, arthritis, and high blood pressure—than those who are not poor and their problems stem largely from a lower standard of living.

• In addition to physical illnesses, serious psychological problems are extremely common in American society. The "medical model" sees mental illness as caused by the same natural forces as physical illnesses. While this view is an improvement over superstitious beliefs about mental illness, there is still no widespread agreement about the nature of mental health or the causes and treatment of mental illness.

• One alternative to the medical model—the personal maladjustment approach—holds that mental disorders arise when someone is unable to deal effectively with his or her personal difficulties, and disturbed behavior is therefore seen to be caused by the same forces that govern other behavior. Another alternative to the medical model—the social deviance approach—is that there are no objective standards by which to judge someone's mental health. From this view, mental illness is a form of social deviance and relative to the norms of the culture in which one lives.

• The most widely accepted classification of mental disorders is the American Psychiatric Association's *Diagnostic and Statistical Manual of Mental Disorders (DSM)* which lists thirteen major categories. The three most common are mood disorders, substance abuse disorders, and anxiety disorders.

• Sociologists are interested in the way mental disorders are distributed throughout society. They are particularly interested in the relationship between social class and mental health. They have generally found an inverse relation between social class and the rate of psychological disorder. Women are more likely to suffer from disorders involving anxiety or depression, while men are more likely to have a substance abuse disorder. Sociologists believe that this is probably due to different gender role expectations. The biological approach to mental disorder explains the roots of depression and related mood disorders as the result of genetic factors. Sociologists argue that while this may be true in some cases, there are many social environmental factors that tend to be overlooked as explanations.

• The earliest social environment theories of mental illness hold early childhood rearing practices responsible. Although these views have been criticized for being overly simplistic,

108

there is evidence that traumatic events such as physical abuse or sexual molestation lie at the roots of many serious psychological problems, such as anxiety, depression, and phobias. A related approach argues that excessively stressful conditions are related to mental disorder. Interactionist theorists argue that mental illness is not a medical condition, but, rather a social role that is learned like any other role that some people are compelled to fulfill.

• Whereas other countries have all adopted broadly based systems of government-supported health care, the U.S. created a medical welfare system for the poor and the elderly, but has left the rest of the health care system privatized. While the U.S. spends more money per person than any other nation, it compares poorly with regard to health statistics. It has the highest infant mortality rate and highest percentage of infants born with a low birth-rate.

• There are three basic parts of the health care system in the U.S. that have come under scrutiny: physicians and other health care professionals, hospitals and mental institutions, and the bureaucracy. One problem is the growing discontent with the performance of physicians for a number of reasons, As medical technology has grown and the health care system more bureaucratic, the doctor-patient relationship has often been depersonalized. There is concern over the poor distribution of physicians. There is a shortage of primary care physicians such as general practitioners, internists, and pediatricians, largely because these are the less lucrative specialty areas. There are still a disproportionately higher number of physicians who are white males, with an under representation of females and other ethnic groups. Physicians are too heavily concentrated in affluent neighborhoods of big cities and suburbs, leaving many low income and rural areas with a shortage. There is lack of sufficient criticism of physicians within the medical profession, which leads to lack of quality control. Nurses, whose jobs require long hours and entail enormous responsibilities, receive little recognition and are under-paid.

• The second part of the health care system that is problematic is the hospital. The trend toward corporate ownership of hospitals in the U.S. has had some beneficial effects, but for the most part it has created problems. Traditional hospitals were usually run by their physicians, but the corporate chains are controlled by professional managers who are likely to have far less understanding of medical practice and the needs of patients, and are likely to be concerned primarily with financial matters. The corporate hospitals have tended to ignore the enormous health care needs of the poor and focus on the people with good health insurance. Further, the skyrocketing cost of medical technology has led to escalating hospital costs.

• Government pays about 43% of the health care bill, insurance companies pay about 33%, and consumers pay about 25%. A problem with this system is that some people are almost entirely protected from the high costs of health care while others have only spotty protection. Another problem is that the private insurance system is extremely wasteful and inefficient, with far larger overhead and administrative costs than government programs. These inefficiencies place an increasing burden on American businesses that pay a large part of employee's health insurance and, ultimately, burden the consumer through higher product costs. The government's health care payments come primarily from Medicare—which buys medical services for the elderly—and Medicaid—which helps the poor and the disabled.

• The American health care system is failing the poor, women, and the elderly, at the same time that its overall cost continues to escalate out of control. There are at least three reasons health care is so expensive in the U.S. The first is the way the health care industry is organized and financed. Because most physicians are paid on a fee-for-service basis, it is in their financial interests to perform as many medical procedures as possible. The second reasons is the increasing costs of new drugs and medical techniques. The third reasons is the increase of malpractice suits and, thus, the increase in malpractice insurance physicians must pay.

• In all the industrialized nations except the U.S., the government has created a system of national health care with some form of universal coverage. This has three advantages over the American system: it is usually more fair, it provides better service for the less fortunate, it is cheaper. However, systems vary. Britain and Canada, for example, have two very different ways of organizing a national health care system, each with its own advantages and disadvantages.
• There are a number of ethical problems faced by the medical profession. Some of these include whether or not to extend the lives of dying patients through life-sustaining equipment, whether or not to assist in euthanasia, whether or not abortion should be legal, whether or not women should become surrogate mothers, and other issues.

• There are two approaches to the problems of the sick. The first is to try to prevent health problems by changing life styles and eating habits, reducing pollution, and increasing the use of preventive medicine. The second aims at improving care for people after they become sick. The second approach includes proposals designed to create equal access to health care and to improve the quality of health care services at less cost. One proposal is to train more general practitioners, pediatricians, and nurses, and offer higher pay and more professional authority to nurses. The second proposal involves restructuring the health care system to control costs and provide universal coverage.

• Restructuring the health care system involves two fundamental issues: how to organize the health care system and how to pay for it. From an administrative standpoint, the most efficient approach is a "single -payer system" in which one government agency pays the bill. This approach is opposed intensely by the insurance industry. The original proposal by Clinton is to encourage the existing insurance companies to band together to form "health care alliances," a plan also opposed by the insurance industry. The strongest debate in restructuring the health care system concerns the best way to pay for universal coverage: direct payments by individuals, payments from employees, or general tax revenues. Each approach has come under political attack from one group or another.

• From the functionalist perspective, the U.S. health care system is disorganized because it has grown rapidly and haphazardly, without proper planning. The solution, functionalists feel, is reorganization. Some functionalists argue for a return to complete free enterprise in the health care business, others believe that we should stick with the present system and work to make it more efficient, and still others hold that the best way is to create a centralized government run system.

• From the conflict perspective, the problems of the health care system have arisen because it is designed to serve the needs of the rich and the powerful, including doctors themselves, thus neglecting the needs of low-income groups. Conflict theories contend that the best way to resolve the health care problem is to reduce the medical profession's control over the financing and origination of the health care system and transfer it to the government.

• The feminist perspective concurs with the conflict perspective regarding the exploitation of the poor and the working class. In addition, feminists also see a systematic repression of women. Until very recently, women were grossly underrepresented in our medical schools and were exluded from many of the highest paying most prestigious medical positions. Further, for generations the medical profession, dominated by males, focused more on the needs of men than women. So, in addition to reforms to provide better medical care for the porr, feminists call for an end to the discrimination against women in medical careers and new concenr for the special

110

health care needs of women and children.

• The interactionist perspective does not deal directly with the organization of health care services but, rather, with the relationship between aspects of the health care system and individuals. For example, social psychologists have examined how the socialization of doctors in medical school often has a negative impact on the way doctors practice medicine. They are also concerned with the way people develop unhealthy habits and life styles. From their view, improvements can be made in public health through strong education and social change.

NOTES:

KEY TERMS

The following key terms are found in your textbook on the page number indicated in parentheses. In the space provided, write a brief definition of the key term **in your own words**. Then **provide an example** of the term, such as a culture in which the practice takes place, or people that you might know whose behavior illustrates the term, a current event that illustrates the term, how a term could be used to shed light on or help solve a particular social problem, and so on. You could include examples from the news, books, movies, or anything else that will illustrate the term and help you remember it. Include any comments from your class discussions or textbook that might help you remember and understand these key terms. Use additional paper if necessary, but keep it with your study guide to help you review for exams.

health (P. 168)

_____

_____

_____

_____

contagious diseases (p. 172)

_____

_____

_____

_____

acquired immune deficiency syndrome (p. 173)

_____

_____

_____

_____

mental disorder (p. 176)

_____

_____

_____

personal maladjustment (p. 177)

_____

_____

_____

_____

labeling theory (p. 177)

_____

_____

_____

_____

mood disorders (p. 178)

_____

_____

_____

_____

substance abuse disorders (p. 178)

_____

_____

_____

_____

anxiety disorders (p. 178)

_____

_____

_____

_____

schizophrenia (p. 180)

_____

_____

_____

_____

Alzheimer's Disease (p. 182)

_____

_____

_____

_____

bipolar disorder (p. 183)

_____

_____

_____

_____

psychoanalytic theory (p. 183)

_____

_____

_____

_____

double bind (p. 184)

_____

_____

_____

_____

stress theory (p. 184)

_____

_____

_____

_____

Medicaid (p. 188)

_____

_____

_____

_____

Medicare (p. 188)

_____

_____

_____

_____

deinstitutionalization (p. 189)

_____

_____

_____

_____

fee-for-service (p. 194)

_____

_____

_____

_____

malpractice (p. 194)

_____

_____

_____

_____

surrogate mothering (p. 199)

_____

_____

_____

_____

national health care (p. 195)

_____

_____

_____

_____

preventive medicine (p. 200)

_____

_____

_____

_____

holistic medicine (p. 200)

_____

_____

_____

_____

physician's assistants (p. 201

_____

_____

_____

_____

nurse practitioners (p. 201

_____

_____

_____

_____

NOTES:

PRACTICE TEST

Multiple Choice

1. According to the World Health Organization, a state of complete physical, mental, and social well-being is the definition of:
   a) mental health
   b) health
   c) human wellness
   d) religious fulfillment

2. Which of the following is true about the American diet?
   a) Most Americans now eat high fiber, low calorie diets.
   b) Drugs have reduced most of the risks from eating fatty foods.
   c) Americans' love of high calorie and fatty food has led to much obesity.
   d) High calorie food no longer poses a health risk.

3. One reasons why people appear less healthy around the world is:
   a) a dramatic increase in infant mortality
   b) the greater spread of disease throughout the earth
   c) our standards of judgment about health are higher
   d) greater training of doctors and nurses

4. Which of the following threats to health is almost unavoidable today?
   a) diet
   b) smoking
   c) environmental pollution
   d) stress

5. All of the following are changes taking place in the twentieth century that have hurt health, EXCEPT for:
   a) the development of unhealthy, sedentary life-styles
   b) the increase in environmental pollution
   c) affluence for the many
   d) stress

6. Which of the following is a contagious disease?
   a) heart disease
   b) cancer
   c) AIDS
   d) obesity

7. If someone is so disturbed that coping with routine, everyday life is difficult or impossible, he or she:
   a) has a mental disorder
   b) suffers from mental illness
   c) is personally maladjusted
   d) labeled medically insane

118

8. Which of the following types of persons is most likely to be mentally ill?
   a) men
   b) married persons
   c) rural residents
   d) the poor

9. Poor people have more health problems than others because:
   a) poor people do not care about their health
   b) they cannot keep themselves adequately fed
   c) the federal government provides the wrong kind of support
   d) they differ genetically

10. If someone breaks tacit rules that govern our daily behavior without some socially acceptable reasons, he or she could be:
    a) disorganized
    b) physically ill
    c) labeled mentally ill
    d) eccentric or magical

11. All of the following are environmental explanations of mental disorders, EXCEPT for:
    a) biological theory
    b) learning theory
    c) labeling theory
    d) stress theory

12. Recently, Americans have experienced a rise in the incidence of measles and mini-epidemics due to:
    a) new variations of these diseases
    b) environmental pollution and other hazards
    c) immigration of many unhealthy persons
    d) declining federal support for health programs

13. Which of the following statements about mental disorders is an alternative to the medical model?
    a) Mental disorders represent problems of personal maladjustments.
    b) Mental disorders are caused by demons and devils.
    c) Biological defects cause most forms of mental illness,
    d) Drugs are effective cures of most mental disorders

14, Early childhood development theories of mental disorders:
    a) are now widely accepted
    b) focus on biological causes
    c) have been criticized for being too vague
    d) have been criticized for emphasizing childhood too much

15. American physicians are poorly distributed to help all of the following people except:
    a) people in poor neighborhoods
    b) men with specific medical problems
    c) people in need of primary care
    d) ethnic minorities

119

16. The American health care system is in crisis because:
    a) it fails to provide care to the poor
    b) it fails to provide sufficient primary care
    c) it cannot control runaway costs
    d) all of the above

17. The "working class" of medical professions are:
    a) doctors
    b) physician's assistants
    c) patients
    d) nurses

18. According to Coleman and Cressey, one reason why the costs of medical care are increasing almost uncontrollably is:
    a) the dramatic increase in illness
    b) cheating by doctors
    c) the fee-for-service system
    d) government gifts to medical institutions

19. Which of the following statements bout the American health care system is true?
    a) America's health care system is the best in the world.
    b) Americans are healthier than persons from other countries.
    c) Americans have the longest life expectancies.
    d) The American health system is the most expensive in the world.

20. Most hospitals today are _____ owned.
    a) corporate
    b) government
    c) publicly
    d) church

21. If a woman is hired to take the place of an infertile wife she is called a:
    a) mid-wife
    b) surrogate mother
    c) prostitute
    d) legal mother

22. If a doctor promotes school courses in nutrition and personal hygiene and pushes campaigns against excessive use of tobacco and alcohol, he or she is practicing:
    a) scientific medicine
    b) holistic medicine
    c) traditional medicine
    d) preventive medicine

23. If a doctor focuses on a patient's overall mental, emotional, and physical condition, he or she is taking a _____ approach.
    a) holistic
    b) preventive
    c) traditional
    d) ritualist

120

24. Who pays the biggest share of the health care bill?
   a) doctors
   b) patients
   c) government
   d) hospitals

25. Canada and Britain have:
   a) private health care systems
   b) national health care systems
   c) more disease than America
   d) doctor-sponsored health care

26. Which of the following types of medical practitioner is more needed today?
   a) psychiatrists
   b) surgeons
   c) nurse's aides
   d) general practitioners

27. Which of the following is NOT the type of basic service provided by community mental health centers?
   a) laboratory services
   b) short-term hospitalization
   c) emergency care for special problems
   d) educational services for the community at large

28. Viewed functionally, the jumbled health care system is a result of:
   a) the rapid development of medical technology
   b) its service to the rich and powerful
   c) ignoring emotional needs at the expense of physical needs
   d) unhealthy habits and life-styles

29. Which of the following proposals to change the health care system reflects a conflict perspective?
   a) a concerted campaign of education and social changed
   b) better organization of health care services
   c) the end of the medical model of illness
   d) government-financed health care that is available without charge

30. Social psychological research is the foundation for the popular notion that effective medical care should meet patients' _____ needs.
   a) financial
   b) dietary
   c) emotional
   d) physical

PROJECTS

PROJECT 6.1 Who Will Pay?

As Coleman and Cressey pointed out, the high cost of health care in the United States is a significant social problem. One reason this is important is that the high cost determines the extent to which all members of society can receive adequate health care. Second, the high cost of health care affects the way that other social institutions function and how they meet social needs. third, solving the high-cost issue may have implications for the way in which our entire health-care system operates, thus affecting the medical profession, other health care organizations and businesses, and the economy. The objective of this project is to have you examine the implications of high health care costs, how they affect society, and how various alternatives to our current health care system will affect society.

Journal instructions:

1. Discuss with your parents, spouse, or other family members the percentage of your family's annual income that goes toward health-care insurance. If your family does not have health care insurance, what percentage of its annual income is generally spent on health care? Think about and discuss in your journal how your family has been and will continue to adjust to increasing health care costs.

2. Health care reform is a major political issue. Many policies have been suggested by politicians from both parties regarding how health care will be paid for and the organization of the health care system itself. Look through current and past issues of newspapers, magazines, and journals (use your library's indexes to help you locate appropriate articles) to identify at least two policies that have been proposed to deal with the cost of health care in the United States during recent years. In your journal, briefly outline what each of these policies proposes and where the proposal comes from.

3. For each policy, think about and discuss in your journal what the implications are for your family, for the medical profession, and for health care in general if it were adopted.

4. Interview two physicians and two federal, state, or local politicians (on Republican and one Democrat) about the high cost of health care. Ask them what they think about the policies that you identified and discussed above. Also, ask them what they think could be done to deal with the high cost of health care in the United States. Finally, ask them if they think that there is a health care crisis in the U.S. and if so, what should be done about it. Record all of their responses in your journal.

5. Review the sociological perspectives on health care as discussed in chapter 8. In your journal, discuss the relevance of each perspective to each of the policies you identified (above).

Option: essay

Write an essay (around four pages, typed) in which you evaluate the merit of each of the policies you identified (above). Be sure your discussion includes each of the following items:
    a) an explanation of each of the policies you identified (above);
    b) how the sociological perspectives are relevant to each theory;

PROJECT INSTRUCTIONS ARE CONTINUED ON THE FOLLOWING PAGE.

c) the views of those you interviewed;

d) your position, **based upon your research**, on which health care policy should be adopted.

Option: bibliography

Use your library's indexes (or any other indexes, such as computerized searches) to develop a bibliography of ten to fifteen articles from popular periodicals and sociology journals and/or sociology books that discuss the health care crisis in American society and/or health care reforms that have been accomplished in other countries. Additionally, locate two or three seb sites that deal with issues related to health care problems in the US and/ or globally. Try to find articles that provide arguments for and/or against the policies you identified in your journal (above). Type your bibliography following the format found in one of the sociology journals.

Option: research paper

Write a paper (around seven pages, typed) in which you use the results of your field journal, essay, and bibliography in which you:

a) discuss each health care policy you identified;

b) present the arguments for and against each policy, including a discussion of the implications for society and the health care system;

c) support a position about one or more of the policies;

d) integrate at least five items from your bibliography and material from your field journal;

e) provide proper documentation of your sources throughout your paper and include a reference page.

HINT: If you have already written the essay portion of this project, use it as a rough draft for your research paper. Use items from your bibliography to develop the arguments and discussions you already began in your essay.

PROJECT 6.2 A Cross Cultural Look at Health Care Systems

The United States is one of the wealthiest countries in the world and spends the most on health care than any other country, yet more than thirty percent of its population does not get they health care they need. The objective of this project is to look at health-care systems in other countries and to evaluate whether or not they are useful models that can be applied to the U.S.

Journal instructions:
1. Interview two people who are visiting or who has moved to the U.S. from a foreign country in which government plays a greater role in health care than in the United States (for example, Great Britain, Canada, China, Japan, or Sweden): international exchange students, visiting professor on your campus, or someone you know. Discuss with the person the way in which the health care system in his or her country operates. Keep notes about your discussion in your journal. Here are some question to help get your started:

      a) How expensive is health care in your country? (Discuss some specific types of health care, such as the cost of having a baby, a pediatric exam, a physical, a dental visit, and so on, and compare with the U.S.)

      b) Do people have to pay for health care insurance? What portion does the government pay? Who pays?

      c) Is health care operated on a fee-for-service basis?

      d) To what extent is health care operated by private health-care practitioners and by the government?

      e) In general, how is the quality of health care?

      f) How long do you have to wait in order to obtain health care for an immediate problem or illness?

      g) How long do you have to wait to obtain health care for an elective procedure such as cosmetic surgery?

      h) In general, how is the cost and quality of health care perceived by the people who live in that country?

Option: essay
Using material you obtained from your interview, write an essay (around four pages, typed) in which you evaluate and compare the way in which health care is practiced in the U.S. with that of countries where the government plays a larger role.

Option: bibliography
Develop a bibliography of around ten articles and/or books, and two or three web sites, about health care in the countries of the people you interviewed for your field journal (above). Make sure that at least five of the items are articles from sociology journals or books written by sociologists. Type your bibliography following the format found in one of the sociology journals.

Option: research paper
Write a paper (around five to seven pages, typed) in which you compare health care systems in the U.S. with countries in which government plays a larger role in health care. Some things you might discuss include the following: Describe the way the health care systems in the U.S. work and the health care systems in the other countries you selected. What are the advantages and disadvantages of each for individuals, society, health care practitioners, and so on? What are the functions and dysfunctions of each? Would the other health-care systems work in the U.S? Why or why not? What types of changes would occur in our present system if the other ones were enacted here?

PROJECT 6.3 Comparing Different Types of Healing

Besides the dominant health care system in the United States made up of physicians, hospitals, nurses, and other supporting staff, there are a variety of other health care practitioners—such as chiropractors, osteopaths, Christian Science practitioners, mid-wives, acupuncturists, Native American healers, and others—that take a different approach to healing. The objective of this project is to have you examine some of these alternative forms of health care.

Journal instructions:
1. Interview four health care practitioners who are not part of the dominant health-care system in the United States, such as those mentioned above. Ask each to discuss what their views on health an illness are, how their views and practices are different from the dominant health care approach and some examples of how they would treat various types of illness and disease. Record their responses in your journal.

2. As the people you interview for any brochures, pamphlets, or other literature that they may have that describes their approach to health cares. Keep this material with your journal.

3. Interview a physician who is around forty years of age, one who is around fifty years of age, and one who is around sixty or older. Ask them to respond to and discuss the approaches and views of the above health care practitioners whom you interviewed. Record their responses in your journal.

Option: essay
Write an essay (around five pages, typed) in which you use the functionalist, conflict and social psychological perspectives on health and illness to discuss and compare the various types of health care for which you obtained information through your interviews, above.

Option: bibliography
Develop a bibliography of ten to fifteen articles from sociology journals and/or sociology books that discuss one of the alternative forms of healing (that is, other than the dominant health care system) that you discussed in your journal. Additionally, locate two or three web sites that deal with alternative forms of healing. Type your bibliography following the format found in one of the sociology journals.

Option: research paper
Write a paper (around five to seven pages, typed) in which you discuss a brief history of an alternative form of healing, the way in which it is practiced and organized, the types of practitioners who are involved, the social context out of which it emerged, the way in which practitioners are socialized into the practice, and how it could possibly be a means of addressing health-related social problems today. Provide proper documentation throughout your paper and include a reference page.

PROJECT 6.4 Using Sociological Perspectives to Explore Controversial Health Care Issues

The battle between "pro-choice" and "pro-life" advocates (political and civic leaders, religious leaders, members of activist groups, and so on) has become intense and emotionally charged. When an issue becomes emotionally charged, people often have a difficult time examining it from any perspective other than their own. The objective of this project is to put your personal and emotional views aside and to look at the various sides of the abortion controversy from sociological perspectives.

Journal instructions:
1. Interview three "pro-live" and three "pro-choice" advocates on your campus or in your community. For each find out their gender, race, highest level of education, religion, occupation, marital status, age, political party, and (if possible) income level. Ask them the following questions and record the responses in your journal:
    a) Why do you feel abortion should be (legal) (illegal)?
    b) What do you feel are the major considerations in the debate over legalized abortion?
    c) Why do you think the debate is so controversial and why does it persist?
    d) What are your views about pre-marital sex?
    e) Do you feel that sex is primarily for procreation or for pleasure?
    f) Do you feel that women should have the same employment opportunities as men?
    g) Do you feel that women should be equal to men in rights and responsibilities in the family?
    h) Who do you think should be primarily responsible for taking care of the children in a family: mother, father, both?

2. In your journal, analyze the responses to the questions from the point of view of the functionalist, conflict, feminist, and interactionist perspectives. How would each explain or approach the issue? What would each say the controversy is really about and why it exists?

Option: essay
Write an essay (around four pages, typed) in which you discuss the abortion debate from the point of view of each of the four major sociological perspectives: functionalist, conflict, feminist, and interactionist. Use information, quotes, and ideas that you collected in your field journal (above) to help you illustrate your ideas and to help you get your point across.

Option: bibliography
Develop a bibliography of six articles from popular periodicals (newspapers, magazines, and so on) and six articles from sociology journals and/or sociology books within the past decade that contain debates or discussions about the abortion controversy. Include an equal number of articles that support and oppose abortion. Use the *Reader's Guide to Periodical Literature*, the *Social Science Index*, or other library or computerized indexes to help you find your sources. Additionally, identify two or three web sites that deal with the abortion controversy. Type the bibliography following the format found in one of the sociology journals.

Option: research paper
Using the information from your field journal, library research, and essay (above), write a paper (around five to seven pages, typed) in which you present well-organized, balanced arguments for keeping abortion legal and for making abortion illegal. Use the sociological perspectives as a framework to organize the data that you have collected and to develop your positions for and against legalized abortion. Use at least six sources from your bibliography. Be sure to leave your personal feelings and emotions out of the positions for and against legalized abortion.

CHAPTER 7

THE POOR

CHAPTER OUTLINE

The Rich and the Poor: A Widening Gap

Measuring Poverty
> Who Are the Poor?
> The Trends in Poverty

The Life of Poverty
> The Homeless
> The Underclass
> The Working Poor

Understanding the Welfare System
> Attitudes Toward the Poor
> The History of the Welfare System
> The Attack on Welfare
> The Current Welfare System

Explanations of Poverty
> Economic Explanations
> Political Explanations
> Cultural Explanations

Solving the Problems of Poverty
> More and Better Jobs
> Improving Welfare
> Distributing the Wealth More Fairly
> Organizing the Poor

Sociological Perspectives on the Problems of the Poor
> The Functionalist Perspective
> The Conflict Perspective
> The Feminist Perspective
> The Interactionist Perspective

CHAPTER LEARNING OBJECTIVES AND ESSAY QUESTIONS

After studying this chapter, you should be able to:

• Explain how the modern industrial economy produces both fantastic wealth and extensive poverty.

• Discuss the increasing gap between the rich and the poor.

• Analyze how sociologists measure poverty and determine who are the poor.

• Describe the profound psychological and sociological consequences of being poor in American society.

• Outline and discuss components of the welfare system, including attitudes toward the poor, the structure of the welfare system, and the recent changes to the welfare system.

• State and compare the several explanations of poverty.

• Contrast and compare sociological perspectives on problems of the poor.

KEY POINTS FOR REVIEW

• The American industrial economy has produced huge wealth for some while at the same time leaving a large amount of poverty. The gap between the "haves" and the "have-nots" has been steadily and significantly growing in American society since the 1970s. The United States has the biggest gap between the rich and the poor and the highest poverty rate of any developed nation. There are a number of reasons. First, the recent stagnation of the economy has prevented the poor from improving their standard of living. Second, foreign competition has placed the U.S. worker in direct competition with workers who receive far lower wages. Third, the use of technology has reduced well paying jobs for skilled laborers. Fourth, taxes on the rich have been substantially reduced.

• There is some disagreement over the definition of poverty. The relative approach holds that people are poor if they have significantly less income and wealth than the average person in their society—that is, they are psychologically and sociologically excluded from the mainstream of society. The absolute approach—the most widely used approach by government agencies and social scientists—divides the poor from the non-poor by using some fixed standard such as the lack of money to purchase a minimum amount of living essentials.

• Definitions of poverty are used to discover which segments of society are the poorest and to measure changes in the poverty population. Currently, single mothers with children are the fastest growing segment of the poverty population. Poverty declined sharply in the 1960s, due to national economic prosperity and the government's War on Poverty, but has increased again today.

• There are numerous psychological and sociological consequences of poverty including feelings of inadequacy, lack of education, limited vocabulary, psychosomatic illnesses, violent crime, economic uncertainty, higher rates of family instability, second-rate health care, deficient

128

diets, inadequate shelter, higher rate of infant mortality, a shorter life span, and homelessness. While it is impossible to know how many people are homeless at any one time, homelessness appears to be increasing especially among families. Almost one half of all homeless people have a substance-abuse problem, but one in five has a full or part-time job. Some reasons for homelessness include the de-institutionalization of the mentally ill, inadequate income from dead-end jobs, a reduction of government-subsidized housing, and increases in the cost of rental housing.

• North Americans have a history that includes a tremendous faith in the value of hard work and competition which led to an ideology of individualism that holds each person responsible for his or her own economic destiny. Thus, most people explain poverty by blaming the poor themselves rather than with possible structural structural explanation. The ideology of individualism has had enormous implications on the way the welfare system has been shaped, the way it is perceived by the public and the government, and the types of reforms it is currently undergoing.

• There are three categories of explanations of poverty: those based on an analysis of economic structures, those based on an analysis of the culture of the poor, and those based on an analysis of political relationships among power groups. Explanations based on an analysis of economic structures focus around the simple fact of low wages and too few jobs for those at the bottom of the social hierarchy. Despite fluctuations in the economy, the trend is toward increasing unemployment. Further, upswings in the economy benefit the poor much less than the higher social classes. The structure of capitalism and an open competitive market inevitably creates a huge gap between the rich and the poor.

• Political explanations contend that poverty is as much a political problem as it is an economic one. From this view, a high degree of inequality exists because many Americans—with their ideology of individualism—seem to have little concern about the conditions of the poor, and those who do are not politically organized. Politicians win votes more by promising to eliminate crime and curtail taxes rather than by promising to develop programs to eliminate poverty.

• The cultural explanations of poverty hold that a culture of poverty, passed down from generation to generation, provides people with values and attitudes that make it very difficult for them to escape their condition.

• While it may not be possible to eliminate poverty in an absolute sense, many other industrialized nations have made much greater progress than the United States. Some responses to the problem of poverty include creating more jobs that pay a living wage, new education and job training programs, improving the welfare system in such a way that it helps people get off of welfare without penalizing them, keeping track of absent fathers, improving the welfare system through administrative reforms, and organizing the poor so that they have some political power.

• The functionalist perspective sees poverty as the result of malfunctions in the economy. Specifically, rapid industrialization has disrupted the economic system leaving it disorganized and unable to perform many of its essential functions. The ultimate consequence is that people lack the job skills to perform new jobs or they become unnecessary. Functionalists argue that the best way to deal with poverty is to reorganize the economic system and the social service agencies so they operate more efficiently and integrate the poor into the mainstream of economic life.

• The conflict perspective sees poverty as a result of the middle and upper classes wanting it to exist. That is, the working poor are exploited so that their employers can make fatter profits. The middle and upper classes also rely on the ideology of individualism to exploit and blame the poor for their condition. From the conflict perspective, the way to deal with poverty is through political action which gives a stronger voice to the poor.

• Feminists were among the first to point out what has been termed the "feminization of poverty." The feminist perspective sees this long-term trend in our society for poverty to be concentrated among women and children as a result of the instability of the family and increases in the number of single mothers raising their children alone.

• The interactionist perspective holds that poor people learn to behave in the ways society expects of them and that the culture of poverty is passed on to children thus directing them into lives of poverty. This perspective also studies the psychological effects of being poor in a wealthy society. Interactionists agree that in order to overcome the psychological and cultural consequences of poverty, there must be more opportunities of the poor and their children and the poor must be encouraged to redefine their social environment and develop positive self images.

NOTES:

KEY TERMS

The following key terms are found in your textbook on the page number indicated in parentheses. In the space provided, write a brief definition of the key term **in your own words**. Then **provide an example** of the term, such as a culture in which the practice takes place, or people that you might know whose behavior illustrates the term, a current event that illustrates the term, how a term could be used to shed light on or help solve a particular social problem, and so on. You could include examples from the news, books, movies, or anything else that will illustrate the term and help you remember it. Include any comments from your class discussions or textbook that might help you remember and understand these key terms. Use additional paper if necessary, but keep it with your study guide to help you review for exams.

income (p. 217)

_____

_____

_____

_____

wealth (p. 217)

_____

_____

_____

_____

poverty (p. 219)

_____

_____

_____

_____

absolute approach (p. 219)

_____

_____

_____

relative approach (p. 219)

_____

_____

_____

_____

underclass (p. 224)

_____

_____

_____

ideology of individualism (p. 228)

_____

_____

_____

_____

Aid to Families with Dependent Children (AFDC) (p. 229)

_____

_____

_____

_____

Social Security (p. 231)

_____

_____

_____

_____

132

Temporary Aid to Needy Families (p. 231)

_____

_____

_____

_____

Supplemental Security Income (SSI) (p. 232)

_____

_____

_____

_____

food stamp program (p. 232)

_____

_____

_____

_____

Medicare (p. 232)

_____

_____

_____

_____

Medicaid (p. 232)

_____

_____

_____

_____

family allowance (p. 233)

_____

_____

_____

_____

culture of poverty (p.235)

_____

_____

_____

_____

noncategorical programs (p. 239)

_____

_____

_____

_____

feminization of poverty (p. 240)

_____

_____

_____

_____

situationalists (p. 236)

_____

_____

_____

_____

PRACTICE TEST

Multiple Choice

1. Which of the following statements about the modern industrial economy is true?
   a) Few Americans actually live in poverty.
   b) The modern industrial economy has virtually eliminated poverty as it is defined by social scientists and the government.
   c) Poverty is a basic characteristic of industrialized society.
   d) Americans provide widespread support for the poor.

2. Examining the distribution of wealth in American society is difficult because:
   a) the numbers of people who have wealth is too large to measure
   b) some types of wealth are hard to measure
   c) wealth is not reported on in a regular way
   d) it is concentrated in the hands of a few

3. The value of a person's total assets is that person's:
   a) wealth
   b) income
   c) level of affluence
   d) relative worth

4. Wealth is more unequally distributed than income because:
   a) most wealth is held in secret
   b) America has little wealth left
   c) most people are not interested in accumulating wealth
   d) wealth is passed on from one generation to another

5. The distribution of income in the United States is:
   a) relatively equal when compared with other industrialized nations
   b) not measurable
   c) extremely unequal and becoming increasingly so
   d) more equal than most other societies

6. All of the following statements about the distribution of wealth in the U.S. are true, EXCEPT that:
   a) the distribution of wealth and income does not constitute a social problem
   b) the gap between the rich and the poor widened during the 1980s
   c) the United States has the biggest gap between rich and poor of all industrialized countries
   d) the infant mortality rate is higher in the U.S.

7. Which of the following is a force that contributes to the inequality of American society?
   a) the reduction of taxes on the rich
   b) foreign competition
   c) economic stagnation
   d) all of the above

135

8. Contrary to popular stereotypes, most poor people in the U.S. are:
   a) white
   b) black
   c) urban
   d) old

9. The _____ approach of defining poverty emphasizes whether one has significantly less income and wealth than the average person.
   a) relative
   b) absolute
   c) sociological
   d) industrialized

10. About two-thirds of all families below the poverty line are:
    a) black
    b) headed by single parents
    c) elderly
    d) headed by two parents

11. Most critics feel that the figure used by the government to measure poverty:
    a) is a little low
    b) is accurate in most but not all cases
    c) significantly underestimates the amount of poverty
    d) significantly overestimates the amount of poverty

12. While there is less poverty in the U.S. than thirty years ago:
    a) children as a whole do not suffer the effects of poverty
    b) being poor in America is not as difficult as before
    c) many more older people are now poor
    d) the problems associated with poverty have gotten far worse

13. The poorest of poor people are called:
    a) lower class
    b) homeless
    c) working poor
    d) underclass

14. All of the following are reasons why homelessness has increased, EXCEPT:
    a) a massive increase in poverty
    b) de-institutionalization of the mentally ill
    c) indifference of the federal government
    d) increases in the cost of rental housing

15. Many people believe that economic failure is an individual's own fault. This belief is part of America's:
    a) empathy toward the poor
    b) explanation of structural explanation
    c) ideology of individualism
    d) structure of industrialization

136

16. Counting the number of homeless persons is difficult because:
    a) homeless people move all the time
    b) few people see an importance in knowing the total number
    c) by definition, we do not know where the homeless live
    d) political groups have tried to influence estimates

17. Many people who work full-time are officially poor because:
    a) they cannot mange their funds
    b) the minimum wage is not enough to keep a family out of poverty
    c) taxes are too high to escape poverty
    d) they have too many children to support

18. All of the following are economic explanations of poverty, EXCEPT:
    a) low wages
    b) too few jobs for the poor
    c) a variety of local conditions
    d) the culture of poverty

19. Which of the following is a myth about the welfare system?
    a) Welfare benefits are meager and getting worse.
    b) Many poor people get nothing at all from the welfare system.
    c) Welfare programs in all states bring people to the poverty line.
    d) The U.S. is third from the bottom in percent of national spending on welfare programs.

20. Which of the following is part of the 1960s part of the history of welfare?
    a) meeting the crisis of the Great Depression
    b) a modest increase in welfare support for the poor
    c) the War on Poverty
    d) a drop in federal welfare spending

21. Those social scientists who feel that Jane is poor because she grew up in a poor neighborhood, had sexual relations and was married at an early age, and lived in a weak an unstable family unit are using WHICH explanation of poverty?
    a) structural unemployment
    b) the culture of poverty
    c) the functions of poverty
    d) the homeless problem

22. Programs of mandatory employment for welfare recipients is called:
    a) the culture of poverty
    b) employer of last resort
    c) workfare
    d) welfare

23. One of the reasons why many middle class and wealthy people do little about poverty is because, for them, poverty is:
    a) valuable
    b) invisible
    c) non-existent
    d) inevitable

137

24. One way to reduce administrative waste in welfare is to:
    a) institute tougher investigations
    b) develop elaborate workfare programs
    c) use more computers
    d) provide some services for all citizens

25. European countries widely use _____ to reduce unemployment.
    a) stimulation of the national economy
    b) political protest
    c) welfare payments
    d) job retraining

26. Which of the following is a program designed to guarantee annual income?
    a) employer of last resort
    b) negative income tax
    c) positive income tax
    d) workfare

27. Sociological research has shown that programs to help the poor are created only when:
    a) the middle class begins to care
    b) the poor help themselves
    c) the poor organize and demand more
    d) welfare employees decide to raise benefits

28. From the social psychological point of view, poverty is clearly:
    a) the result of exploitation
    b) a failure of socialization
    c) the result of disorganization
    d) not a personal problem

29. According to the functionalist perspective, the major problem with welfare is:
    a) the undeserving poor
    b) too few resources
    c) disorganization
    d) failure to follow a political mandate

30. The argument that poverty exists because the middle and upper classes want it to exist is consistent with WHICH sociological explanation?
    a) the functionalist perspective
    b) the conflict perspective
    c) the interactionist perspective
    d) the feminist perspective

PROJECTS

PROJECT 7.1 How Much Does it Cost to Live? Why is There Poverty?

Many Americans believe that the poor are responsible for their own poverty. However, a significant number of poor people work, but earn too little to bring them out of poverty. In 1991, the U.S. Government defined the poverty level at $12,812 and in 1995 changed it to $14,333 for a family of four. Besides being an indicator of the number of people who are officially poor in the United States, this figure is one of the measures used to determine if people are eligible for particular forms of government assistance. Does this figure reflect what it costs a family of four to live in today's society? Are people poor because they do not work hard enough? The objective of this activity is to have you explore answers to these questions and to examine how much it costs for a family to live.

Journal instructions:
1. Prepare a budget of expenses for a family of four to live in the city in which you currently reside. Proceed as follows:
    a) Make three columns on a sheet of paper in your journal or notebook.
    b) Label the first column "budget items." In this column, list all of the items that have to be paid for each month. These include, but are not limited to, the following: housing (rent or mortgage), utilities (gas, electric, water), telephone, medical care (office visits, drugs, insurance), food, clothing, transportation (car payments, insurance, gas, other transportation expenses), education, and so on. Think about this list carefully and include any other items that should be on the list. You may want to ask your parents or someone who pays their family's bill for suggestions of what to include on this list.
    c) Label the second column "minimum monthly expense." In this column, estimate for each item in the first column what you think the absolute minimum monthly expense for that item would be. That is, what is the bare minimum that you think a family of four could spend on that item.
    d) Label the third column "projected monthly expense." In this column, take a more realistic approach. Estimate the expense that you think a family of four of which you are a member is <u>likely</u> to incur each month.

2. Using your monthly budget estimates, calculate the total annual expense. (That is, add up each column and multiply by twelve.) Based upon your budget estimates, these figures indicate the net income, that is income after taxes are taken out, that a family of four needs to meet their minimum living expenses and your projected living expenses.

3. Considering these estimates, how appropriate is the government's figure for the poverty level?

4. How many full time, minimum wage jobs would it take to meet the needs of each of the budgets you estimated?

5. Based upon your budget, what would the minimum wage per hour have to be for a person to support a family of four? What would it have to be for two people to support a family of four?

PROJECT INSTRUCTIONS ARE CONTINUED ON THE FOLLOWING PAGE.

6. <u>In light of your findings</u>, think about and discuss in your journal why people are poor. Are people poor, as many Americans believe, because they are not determined enough to work?

Option: essay
Reread the sections in chapter 7 about explanations of poverty. Write an essay (around three to five pages, typed) in which you use your journal material and information found in chapter 6 to discuss why there are so many poor families in the United States.

Option: bibliography
Develop a bibliography of ten to fifteen articles from sociology journals and/or sociology books that discuss the causes of poverty. Type your bibliography following the format found in one of the sociology journals.

Option: research paper
Write a paper (around seven pages, typed) in which you use material from your field journal (above) and at least four items from your bibliography to discuss the reasons for poverty in the U.S. today. As part of your paper, evaluate the different explanations of poverty discussed in your text and discuss the relationship between poverty and the nature of employment in the U.S. Be sure to base your analysis on your journal observations and items in your bibliography. Use proper documentation throughout your paper and include a reference page.

PROJECT 7.2 Life Chances and Inequality

A person's social class position can greatly his or her life chances—the opportunities one has to improve his or her income or lifestyle. Whether one is poor or wealthy often is greatly affected by their social class. The objective of this activity is to have you examine how social class position of a family affects its members' life chances.

Journal instructions:
1. Locate two or three introduction to sociology textbooks. If you do not have one, look in your college or local library, ask a sociology professor if you can borrow a few, or ask to borrow one from students who have taken introduction to sociology. Read the chapter in the introduction to sociology textbook on social stratification and pay particular attention to the sections that discuss the relationship between social class position and life chances. Most introductory sociology books discuss this. Additionally, reread the section in Coleman and Cressey in chapter one that discusses social class.

2. Think about and list in your journal all of the ways in which peoples' social class positions can affect (positively or negatively) their life chances and opportunities (for example, housing, medical care, life expectancy, education, employment, mate selection, family stability, justice, and so on).

3. For each item in your list, write two or three sentences on how a family's social class position can affect a person's life chances. Then, discuss how your family's social class position has affected your life chances.

4. After you complete the above steps, identify and locate a lower class, middle class, and an upper class neighborhood in the area where you live. By yourself or with one of your classmates, observe each neighborhood for two or three hours. Try to observe each neighborhood at approximately the same time of day. (If possible, do your observation with someone who is from a different social class position than you. You will be able to share important insights with each other that you might not see if you were on your own). Keep a journal in which you record your observations about everyday life in the neighborhoods. The following is a list of some items you can focus on, but do not feel limited to this list:
    a) the types and conditions of the houses;
    b) the types and conditions of the automobiles;
    c) the condition of the schools, inside and out;
    d) the condition of the public parks;
    e) the condition of the roads;
    f) the types of stores, their condition, the types of products available, and the quality of the products;
    g) the hospitals and medical facilities;
    h) the amount of police protection or police surveillance.

5. After you complete your observations, discuss the impact of social class position on people's life chances and opportunities in both communities that you observed.

PROJECT INSTRUCTIONS ARE CONTINUED ON THE FOLLOWING PAGE.

Option: essay
Read the chapters on socialization from one or two of the introduction to sociology textbooks that you located. Using information from those chapters (theories about socialization and other ideas) and examples from your journal observations (above), write an essay (around five pages, typed) in which you discuss how social class position affects a person's life chances, opportunities, and sense of self. If you wish, you can make your self the focus of this essay.

Option: bibliography
Using the library's indexes, construct a bibliography of fifteen to twenty articles (primarily from social science journals) and books about how social class position affects people's life chances and opportunities. Use key words, phrases, or ideas such as stratification, housing, educational attainment, family stability, life expectancy, and others in your search through the library's references, indexes, and other resources. Additionally, locate two or three web sites that deal with these issues. Type your bibliography using the style found in the journals or in your textbook.

Option: research paper
Write a paper (around seven to ten pages, typed) in which you integrate your journal discussions (above) and at least four items from your bibliography to discuss how **your** family's position in the stratification system has affected your life chances, your socialization, and your sense of self. You can use the bibliographic material in a variety of ways. For example, use it to help you explain how various aspects of social class position have affected your life; or you might use examples from your life to illustrate some of the ideas found in your library research material. Be sure to cite all of your bibliographic references properly in your paper, and include a reference (works cited) page.

PROJECT 7.3 Homelessness

There are a number of perspectives and explanations about homelessness, as you have read in Chapter 7. The objective of this activity is to help you gain some insights about why people are homeless and to help you overcome some of the myths about homelessness.

Journal instructions:
1. Interview five people who are not experts in understanding the nature of homelessness. For example, interview some of your friends, your parents, neighbors, and so on. Ask them the following questions and record their answers in your journal:
   a) Do you personally know anyone who is homeless, that is, who sleeps on the streets, in a homeless shelter, in a car, or somewhere else besides a home?
   b) Why do you think that most people who are homeless are so?
   c) What do you think are some typical characteristics of homeless people?
   d) Do you think that all people could find a place to live if they really wanted to?

2. Locate and read four or five articles, essays, or letters to the editor about homelessness that appeared in newspapers or news magazines during the past year. In your journal, summarize the views about homelessness portrayed in the articles, essays, or letters.

3. Visit a homeless shelter in your area. Observe it for one or two hours on three separate occasions and at different times of the day (morning, midday, and night). Talk to as many of the people there as you can. Ask them why they are there and what conditions led them to become homeless. Also, talk to the director of the homeless shelter. Ask the director if homelessness is increasing in the area and the reasons for the increase or decrease in homelessness. Record these discussions in your journal.

4. In your journal, compare the views of the people that you first interviewed about homelessness, the views you found in the newspapers, and your observations and discussions at the homeless shelter.

Option: essay
Write an essay (around four to five pages, typed) in which you discuss popular conceptions about homelessness with the realities of homelessness that you observed.

Option: bibliography
Use bibliographic indexes (from your library, computer databases, and so on) to construct a bibliography of fifteen to twenty articles from sociology journals and/or books that discuss the extent of homelessness in the United States today and the reasons for it. Since there are many excellent current sociological articles that discuss homelessness, you should begin your search starting with the present and working your way back. Type your bibliography in proper bibliographic style.

Option: research paper
Write a paper (around seven pages, typed) in which you discuss the nature of homelessness today, the reasons for it as offered by social scientists, and a comparison of social science explanations for homelessness and popular views about homelessness. Use at least five of the articles and/or books from your bibliography (above). Be sure to provide proper documentation throughout your paper and include a reference page.

PROJECT 7.4 The Relationship Between Sociological Perspectives on Poverty and Political Viewpoints

Sociological perspectives on poverty and inequality—functionalist, conflict, and social psychological—provide very different explanations about the nature of inequality in the United States and why it exists. Some practical applications of these theories seem to exist within American politics. Although the political views of Republicans, Democrats, conservatives, and liberals are not necessarily based upon these theories precisely, there does seem to be a great deal of similarity between the political views and the theories. The objective of this project is to have you examine the theoretical bases of the different political views regarding inequality and to help provide you with a greater understanding of the theories that underlie government policies that affect the poor.

Journal instructions:
1. Review the sections in chapter seven of Coleman and Cressey's text about sociological perspectives on poverty. Additionally, review the sections in chapter 2 (problems of the economy) and chapter 3 (problems of government) that discuss the sociological perspectives. Finally, read the sections on theories of inequality from the chapter on inequality (stratification) from any current introduction to sociology text. In your journal, summarize the major arguments and explanations about poverty and inequality of each theoretical perspective.

2. Interview two people who are involved in or are knowledgeable about politics, for example, political science professors at your college and/or a local, state, or federal politicians. Discuss the following items with them and record their responses in your journal.
   a) Explain the functionalist, conflict, and social psychological perspectives on poverty to them.
   b) Ask them how each of these theories relates or compares to the views of Democrats and Republicans, and liberals and conservatives.
   c) Ask them for an example of an issue related to economic inequality or poverty in which Democrats and Republicans, or liberals and conservatives, have deeply divided views (for example, taxes, welfare reform, funding for education, minimum wage, and so on).

Option: essay
Write an essay (around four pages, typed) in which you use the information you gathered in your journal (above) to discuss some parallels between the views of the political parties (Democrat and Republican) or the political ideologies (liberal and conservative) and the sociological perspectives on poverty and inequality. Suggestion: Begin your essay with a general discussion of the similarities of each sociological perspective with each political position. Then you might want to briefly discuss how each perspective and each political position looks at two or three controversial issues regarding poverty and inequality.

Option: bibliography
Select one controversial issue regarding poverty or inequality that you wrote about in your essay or discussed in your journal (above). Develop a bibliography of fifteen to twenty articles, and two or three web sites, about the issue. Make sure that you bibliography contains a good balance between:
   a) items from popular periodicals (newspapers, new magazines, commentary magazines, and so on) that express represent each political viewpoint;

PROJECT INSTRUCTIONS ARE CONTINUED ON THE FOLLOWING PAGE.

b) articles from sociology journals and/or books (excluding the ones you used in your journal, above).

Type your bibliography following the format found in one of the sociology journals.

Option: research paper
Using your bibliographic research, your essay (above), and your journal (above) write a paper (around seven pages, typed) in which you:
   a) discuss and compare how each of the sociological perspectives views, explains, and would resolve the particular problem or issue related to poverty about which you developed your bibliography;
   b) discuss the relationship between the sociological perspectives about the issue you selected and the different political views toward that issue;
   c) illustrate your ideas and analysis with quotes and excerpts from your bibliographic sources and the interviews you conducted for your journal work (above).

Be sure to document all your sources throughout your paper and include a reference page.

CHAPTER 8

THE ETHNIC MINORITIES

CHAPTER OUTLINE

Ethnic Groups

        Patterns of Ethnic Relations
        A Melting Pot or a Salad Bowl?

Ethnic Minorities in North America
        Historical Background
        Institutional Inequality
                Education
                Employment
                Law and Justice
        Problems and Prospects
                Native Americans
                Europeans
                Jews
                African Americans
                Latinos
                Asians
                Mixed Backgrounds
        The Impact of Immigration

Explaining Ethnic Inequality
        Conflict and Competition
        Prejudice and Discrimination
                Cultural Theories
                Structural Theories
        Class

Solving the Problems of Ethnic Minorities
        Political Activism
        Reforming the Educational System
        Fair Employment
        Economic Justice

Sociological Perspectives of Ethnic Minorities
        The Functionalist Perspective
        The Conflict Perspective
        The Feminist Perspective
        The Interactionist Perspective

CHAPTER LEARNING OBJECTIVES AND ESSAY QUESTIONS

After studying this chapter, you should be able to:

• Discuss how ethnic violence and exploitation alarms many people.

• Define the concept of ethnic group and outline patterns of ethnic relations.

• Summarize the experiences of ethnic minorities in the United States.

• Outline and discuss the several ways sociologists have tried to explain ethnic inequality.

• Explain how American society is responding to the problems of ethnic minorities.

• Discuss how each of the different sociological perspectives explains the problems of ethnic minorities.

KEY POINTS FOR REVIEW

• Ethnic clashes have been part of every nation that has more than one ethnic group. While most industrialized nations today have a relatively stable system of ethnic relations, much ethnic injustice still exists below the surface.

• Ethnic group members—people who share a common set of cultural characteristics or a common national origin—tend to form an intense loyalty to the group. This is largely because their economic and social destiny is often tied up with that of their ethnic group and because they psychologically identify with the group.

• An ethnic group is considered a minority group when it suffers prejudice and discrimination at the hands of the dominant group in their society, not necessarily because it may be smaller in number than the dominant group.

• While a racial group may be an ethnic group, the concept of race is more a social idea than a biological fact. That is, the way a group's physical characteristics are classified and the meanings they are given are socially determined.

• Ethnocentrism—the attitude that one's own ethnic group is superior to others—is concerned with cultural differences between people and racism—the attitude of ethnic group superiority that leads to prejudice and discrimination—is concerned with physical differences between people.

• Three models of the general patterns of ethnic relations are domination, integration, and pluralism. Domination occurs when one ethnic group holds all the power, economically and politically dominating the others. Integration occurs when ethnic groups are basically equal, attending the same schools, working in the same businesses, and living in the same neighborhoods. In pluralism, different ethnic groups are equal, but are more separate and distinct in the living and working patterns.

• Each system of ethnic relations has its own source of instability. A system of domination must keep minorities weak and divided. When the balance of power changes, ethnic conflicts and violence can erupt. A pluralistic system can also lead to ethnic conflicts when one group feels it is not being treated fairly. With integration, distinctive ethnic characteristics may gradually be eroded.

• Three theories of what the relationship between immigrants to the U.S. are assimilation, the melting pot, and the salad bowl. Those who advocate assimilation feel that immigrants should conform to the standards of Anglo-American culture. The melting pot approach contends that immigrants should blend into a distinctively new culture blending their various ethnic backgrounds. The salad bowl idea holds that the U.S. works best as a diverse blend of "unmelted" subcultures, thus allowing each ethnic group to hold onto to its individual characteristics.

• Ethnic minorities have a long history in the United States. Native Americans (the Indians) inhabited North America when the first three groups of colonists from France, Britain, and Spain arrived. At first, relations between the Native Americans and the colonists were peaceful, but as the European colonists came to dominate the Indians, conflict developed. Conflict developed not only between Native Americans and the colonists, but between the colonists from different countries. The British came to dominate the other European and Native American minorities. The Native Americans suffered the most, losing most of their land and their population. By the turn of the nineteenth century, immigrants from Italy, Ireland, and the eastern European countries arrived. When they did not assimilate into British Protestant culture, ethnic tensions and hostilities arose.

• The history of Africans in North America is unique since they did not arrive of their own will and arrived in chains. Slave holders tried to extinguish the culture of the immigrant Africans by breaking up families, forbidding Africans from speaking their own language, and forcing them to abandon their native religions. When slavery finally was abolished, a system of rigid segregation existed in the Southern states and informal segregation existed in the rest of the country. By the 1960s, the system of formal segregation had been dismantled, but much informal segregation and prejudice remained.

• Ethnic minorities face a high degree of institutional inequality in North America, especially in education, employment, and the law. Blacks, Latinos, and Native Americans receive significantly less education than others. This is the result of economic and cultural domination. Many students still attend segregated classes as a result of segregated housing patterns in American cities. The cultural assumptions of the white middle class are built into today's schools—in standards of discipline, course materials, and language—creating behavioral as well as learning problems for some minority students. Additionally, differences in the value placed on education in the family structure of various ethnic groups affects student achievement.

• Members of minority groups are far more likely to have low-status and low-paying jobs. This may be explained by educational differences and as a result of cultural discrimination.

• Minorities have a history of being treated unfairly by the legal system, beginning when slaves were counted by the Government as only two-thirds of a person for congressional appointment and tax purposes. Blacks are more likely than whites to be arrested, brutalized by police, indicted, convicted, and committed to an institution.

148

• Despite the institutional inequality that ethnic minorities in general face, it would be misleading to lump all ethnic groups together. Each of North America's ethnic groups—the Native Americans, Anglo-Protestants, Irish, Italians, Jews, Polish, African Americans, Latinos, and Asians—has its own distinct problems and concerns.

• The large increase in immigrants and a major shift in the countries they come from is significantly changing the nature of ethnic relations in North America. Until the 1950s, most immigrants were from Europe or Canada, but in the last decade 85% came from Asia or Latin America. This influx—which is largely the result of immigrants seeking to escape the poverty of the Third World and likely to continue—is the topic of much controversy. On the one hand, new immigrants can provide labor and skills needed for today's economy. On the other hand, new immigrants often come into conflict with already established groups.

• Sociologists generally see three major factors that can explain ethnic inequality: conflict and competition, prejudice and discrimination, and class. Competition for control or resources, power, and prestige is likely to occur early in the history of relationships between most ethnic groups early in their co-existence. Military advantages often are transformed into economic and political advantages and, as time goes by, people may begin to accept the resulting inequality as the natural order of things.

• Prejudice and discrimination can be explained through psychological theories, cultural theories, and structural theories. Many psychologists believe that people with an authoritarian personality—people who are rigid, inflexible, and have a low tolerance for uncertainty—are the most likely to be prejudiced. Another psychological theory focuses on the use of minority groups as scapegoats for other people's problems. Cultural theories focus on how people learn prejudice—especially ethnic stereotypes—within the culture in which they are socialized. Structural theories focus on the way institutional discrimination takes place through a society's economic, political, and social activities, even when the individuals working in that system are not prejudiced.

• A third explanation of ethnic inequality says that ethnic inequality is not the result of prejudice and discrimination but the result of having a class system that passes along the burdens of past discrimination to minority children.

• There are a number of proposals aimed at achieving justice and fair treatment for ethnic minorities. One way is through political activism that places pressure on the government to help minorities. This has been especially evident for African and Native Americans. A second proposal is to reform the educational system to improve the academic performance of minority children and to help reduce the prejudices toward minorities that are taught to all students. A third way is to develop fair employment strategies, such as affirmative action programs, to create equal opportunities for minorities. The fourth proposal is to develop programs to reduce economic inequality. Each of these proposals has its adherents and its critics.

• Functionalists feel that although the various ethnic groups in North America have come to share many values, it lacks the unity, consensus, and organization that are essential to a harmonious society. From the functionalist perspective, ethnic discrimination is both a cause and an effect of contemporary social disorganization. The solution, functionalists argue, is to reduce discrimination by reorganizing our social institutions so that there is no discrimination in housing, education, criminal justice, and elsewhere.

• From the conflict perspective, the history of all ethnic relations is the history of a struggle for

149

power. Thus, conflict theorists argue that ethnic equality can be achieved only through struggle, primarily through increased political action.

• From the feminist perspective, there are similarities in the social position of women and ethnic minorities in our society. Both have been negatively stereotyped, subject to discrimination, and excluded from many areas of cultural life. Women of color face double jeopardy. Feminists share the views of minority activists to protect affirmative action programs.

• The interactionist perspective has focused primarily on the causes of prejudice and discrimination and their effects on individuals. The interactionists' proposals for reducing ethnic discrimination and prejudice fall into two broad categories. The first calls for efforts to eliminate ethnic stereotypes through greater ethnic contact and attacks on stereotypes through media and in schools. The second category includes proposals that attempt to go to the roots of the problem by recommending long-term changes to reduce ethnic competition and conflict such as developing more contacts and communication among ethnic groups of equal status.

NOTES:

KEY TERMS

The following key terms are found in your textbook on the page number indicated in parentheses. In the space provided, write a brief definition of the key term **in your own words**. Then **provide an example** of the term, such as a culture in which the practice takes place, or people that you might know whose behavior illustrates the term, a current event that illustrates the term, how a term could be used to shed light on or help solve a particular social problem, and so on. You could include examples from the news, books, movies, or anything else that will illustrate the term and help you remember it. Include any comments from your class discussions or textbook that might help you remember and understand these key terms. Use additional paper if necessary, but keep it with your study guide to help you review for exams.

ethnic group (p. 249)

_____

_____

_____

_____

ethnic minority (p. 250)

_____

_____

_____

_____

race (p. 250)

_____

_____

_____

_____

ethnocentrism (p. 250)

_____

_____

_____

racism (p. 250)

_____

_____

_____

_____

segregation (p. 251)

_____

_____

_____

_____

domination (p. 251)

_____

_____

_____

_____

integration (p. 251)

_____

_____

_____

_____

pluralism (p. 251)

_____

_____

_____

_____

assimilation (p. 252)

_____

_____

_____

_____

melting pot theory (p. 252)

_____

_____

_____

_____

salad bowl theory (p. 252)

_____

_____

_____

_____

prejudice (p. 268)

_____

_____

_____

_____

discrimination (p. 268)

_____

_____

_____

_____

authoritarian personality (p. 268)

_____

_____

_____

_____

scapegoat (p. 269)

_____

_____

_____

_____

ethnic stereotype (p. 270)

_____

_____

_____

_____

institutional discrimination (p. 270)

_____

_____

_____

_____

contrast conceptions (p. 270)

_____

_____

_____

_____

civil rights movement (p. 272)

_____

_____

_____

_____

eurocentric view (p. 273)

_____

_____

_____

_____

multicultural education (p. 274)

_____

_____

_____

_____

affirmative action (p. 274)

_____

_____

_____

_____

white backlash (p. 274)

_____

_____

_____

_____

155

reverse discrimination (p. 274)

_____

_____

_____

_____

NOTES:

156

PRACTICE TEST

Multiple Choice

1. The members of a group with a common set of cultural characteristics is called a
   _____ group.
   a) national
   b) minority
   c) ethnic
   d) racial

2. For sociologists, an ethnic minority is a:
   a) group that has fewer members than a majority group
   b) culturally distinctive group
   c) group that suffers prejudice and discrimination at the hands of the majority
   d) group with a common set of physical characteristics

3. The belief in the superiority of one racial group to another is called:
   a) prejudice
   b) racism
   c) ethnocentrism
   d) native stupidity

4. Which of the following is NOT one of the ideal patterns of ethnic group relations?
   a) ethnic assimilation
   b) the melting pot
   c) the salad bowl
   d) cultural separation

5. In a pluralistic system, ethnic groups:
   a) maintain a high degree of independence
   b) practice a policy of treating all individuals alike
   c) behave in opposition to cultural ideals
   d) suffer prejudice and discrimination

6. When different ethnic groups go to the same schools, work in the same businesses, and live in
   the same neighborhoods, they follow a pattern of:
   a) integration
   b) separatism
   c) pluralism
   d) the melting pot

7. As opposed to America, Canadian treaties with Indians were:
   a) rarely honored
   b) usually honored
   c) rarely negotiated
   d) made obsolete

8. Which of the following is NOT true about immigration to America during the 1980s?
   a) Much immigration was illegal and undocumented.
   b) Less than one million immigrants came overall.
   c) The largest number of immigrants came from Asia.
   d) Nearly one out of four Americans are now members of a non-European minority.

9. The history of Africans in North America is unique because these immigrants:
   a) came against their will
   b) were banned in 1924
   c) came from Europe
   d) practiced rigid segregation

10. The Irish, Italians, Jews, and Polish are all examples of:
    a) WASPS
    b) Native Americans
    c) white ethnics
    d) assimilated groups

11. If members of ethnic minorities are more likely to be at the bottom than the top of educational, economic and political hierarchies, they experience:
    a) disorganization
    b) prejudice
    c) cultural inequality
    d) institutional inequality

12. In the near future, the largest ethnic group will probably be:
    a) Asian
    b) European
    c) African American
    d) Hispanic

13. All of the following are ways that discrimination exists in the legal system, EXCEPT that:
    a) in 1857, the Supreme Court ruled that constitutional rights and privileges did not extend to blacks
    b) blacks today are more likely than whites to be arrested, indicted, and committed to an institution
    c) more white than blacks belong to the urban underclass and therefore now commit more crime
    d) expectations of police officers, prosecutors, and judges expect blacks to be criminals

14. The history of the relationship; between different ethnic groups almost always involves a period of:
    a) cultural curiosity and exploration
    b) religious conflict
    c) accommodation, assimilation and sharing of resources
    d) open conflict and competition over control of resources

15. Discrimination refers to:
    a) a theoretical condition
    b) beliefs
    c) attitudes
    d) action

16. If someone is rigid, inflexible, and has a low tolerance for uncertainty, and is therefore prejudiced, that person has a(n):
    a) discriminatory complex
    b) authoritarian personality
    c) scapegoating personality
    d) set of stereotypes

17. If inequality is built into the economic, political, and social activities independently of individuals, it is called:
    a) prejudice
    b) discrimination
    c) institutional discrimination
    d) scapegoating

18. Which of the following is an education reform designed to help most minorities?
    a compensatory education
    b) multicultural education
    c) bilingual education
    d) stricter education

19. A group of people who are thought to have a common set of physical characteristics and a common ancestry is called a(n):
    a) ethnic group
    b) salad bowl
    c) race
    d) people

20. To portray all members of a group as having similar fixed, usually unfavorable characteristics is to use:
    a) ethnic stereotypes
    b) the authoritarian personality
    c) institutional discrimination
    d) cultural scapegoats

21. A negative attitude toward a large category of people is called:
    a) racism
    b) discrimination
    c) prejudice
    d) scapegoating

22. During the 1980s, _____ led to a deterioration of ethnic relations.
    a) TV
    b) hard economic times
    c) actions of the Reagan government
    d) college teachers

159

23. In his influential book, *The Declining Significance of Race*, William Julius Wilson argued that the chief problem facing blacks is:
   a) prejudice
   b) racism
   c) class
   d) self-hatred

24. The attitude that one's own culture is the best and most enlightened is called:
   a) ethnocentrism
   b) racism
   c) prejudice
   d) ethnicity

25. According to Coleman and Cressey, the most important technique to solve ethnic problems is:
   a) prejudice reduction efforts
   b) fair employment laws
   c) multicultural education
   d) organized political pressure

26. Which of the following programs has led to a substantial white backlash against blacks?
   a) the civil rights movement
   b) compensatory education
   c) national job training
   d) affirmative action

27. _____ is probably as important as programs specifically attacking prejudice and discrimination to end ethnic problems.
   a) Education
   b) Immigration
   c) Integration
   d) Economic justice

28. From an interactionist perspective, when members of a minority group are constantly treated as though they were inferior, some members will:
   a) continue to struggle for power
   b) experience a sense of cultural disunity
   c) become convinced they really are inferior
   d) become more ethnocentric

29. From the conflict perspective, the history of all ethnic relations is the history of:
   a) cultural disunity
   b) poor socialization
   c) a struggle for power
   d) religious conflict

30. For functionalists, the best way to reduce discrimination is:
   a) cultural separation
   b) racial domination
   c) socialization
   d) cultural unity

160

PROJECTS

PROJECT 8.1 Using Census Data to Explore Patterns of Ethnic and Racial Group Relations Where You Live

There are a number of patterns that can occur when various ethnic and racial groups reside in the same area. These can be represented by three models:

One model is referred to as **assimilation** or **Anglo-conformity** and can be represented as: o. Here, "A" refers to the dominant Anglo-American culture. In this model, other racial and ethnic groups become integrated into the dominant culture by forsaking their own cultural traditions and adopting the Anglo-American traditions.

A second model is referred to as **the melting pot** and can be represented as: A+B+C=D. Here, racial and ethnic cultures mix to form new cultural traditions, with some elements of each, but distinct from any one of them.

A third model is referred to as **the salad bowl** or **cultural pluralism** and is represented as: A+B+C=A+B+C. In this model, the culture of each racial and ethnic group is recognized as equally valid and practiced in the society.

The objective of this project is to have you learn about these three patterns by examining patterns of ethnic relationships in your area.

Journal instructions:
1. Using census information, determine the extent to which the racial and ethnic population for the city in which you live has changed during the past two decades. For example, how did the percentage of whites, African-Americans, Hispanics, Asians, and so on change within your city? What were the percentages, around twenty years ago, around ten years ago, and most recently? Compile these data and discuss the extent to which the racial and ethnic population has changed in your area.

2. In addition to looking at the whole city, look at the racial and ethnic composition for each census tract within the city. Make a list of the census tracts and indicate the percent of the total population that is white, black, Hispanic, etc. around twenty years ago, around ten years ago, and most recently. Describe the changes that have occurred.

3. In your journal, discuss how the information you collected reflects any of the patterns of interaction (assimilation, melting pot, salad bowl) described above and in chapter 7 of Coleman and Cressey's text.

4. Consider which model of racial and ethnic patterns best represents racial and ethnic relations in our city. In your journal, discuss some things you could observe that would help you determine the pattern that has existed in the past and that currently exists. For example, what could you find out about each of the following in order to help you determine the pattern of racial and ethnic relations in your city: schools, churches, political representation, stores, mutual aid groups, community organizations, recreation centers, parks, and so on? Are there other clues you could look for? Describe them.

PROJECT INSTRUCTIONS ARE CONTINUED ON THE NEXT PAGE.

Option: essay
Write an essay (around three to five pages, typed) in which you discuss the extent to which the racial and ethnic population has changed within your city, the pattern of ethnic and racial relationships that exists, and the impact of any changes in population and/or patterns or relationships.

Option: bibliography
Develop a bibliography of ten to fifteen articles from sociology journals or sociology books that discuss patterns of ethnic and racial groups relationships. Type your bibliography following the format found in one of the sociology journals.

Option: paper
Write a paper (around five to seven pages, typed) in which you integrate material from your field journal (above) and at least five sources from your bibliography to discuss the changing racial and ethnic population in your area, the way patterns of relationships have changed (or why they have not changed), and the social impact of such changes (or lack of changes). Be sure to document your sources throughout your paper and include a reference page.

PROJECT 8.2 Patterns of Racial and Ethnic Relations at Your College

One way of exploring the changing nature of ethnic and racial patterns of relationships can be found at the college you attend. The objective of this project is to have you using observational techniques to explore these patterns of relationships at your college.

1. Make sure you read the introduction to Project 8.1 above and the sections in chapter 7 of Coleman and Cressey's text that discuss patterns of ethnic and racial group relationships.

2. Think about and write down in your journal some things you could observe to assess the type of racial and ethnic patterns that exist at your college. Here are some examples, but do not confine yourself to these:

   a) Attend meetings of different racial and ethnic organizations (Black Cultural Society, the Italian Club, and so on).
   b) Interview members of various ethnic and racial groups and discuss with them if they think the campus follows the assimilation, melting pot, or salad bowl model?
   c) Ask them if they would like the pattern that exists to be different and, if so, which one they would prefer.
   d) Interview faculty members who are white and faculty members who are members of racial or ethnic minorities and discuss the issue with them.
   e) Observe patters of interaction in daily life. For example, do members of the same racial or ethnic groups tend to sit together in classrooms and in the cafeteria?
   f) Do racial and ethnic group members have their own fraternities, sororities, and other organizations? Are they adequately represented in other fraternities, sororities, and campus organizations?

3. Once you complete your list, spend around a week conducting your observations and writing your results in your journal.

Option: essay
Write an essay (around three to five pages typed) in which you discuss the patterns of ethnic and racial group relationships that exist at your college. Identify the model which you think represents relationships at your college and illustrate why you think so by using examples from your journal. What is the social impact of the existing model on your college?

Option: bibliography
Develop a bibliography of ten to fifteen articles from popular periodicals, sociology journals, and sociology books about the racial and ethnic composition at American colleges today. Type your bibliography following the format found in one of the sociology journals.

Option: research paper
Write a paper in which you integrate ideas from your journal (above) and at least five sources from your bibliography to discuss the nature of racial and ethnic group relationships in American colleges today. Be sure to document your sources throughout the paper and include a reference page.

PROJECT 8.3 Observing Stereotypes, Prejudice, and Discrimination in Everyday Life

Each of us is a member of an ethnic and a racial group, either a dominant one or a minority one. Whether we like it or not, we hold stereotypes of people in other ethnic and racial groups. And it is likely that others hold stereotypes of us. Stereotypes are often the basis for prejudice and discrimination. The objective of this project is to have you examine the way stereotypes occur and are reinforced in everyday, and to examine the extent to which they are true.

1. For one week, keep an extensive journal in which you record racial and ethnic stereotypes and prejudices that you observe, hear, witness, express personally, or are the object of. These can occur anywhere: interactions between friends, in your family, by teachers or students in or out of the classroom, on television programs, in advertisements, in newspapers, in magazines, on MTV, in the movies, and so on. Be sure to keep your journal with you at all times for one week so that you can record the stereotypes when you observe them.

2. In your journal, describe each of your observations of racial or ethnic stereotypes.

3. On what basis (for example, myth, personal experience, and so on) do you think each of these stereotypes was made?

4. Do the stereotypes represent accurate FACTS about the group about which they were made? Support your answer with evidence. (Be careful not to use a stereotype that you hold as your evidence.)

5. Using explanations of prejudice that you read about in chapter 7, discuss some of the reasons for each of the stereotypes and prejudice that you observed.

6. Discuss some of the problems each of the stereotypes and prejudices that you observe. For example, what can happen to people as a result of being stereotyped in a particular way? Discuss what each of the sociological perspectives would say about the causes and consequences of the stereotypes.

Option: essay
Write an essay (around three to five pages, typed) in which you use information compiled in your field journal (above) to discuss the nature and extent of stereotypes in everyday life and their consequences.

Option: bibliography
Develop a bibliography of ten to fifteen articles from sociology journal and/ or sociology books about the ways in which ethnic and racial stereotypes and prejudices are created and the consequences of them. Type your bibliography following the format found in one of the sociology journals.

Option: research paper
Write a paper (around five to seven pages, typed) in which you integrate material from your field journal and at least four items from your bibliography to discuss how TWO of the sources of stereotypes you identified in your field journal (for example, television, movies, MTV, and so on.) Discuss things such as specific examples, the stereotypes that they perpetuate, the reasons for the stereotypes or prejudice, the consequences, and so forth. Use each of the sociological perspectives to explain the consequences of the stereotypes. Be sure to document your sources throughout your paper and include a reference page.

164

PROJECT 8.4 Observing Institutionalized Discrimination

As Coleman and Cressey discuss in chapter 8, **institutionalized discrimination** still exists to a large degree in American society.   The objective of this activity is to have you examine and become more sensitive to the subtle ways in which institutional discrimination exists.

Journal instructions:
1. Identify FOUR situations or organizations in your community (and/ or college) where it might be **possible** for institutionalized discrimination to take place (for example, colleges, country clubs, other types of private clubs, campus groups, housing developments, and so on).

2. In your journal, speculate and discuss how institutionalized discrimination might occur in such situations or organizations.

3. Examine the admission or entrance criteria or policies of two of these organizations or situations.   There area number of ways that you can find out this information legally.   Here are some examples, but **do not feel limited to these:**
>   a) Call or visit a private country club in your area. Ask to speak to the person who is in charge of membership. Once you contact the appropriate person, tell him or her that you are interested in obtaining an application and information for a friend who is moving in the area about how to become a member of the club.
>   b) Find out the criteria that the various fraternities and sororities at your college have for becoming a pledge. You can obtain this information directly from the Greek organization itself, or ask the office of student affairs how you can obtain this information.
>   c) Ask a local real estate agent about the new housing developments in your area. As them to provide you with the criteria necessary for building a house in that area (for example, size of lot, size of house, and so on).

3. Once you obtain the criteria for membership in the organizations or situations you selected, read and/or examine them carefully. Are there any racial and ethnic groups that are LIKELY to be excluded or deterred from joining or seeking membership because of some of the criteria for membership? Explain.

Option: essay
Write an essay (around three to five pages, typed) in which you discuss institutional discrimination in the two situations you observed above.

Option: bibliography
 Use your library's indexes to develop a bibliography of ten to fifteen articles from sociology journals and/or sociology books about institutional discrimination. If possible, Try to find sources that discuss institutional discrimination in the situations you observed in your journal. Type your bibliography following the format found in one of the sociology journals.

Option: research paper
Using at least five sources from your bibliography and material from your field journal (above), write a paper in which you discuss the types of situations in which institutionalized discrimination exists, how it is perpetuated, and its consequences. Tie in the sociological perspectives on race and ethnic minorities whenever possible. You can use your field journal to illustrate ideas found in the sociology articles or books, use ideas found in the articles or books to explain your observations, or both. Be sure to document your sources throughout the paper .

165

CHAPTER 9

THE OLD AND THE YOUNG

CHAPTER OUTLINE

Aging and the Life Cycle

Problems of the Young
        Childhood
        Adolescence

Problems of the Elderly
        Health
        Physical and Psychological Abuse
        Money
        Housing
        Problems of Transition

The Graying of America

Solving the Problems of the Young and the Old
        Employment
        Social Welfare
        Cultural Change

Sociological Perspectives on Problems of the Life Cycle
        The Functionalist Perspective
        The Conflict Perspective
        The Feminist Perspective
        The Interactionist Perspective

CHAPTER LEARNING OBJECTIVES AND ESSAY QUESTIONS

After studying this chapter, you should be able to:

• Explain how aging is both a biological and a social process.

• Discuss the relationship of aging to the life cycle.

• Identify and analyze several problems experienced during childhood and adolescence.
• Outline and discuss some of the problems faced by the elderly in American society.

• Discuss the ways of responding to the problems of the young and the old.

• Explain the different sociological perspectives on the elderly.

KEY POINTS FOR REVIEW

• Aging is a social phenomenon as well as a biological process. Although the problems of aging are rooted in physiological changes people undergo, society says what these changes mean and what is expected of people of any particular age group. These meanings and expectations can create many social problems related to aging for people of all ages.

• Social factors, such as diet, exercise, medical care, and lifestyle, have a profound influence—sometimes positive, sometimes negative—on people's mental and physical health as they age. Additionally, passages through socially constructed age grades—most notably, childhood, adolescence, adulthood, and old age—presents people with a predictable set of new social expectations and a new set of problems to go with them. While most sociologists have focused mostly on the problems of the young and the old, they recognize that people in the middle years—despite having higher incomes, more prestige, and more power—have age-related problems as well. Heavy responsibilities for supporting both children and aging parents, and the mid-life crisis are two such problems they face.

• While childhood appears to be an age of innocence, children face some very real social problems. Child abuse and molestation receive national attention, but there are other serious problems as well. Increased rates of poverty, divorce, single mothers, single parent homes, dual-career parents, parental abuse of alcohol and drugs, combined with decreased government social programs and the lack of adequate child care are at the root of many social problems for children. Additionally, the once specially protected status of childhood has been eroding through increased social expectations for education, success, materialism, and television.

• The contradictory social expectations adolescence experience as a result of no longer being a child but not yet an adult leads to the identity crisis, the central problem of adolescence according to Erik Erikson. A sense of powerlessness and confusion among adolescence has led to the development of a youth culture which reflects a pressing need to create a viable identity. The symbolic rejection of the adult world, the use of alcohol and other drugs, and delinquency often combine to create serious problems, often leading to crime. Adolescence often face problems of depression and other mental disorders; there has been a sharp increase in suicide among adolescence. Coming to terms with their sexuality is one of the most difficult problems

167

faced by all adolescents; once again, this is often the result of confusing social expectations. Finally, adolescents have a higher poverty rate than any other age group in the U.S.

• The breakup of the extended family has led to a severe decline in the status of the elderly, leaving the elderly increasingly isolated and alone. Additionally, the rapidly increasing size of the elderly population has led to many social problems. First, the elderly have more severe health problems than any other age group, yet have trouble getting the care and treatment they need for their ailments. A second problem is elder abuse—including physical violence, psychological threats, verbal attacks, and social humiliation—usually by the people they live with. The third problem is money. Poverty among the elderly is higher than it is for those in their middle years, and there are some serious pockets of poverty among elderly widows and members of minority groups. The elderly are less likely to be employed, less able to have new technological skills necessary for employment, face discrimination in hiring and promotion, and are often have inadequate pensions. Fourth, the elderly face housing problems related to lack of adequate housing that serves their special needs, mortgage payments while living on a fixed income, and expensive private retirement communities. Fifth, the elderly have problems of transition related to retirement, the loss of friends and loved ones, and their own death.

• There are many proposals for action that could benefit the young and the old alike. First, improve the economic condition of all workers by passing laws that deal with problems of age discrimination. Second, increase the government's support for children and their families through better school lunch programs, an increase in the tax exemption allowed for dependent children, a national system of top-quality day care at not cost to middle and low income parents, a better system of education, and improved public recreational needs for the young. For the elderly, there can be better government sponsorship of social security, subsidized housing, deferred property taxes, and a universal program of national health insurance. Third, combat negative age-related stereotypes by encouraging the elderly to participate in community life, provide clear-cut expectations for adolescents, and find more worthwhile things for them to do such as jobs and community-service activities.

• From the functionalist perspective, age-related social problems are rooted in our society's inability to adjust to rapid social changes such as the rapid increase of the elderly population and the breakdown of traditional family. Functionalists believe it is necessary to reorganize the social institutions that traditionally cared for the young and the elderly or to develop new agencies that can do so more effectively.

• From the conflict perspective, the government's seeming indifference to age-related social problems is a result of class conflict. Conflict theorists believe that the wealthy and powerful have blocked efforts to help the young since they do not need government assistance for their children or in their old age. Further, our ideology of individualism blames the elderly for their poverty and single parents for their failure to follow traditional family patterns. Thus, conflict theorists feel the most effect response to age-related social problems is through political action through lobbies such as the American Association of Retired Persons, and others.

• The feminist perspective points to the critical role women play in the problems facing the young and the old. Since women live longer, problems of the elderly pertain largely to women. Further women are assigned a disproportionate share of the responsibility for dealing with the problems of the young and old. As solutions to problems related to aging, feminists advocate that men pitch in and provide more help in child rearing and care of elderly relatives. Recognizing the burdens placed upon men, though, feminists feel that the government could provide more assistance with things such as increased welfare support for poor families with dependent children, tax breaks for those caring for children or the elderly, and more day care centers and nursing homes.

• The interactionist perspective is concerned with the social process of aging and the way the social definition we hold for people of different ages shape their attitudes and their behavior. Transitions to to new roles associated with different ages can be particularly problematic for people, especially the roles related to adolescence and old age. Identity crises, conflicting ideals and expectations, aimlessness and apathy often result from such transitions. Interactionists recommend that supportive social groups that offer a constructive role to play in society can help both adolescents and the elderly.

NOTES:

KEY TERMS

The following key terms are found in your textbook on the page number indicated in parentheses. In the space provided, write a brief definition of the key term **in your own words**. Then **provide an example** of the term, such as a culture in which the practice takes place, or people that you might know whose behavior illustrates the term, a current event that illustrates the term, how a term could be used to shed light on or help solve a particular social problem, and so on. You could include examples from the news, books, movies, or anything else that will illustrate the term and help you remember it. Include any comments from your class discussions or textbook that might help you remember and understand these key terms. Use additional paper if necessary, but keep it with your study guide to help you review for exams.

age grades (p. 287)

_____

_____

_____

_____

life cycle (p. 287)

_____

_____

_____

_____

baby boom generation (p. 300)

_____

_____

_____

_____

rites of passage (p. 287)

_____

_____

_____

childhood (p. 287)

_____

_____

_____

_____

adolescence (p. 287)

_____

_____

_____

adulthood (p. 287)

_____

_____

_____

_____

old age (p. 287)

_____

_____

_____

_____

mid-life crisis (p. 288)

_____

_____

_____

_____

identity crisis (p. 290)

_____

_____

_____

_____

youth culture (p. 291)

_____

_____

_____

_____

elder abuse (p. 295)

_____

_____

_____

_____

retirement communities (p. 297)

_____

_____

_____

_____

activity theory (p. 307)

_____

_____

_____

_____

disengagement theory (p. 398)

_____

_____

_____

_____

erosion of childhood (p. 398)

_____

_____

_____

_____

NOTES:

PRACTICE TEST

Multiple Choice

1. Which of the following is NOT a social dimension of aging?
   a) decline of lung capacity
   b) medical care
   c) life-style
   d) diet and exercise

2. Sociologists call groups of people of similar age:
   a) age groups
   b) age grades
   c) life cycle stages
   d) generations

3. The _____ consists of a series of passages between the social roles expected of people as they age.
   a) age cycle
   b) rite of passage
   c) age stages
   d) life cycle

4. Herman was fourteen and completed a year of religious training. He and his fellow students attended a special religious service to mark their acceptance as adult members of their religion. Sociologists would refer to this service as a:
   a) part of the life cycle
   b) part of human change
   c) rite of passage
   d) resolution to an identity crisis

5. An acute psychological predicament that typically occurs in the middle years of life is called:
   a) age grading
   b) senility
   c) a mid-life crisis
   d) an identity crisis

6. Sociologists tend to label all of the following as the broad age grades EXCEPT for:
   a) infancy
   b) childhood
   c) adolescence
   d) old age

7. During the 1980s, the government:
   a) turned its back on the needs of the elderly
   b) neglected the needs of children
   c) provided additional assistance to schools and poor families
   d) developed many new social programs for the elderly

174

8. One way adolescents respond and adjust to their unique problems and experiences is to:
   a) rebel
   b) work harder
   c) develop a youth culture
   d) revert to childhood ways

9. Which of the following social factors has probably contributed the most to the "erosion of childhood"?
   a) childhood illnesses
   b) the number of children in the family
   c) television
   d) child abuse

10. The central problem of adolescence is:
    a) money
    b) establishing an identity
    c) sexuality
    d) assuming adult roles

11. Adolescents derive their economic status from:
    a) borrowing
    b) working
    c) membership in school
    d) their family's economic status

12. Which of the following statements about society's norms and expectations for adolescent sexual behavior is TRUE?
    a) Society has a clear and constructive set of sexual norms that adolescents must come to grips with.
    b) Most adolescents experience much confusion in coming to terms with their sexuality.
    c) Society protects adolescents by isolating them from conflicting demands of sexuality.
    d) American adolescents are encouraged to use birth control and as a result have the lowest birthrate in the industrialized world.

13. With the breakup of the extended family:
    a) the elderly have been turned to uphold cultural ideals of youth and vigor
    b) the elderly have more freedom to continue working and more freedom in general
    c) the status of the elderly has dramatically increased
    d) the status of the elderly has severely declined

14. Which of the following is a chronic disease faced by the elderly?
    a) heart disease
    b) tuberculosis
    c) AIDS
    d) common colds

15. Approximately how many Americans are now elderly?
    a) 5 million
    b) 15 million
    c) 30 million
    d) 70 million

175

16. The major reason that fewer elderly persons live in poverty today is:
    a) higher saving rates
    b) indexing social security to inflation
    c) more government grants
    d) fewer elderly persons competing for funds

17. The problem of most concern to the elderly is:
    a) health
    b) escaping poverty
    c) managing their money
    d) housing

18. Which of the following is a major reason for financial problems of the elderly?
    a) an inability to work
    b) poor health
    c) age discrimination
    d) greater expenses

19. One problem American culture has with dying is a:
    a) conspiracy of silence about dying
    b) planning a convenient death
    c) avoiding death entirely
    d) dealing with estates and inheritance

20. All of the following are problems of elderly transition, EXCEPT:
    a) the stopping of sexuality
    b) facing the inevitability of death
    c) the shrinking of one's social world
    d) adjusting to retirement

21. One reason why housing is so important to the elderly is because the elderly:
    a) they feel it is the last place they will live before they die
    b) spend so much time at home
    c) have a special need for security
    d) are the centers of their families and need a place to entertain

22. Coleman and Cressey argue that the best way to deal with the problem of high unemployment among adolescents and elderly persons is to:
    a) improve the economic conditions of all workers
    b) develop quotas for the young and the old
    c) create ways for the young and the old to start their own businesses
    d) prohibit age discrimination

23. Which of the following is a way to reaffirm our commitment to the young?
    a) increasing government support for children
    b) increasing employment opportunities for children
    c) taking support away from the elderly
    d) giving children more tax breaks

24. Which of the following is probably the best way to break down stereotypes of the elderly?
    a) changing the behavior of the elderly
    b) developing more residential communities restricted to the elderly
    c) helping the elderly to organize together
    d) encouraging elderly participation in community life

25. Which of the following is the major problem facing social security today?
    a) how to manage your recipients
    b) running out of money
    c) encouraging more donations to the fund
    d) extending benefits to more people

26. All of the following are ways of helping adolescents, EXCEPT:
    a) providing a clear set of expectations for their age grade
    b) providing an adult status to the young
    c) providing jobs for young workers
    d) encouraging and channeling youthful idealism

27. Which of the following is part of the cultural traditions of America?
    a) support for social services
    b) high statuses for the elderly
    c) strong negative stereotypes of elderly people
    d) strong beliefs in the extended family

28. Sociologists who believe that rapid economic and social change led to the decline of the extended family and a reduction in the status of the elderly are most likely to adhere to which perspective?
    a) conflict
    b) functionalist
    c) feminist
    d) interactionist

29. The view that old age is best handled by accepting the inevitable contraction of one's social world and gradually ending social involvement's and responsibilities as death comes nearer is consistent with:
    a) activity theory
    b) subcultural theory
    c) conflict theory
    d) disengagement theory

30. Conflict theorists are convinced that the young and the elderly suffer because:
    a) this suffering is functional for society
    b) the wealthy and powerful profit from policies that add to the misery of the elderly
    c) they are improperly socialized
    d) American society is very disorganized

PROJECTS

PROJECT 9.1 Stereotypes About Age Grades

Coleman and Cressey discuss how various stereotypes affect people in age grades, especially adolescence and old age. Many of these stereotypes are based upon myths. While it may be true that many people live up to these stereotypes, often they unfairly depict the entire age grade as having those stereotypical characteristics. This can lead to prejudice and discrimination (ageism) against people. The objective of this activity is to have you examine the extent to which some of these stereotypes exist, how they are created and perpetuated, and what the results of them.

Journal instructions:
1. For one week, keep an extensive field journal in which you record your observations of stereotypes and prejudices toward adolescents and toward the elderly. Some things to look for: How are they portrayed in television programs and commercials? How are they talked about by members of other age grades? How are they portrayed in movies? How are they portrayed in newspaper and magazine advertisements? What are your spontaneous reactions to members of age grades of which you are not a member? And so on.

2. What myth(s) is each stereotype and prejudice you observed based upon and what myth(s) do they reinforce?

3. Do your observations refute any particular myths about people in these age groups?

4. What are some dysfunctions (negative consequences) of each of the stereotypes and prejudices that you observed?

5. Interview at least five adolescents and five elderly people. Use a variety of sources. For example, don't have all of your interviews from members of your family or friends or teachers, and so on. Try to limit your interviews for each grade to one per source. Discuss the following items with them and record their responses in your field journal:
    a) Discuss with them the list myths, stereotypes, and prejudices relevant to their age grade that you have recorded (above). That is, discuss elderly stereotypes with the elderly and adolescent stereotypes with adolescents. Share your observations with them. Ask them to discuss with you the extent to which each of these myths, stereotypes, and prejudices accurately represent them and people in their age grade in general.
    b) Ask them if they or any of their friends or relatives have ever been the target of prejudice or discrimination because of their age status. If so, ask them to explain.
    c) Ask them if they think the prejudice or discrimination was justified.
    d) Ask them what the effect of the prejudice or discrimination was on their, or their friends', lives. For example: Did they lose a job? Were they denied a job or an opportunity? Did it affect their sense of self? Did it affect their relationships with others? And so on.

6. Reread the sections in chapter 8 (The Ethnic Minorities) about prejudice and discrimination as explanations of ethnic inequality. In your journal, discuss which theories of prejudice and discrimination toward minority groups can also be used as explanations of some of the stereotypes and prejudices you have been examining in the field journal for this project.

PROJECT INSTRUCTIONS ARE CONTINUED ON THE FOLLOWING PAGE.

Option: essay
Using the results of your field journal (above), write an essay (around five pages, typed) in which you discuss and analyze the types of stereotypes, prejudice, and discrimination that against adolescents and against the elderly that occur in everyday life. There are many different things you can choose to discuss in your essay. For example, you might examine one or more of the issues you discussed in your interviews and field journal. Additionally, you could consider any of the following topics: Does each age grade equally from stereotypes or is one group hurt more? Why? How? How do age grade stereotypes, prejudice, and discrimination compare with that of ethnic minorities. Think about this topic carefully before you write your essay. Rather than take a "shotgun" approach to your essay and write a little about many topics, come up with a specific angle that you will focus on.

Option: essay
 Watch the movie *Harold and Maude* (1971). It is available on VHS at most rental video stores and possible in your college's library. Write an essay (around five pages, typed) in which you discuss how the myths, stereotypes, and prejudices about age grades that you discussed and observed in your field journal (above) form the basis for much of the humor in this movie.

Option: bibliography
Develop a bibliography of around fifteen articles from both popular periodicals and sociology journals that discuss problems and issues dealing with age-related stereotypes, prejudice, and discrimination. Make sure that at least seven of your bibliographic items are articles from sociology journals or books written by sociologists. Additionally, identify two or three web sties that address issues related to aging. Type your bibliography following the format found in one of the sociology journals.

Option: research paper
Write a paper (around seven to nine pages, typed) using material you developed in your field journal and/or either of the above essays and at least five sources from your bibliography (at least three from sociology journals or books) to discuss an idea related to stereotypes and discrimination toward age grades. *Suggestion:* You have already discussed many ideas in your field journal and essay (above). Rather than come up with a new idea altogether, try using that material as a rough draft of your research paper and then integrate bibliographic material throughout in order to strengthen your discussion.

Be sure to document your sources properly throughout your paper and include a reference page.

PROJECT 9.2 Using Sociological Perspectives to Examine Social Issues About the Elderly

Gerontology has become one of the most rapidly-growing areas of sociology. There are many issues and problems that the elderly face as a result of the rapidly increasing population elderly in the Unites States (as discussed in chapter 9): abuse, diminishing social security benefits, economics, housing, discrimination, health care, loss of family and friends, and so on. The objective of this project is to have you examine some of the problems and issues of the elderly using the sociological perspectives.

Journal instructions
1. Attend a meeting and/or interview four members of an interest group or organization for the elderly: Gray Panthers, National Retired Teachers Association, American Association of Retired Persons, National Council of Senior Citizens, or any others that may be represented in your area. Ask them to identify and discuss what they think are the five most important issues that the elderly face today. Record their comments in your journal and write a paragraph about each issue that they identify.

2. Find articles in popular periodicals (newspapers, magazines, and so on)from the past few years about the issues identified above. Obtain two or three articles for each social issue. List these, and the bibliographic information, in your journal. Additionally, locate two or three web sites that pertain to the elderly. Read the articles and summarize in your journal what each of the five issues are concerned with according to the articles. Write a paragraph for each.

Option: essay
Select one of the social issues or problems that you identified (above). Write an essay (around three to five pages, typed) in which you discuss the issue from a sociological approach. Include the following in your discussion:
 a) Use the perspectives on aging that apply to discuss the issue or problem. For example, how would the functionalist, conflict, feminist, and/or interactionist perspectives explain lack of job opportunity for the elderly? What would disengagement theory or activity theory say about this? And so on.
 b) Use other relevant sociological information contained within chapter 9 (or any other chapters that you read) to discuss the issue.

Option: bibliography
Develop a bibliography of around fifteen to twenty articles in sociology journal or books written by sociologists that deal with the issues you identified in your journal (above). Your best bet is to look through the *Social Science Index*, the *Sociological Abstracts*, or any other index your library has that contains social science references. Also, look through, a journal that deals specifically with issues and problems related to the elderly. Type your bibliography in following the format found in one of the sociology journals.

Option: research paper
Select one social issue or problem that you identified in your journal (above) for which you have at least four or five references in your bibliography (above). Write a paper (around five to seven pages, typed) about this topic from a sociological approach. Some items you might address include: What kind of focus does sociological research bring to the issue? What perspectives, theories, concepts and so on are discussed in the sociological references? What types of solutions does the sociological approach offer? Are there differences in the way that the issue or problem is presented and analyzed by sociologists than by journalists, news commentators, or the people you interviewed? Be sure to document your sources properly.

PROJECT 9.3 Social Policies and the Elderly

As the number of social issues and problems the elderly face increases, so does the need for policies to address these issues and problems. There is debate about policies regarding mandatory retirement, pension plans, Social Security, Medicaid, disability provisions, euthanasia, and other areas of concern for the elderly. The objective of this project is to have you examine one policy debate from a sociological approach.

Research paper instructions:
1. Identify one debate or controversy regarding a policy that pertains to the elderly that has appeared in the news within the past year. You may need to go through back issues of newspapers and magazines to identity one.

2.. Conduct library and/or computerized research to find five or six articles—either from popular periodicals or sociological literature—that present arguments for and against the policy. Be sure to collect enough articles and web sites to provide you with enough information to present a balanced discussion of the pros and cons for the policy.

3. Summarize the arguments for and against the policy in question.

4. Interview ten elderly people and ask them what their views are about the particular policy in question. Do they support or oppose it? Why?

5. Write a paper (around five to seven pages, typed in which you:
    a) Summarize what the policy is intended to accomplish and how.
    b) Present a balanced discussion of the arguments for and against the policy. Base these arguments on your library research and illustrate the arguments with comments mad by the people that you interviewed.
    c) Use sociological theories and perspectives of aging discussed in your text to examine both sides of the policy debate.
    d) After you present a balanced discussion of both sides of the policy debate, use sociological theories and perspectives of aging, your library research, and your interviews to take a position for or against the policy.
    e) Be sure to document all of your sources throughout your paper and include a reference page.

PROJECT 9.4 A Cross Cultural Comparison of the Treatment of the Elderly

As Coleman and Cressey pointed out in chapter 9, the elderly did not always suffer from as many of the social problems as they now do. Part of the problem stems from the way elderly are regarded in American culture. Is the lower status that is assigned to the elderly in American society characteristic of other cultures also? Do they have similar social problems elsewhere? The objective of this project is to have you examine the types of problems and issues the elderly face in other cultures.

Journal instructions:
Identify some people at your college or in your community from five countries that have cultures that are very different than yours. Select one from each country whom you can interview or with whom you can discuss the role of elderly in their culture. Try to have a representation of people that are from cultures that you think are very different from each other. conduct an interview with each person and record their comments in your journal. Discuss the following with them:

     a) What is the role of the elderly in families? (For example: Are they taken into consideration when major family decisions are made? How much power do they have in the family's decisions? Ho important is their opinion? What is the grandparent's role with regard to grandchildren? Are the elderly treated with respect? And so on.)

     b) How are the elderly portrayed in the media in that country: on television, movies, newspapers, magazines, and so on?

     c) To what extent is ageism (that is, prejudice and discrimination toward the elderly) a problem?

     d) How is the aging process perceived in that culture? (For example, is getting older valued or de-valued?)

     e) Are the elderly treated with equality?

     f) What specific social problems or issues do the elderly face?

     g) In general, what are the differences between how the elderly are treated in the United States with how they are treated in the other cultures?

Option: essay
Write an essay (around three to five pages, typed) in which you use the material from your interviews to compare treatment of the elderly in American society with that of other cultures.

Option: bibliography
Develop a bibliography of around five articles from sociology journals or books written by sociologists about the issues and problems that the elderly face in one of the cultures you examined above (that is, in your field journal). In addition, find around five articles about similar issues and problems concerning the elderly in your own culture. Topics about the elderly that you might find information on are the role of the elderly, age stratification, government policies related to the elderly, social problems of the elderly, social characteristics of the elderly, and others. Type your bibliography following the format found in one of the sociology journals.

Option: research paper
Using at least five sources from the bibliography you developed (above) and your field journal (above),write a paper (around five to seven pages, typed) in which you compare age and social problems of the elderly between your culture and the culture you selected for your bibliography. Be sure to document your sources properly throughout your paper and include a reference page.

CHAPTER 10

WOMEN AND MEN

CHAPTER OUTLINE

Gender Roles
  Nature or Nurture?
  The Historical Development of Gender Roles

Gender Socialization

Gender Inequality
  Education
  Employment
  Political Power
  Social Life
    The Devaluation of Women
    Language and Communication
    Sexual Harassment
  Men's Problems

Solving the Problems of Gender Inequality
  Political Activism
  Fighting Gender Discrimination
  Changing Gender Roles

Sociological Perspectives on Problems of Gender
  The Functionalist Perspective
  The Conflict Perspective
  The Feminist Perspective
  The Interactionist Perspective

CHAPTER LEARNING OBJECTIVES AND ESSAY QUESTIONS

After studying this chapter, you should be able to:

• Explain why and how gender role expectations have changed.

• Define the concept of gender role and explain the origins of male and female roles.

• Discuss how gender role socialization occurs, and what agents of gender role socialization are involved.

• Elaborate about the extent of gender inequality in education, employment, political power, and social life.

• Outline and discuss the several ways of responding to gender inequality.

• Compare and discuss the four sociological perspectives on gender inequality.

KEY POINTS FOR REVIEW

• One of the most significant developments of modern times is the redefinition of what it means to be a woman or a man. As gender roles began to change, gender inequality came to be seen as a social problem.

• Gender roles are social expectations that are assigned to us on the basis of our biological sex. Traditionally, women have been expected to be passive, warm, supportive, emotionally expressive, and focused on the home and family. Men have been expected to be active, independent, self-controlled, and focuses on work. The movement of women our of the home and into the workplace has shaken some of these notions about the "nature" of men and women.

• An age-old debate is whether gender roles are due to nature (that is, biology) or nurture (that is, social and cultural environment). Clearly, there are biological differences between males and females, but whether or not size, hormones, and brain structure account for gender differences is far from clear. If gender roles are determined solely by biology, it is logical to assume that they should be the same in all cultures. However, anthropological studies have shown enormous differences in the gender roles of different cultures, and historians have found that gender roles change within the same culture over time. The evidence suggests two conclusions about gender roles. First, gender roles are social creations and are determined by society, not biology. Second. the gender roles that society creates are strongly influenced by biological considerations.

• Throughout history, gender roles have been shaped by the environment and the economic system. The earliest societies were highly egalitarian since the respective roles of men and women—men hunted, women gathered and took care of children—were both essential to the survival of the group. As agricultural technology developed, men's responsibilities increased, and the status of women declined. Further changes in gender roles came with the industrial revolution. The decline of the extended family, lower birth rates, and the reduction of importance of physical labor led more women into the work place. Technological and social developments sharply reduced the importance of biological differences between the sexes.

184

• Gender socialization—the process by which we learn the behavior and attitudes that are expected of our sex—begins at the moment of birth. Male and female infants , are given different types of clothing, toys, and rooms. They are spoken to differently and handled differently. They are taught a language which conveys social assumptions about the nature of differences between the sexes. Other agents of socialization include children's programs, prime time entertainment, advertisements, movies, and music videos. Expectations about the way males and females are supposed to think and behave, the devaluation of women, the sexual objectification of women, and the dominance of males are taught and reinforced by all of these agents of gender socialization.

• In Western society, traditional male and females roles are highly unequal, with males in the dominant position. This inequality is reflected in such as education, employment, politics, and others. Open discrimination against women in education no longer exists to the extent that it once did, but there are still much fewer women receiving professional degrees and PhD's and they are still under represented in such fields as the natural sciences, mathematics and engineering. The gap between men's and women's pay has narrowed in recent years. In 1975 women earned about 60% as much as men, but by 1992 they earned around 75%. However, part of this increase is due to a decline in men's wages. Sex-typed jobs tend to result in women being subordinate to men in status and pay, and less possibility for advancement for women. Even among successful female executives an invisible "glass ceiling" often exists. Politics has traditionally been considered a man's business. Even though they have enormous potential, women are still grossly under represented in all areas of the government. There are signs of improvement, though, in each of these institutions.

• Besides being present in most social institutions, sexism is present in many areas of social life. Women are devalued in society in many ways. They are portrayed as overly emotional, expected to repress their desires and ambitions, and expected to repress their sexuality at the same time they are expected to conform to unrealistic standards of sex appeal. Our language reflects and reinforces sexual inequalities in many ways. Words associated with men tend to denote strength and power, while words associated with women are linked with sex, family, or subordination. Further, conversational patterns, both in verbal and non-verbal communication, between men and women reflect inequality and reinforce gender stereotypes. Sexual harassment is another major problem that women face.

• Men also face problems as a result of gender stereotypes. They are expected to repress their "feminine" characteristics and are expected to be economically successful. Today, while they are encouraged to take a greater role in child rearing, there is little social support for them during child custody settlements.

• Political activism is necessary to combat problems of gender inequality. The beginnings of the women's movement in North America are traced to the women who were involved in the abolitionist movement to free the slaves, who realized that they, too, were oppressed. The women's movement regained its strength during the civil rights movement of the 1960s. There are three approaches within the modern feminist movement. Liberal feminism, the predominant approach, draws on the values of freedom and individual liberty and calls for a vigorous government attack on all forms of prejudice and discrimination. Socialist feminism holds that inequality stems from the capitalist system and calls for fundamental changes in economic institutions. Radical feminism calls for a radical change from our patriarchal culture to a women-centered culture. A men's movement has also developed in response to gender problems men face. Generally, this movement focuses on the anxiety men face as a result of being expected to live up to our cultural ideals of masculinity.

185

• Proposals to deal with problems of gender inequality generally fall into two categories: those that aim to eliminate sexual discrimination and those that seek to restructure gender roles. Proposals to eliminate sexual discrimination are widely supported, but proposals that challenge deeply entrenched institutional structures that reinforce traditional gender roles are met with resistance. Our attitudes and expectations about gender are formed early, and continuously throughout the life cycle, through socialization processes and challenging these raises peoples' fears and insecurities.

• From the functionalist perspective, the problems with contemporary gender roles result from changes brought on by the industrial revolution which threw the traditional interrelated male and female gender roles out of balance. Some functionalists advocate a return to a traditional division of labor between men and women, while others advocate a redefinition of gender roles to bring them into line with current social conditions.

• From the conflict perspective, problems of gender inequality originally developed as a result of men using their greater size and strength to dominate women, and later using their economic, political, and social advantages to maintain this domination. The solution, according to conflict theorists, lies in continued political activism.

• The feminist perspective, like the conflict perspective, focuses on gender inequality. As solutions to inequality, liberal feminists call for vigorous government attacks on all forms of prejudice and discrimination, tougher legislation punishing gender discrimination, new initiatives against sexual harassment, and longer sentences sex offenders. Additionally, they call for changes in gender socialization through families, schools, and the mass media. Socialist feminists advocate a more generous human welfare system and argue that the exploitation of women arises from capitalism

• The interactionist perspective argues that problems of gender inequality are the result of gender roles, prejudice, and discrimination that are taught and reinforced through socialization processes. They argue that gender differences are learned and that gender problems can be dealt with through socialization processes that encourage equal development of males and females.

NOTES:

KEY TERMS

The following key terms are found in your textbook on the page number indicated in parentheses. In the space provided, write a brief definition of the key term **in your own words**. Then **provide an example** of the term, such as a culture in which the practice takes place, or people that you might know whose behavior illustrates the term, a current event that illustrates the term, how a term could be used to shed light on or help solve a particular social problem, and so on. You could include examples from the news, books, movies, or anything else that will illustrate the term and help you remember it. Include any comments from your class discussions or textbook that might help you remember and understand these key terms. Use additional paper if necessary, but keep it with your study guide to help you review for exams.

gender inequality (p. 313)

_____

_____

_____

_____

sexism (p. 313)

_____

_____

_____

_____

gender roles (p. 313)

_____

_____

_____

_____

androgynous (p. 314)

_____

_____

_____

gender socialization (p. 318)

_____

_____

_____

_____

sexual stereotyping (p. 318)

_____

_____

_____

_____

homophobia (p. 318)

_____

_____

_____

_____

sexism (p. 321)

_____

_____

_____

_____

double standard (p. 327)

_____

_____

_____

_____

sexual harassment (p. 327)

_____

_____

_____

_____

liberal feminists (p. 335)

_____

_____

_____

_____

socialist feminists (p. 336)

_____

_____

_____

_____

NOTES:

PRACTICE TEST

Multiple Choice

1. The inequality of women is usually referred to as:
   a) male supremacy
   b) gender inequality
   c) sexism
   d) sexual inequality

2. If you believe gender roles are based on the physical differences between men and women, then you believe the are created by:
   a) nature
   b) nurture
   c) socialization
   d) hormones

3. Expectations for behavior based on our biological sex are call:
   a) stereotypes
   b) sex roles
   c) gender roles
   d) social roles

4. The two most significant biological differences between men and women are the female's ability to bear and nurse children, and the:
   a) greater size and strength of the male
   b) healthier existence of the male
   c) greater intelligence of the male
   d) greater strength of the female

5. A role that is made up of a combination of traits traditionally assigned to different genders is called:
   a) sexist
   b) sex
   c) anonymous
   d) androgynous

6. Which statement about the relationship between high levels of the male testosterone and aggressive behavior in adult men is true?
   a) High levels have been proven to cause more violent behavior in men.
   b) How levels have been associated with homosexual, and nonviolent behavior.
   c) Studies of the relation between the two have only produced mixed results.
   d) Castrating violent prisoners significantly prevents future violence.

7. Most sociological and anthropological evidence concludes expectations for genders are:
   a) largely the same in all societies
   b) not influenced by biological considerations
   c) biologically determined
   d) social creations

8. In what kind of society was the relationship between the sexes more egalitarian?
    a) hunting and gathering societies
    b) agricultural societies
    c) industrial societies
    d) patriarchal societies

9. What change created by industrialization has had the greatest impact on gender roles?
    a) agricultural technology
    b) urbanization
    c) the transformation the family
    d) equality in the division of labor

10. Which of the following statements bout gender role expectations for older children is true?
    a) The difference in gender role expectations become greater as children become older.
    b) The difference in gender role expectations lessens dramatically during adolescence.
    c) As children grow older, gender role expectations largely disappear.
    d) Teenage gender roles are largely androgynous.

11. The way we learn the behavior and attitudes expected or our sex is:
    a) sexual training
    b) sexual socialization
    c) sexual stereotyping
    d) gender socialization

12. The mass media impacts on the definition of personal gender roles because they:
    a) teach contradictory gender role expectations
    b) fail to clearly define what gender expectations are normal
    c) tend to reaffirm traditional gender role stereotypes
    d) tend to teach new gender role stereotypes

13. Much of what children begin to learn at birth through activity exposure and language largely involves:
    a) socialization patterns
    b) gender role production
    c) individual role expectations
    d) sexual stereotypes

14. According to one study, which of the following is true about teacher's beliefs about student performance based on gender?
    a) Teachers held strong beliefs in the women's rights movement.
    b) Teachers believed poor female performance on tests was due to discouragement from the family
    c) Teachers believed in the genetic inferiority of women in math.
    d) Teachers believed in the genetic inferiority of men in history and science

15. Research on the contents or popular books, movies, and magazines point to the same conclusion, that:
    a) men are usually portrayed as cruel and inhuman toward women
    b) women are commonly portrayed as sex objects and passive bystanders
    c) women are commonly shown in active, aggressive and dominant roles
    d) sexual stereotypes have largely disappeared from these media

191

16. A woman with a college degree earns:
   a) only a little more than a male high school dropout
   b) only a little more than a college dropout
   c) as much as a man with a collage degree
   d) a fair salary, based on her qualifications

17. All of the following are areas of social life that women are expected to repress, EXCEPT for:
   a) their ambitions to pursue a career
   b) their sexuality
   c) their opposition to the double standard
   d) their expression of emotions

18. All of the following are true about the experiences of men and women in education EXCEPT that:
   a) men receive more professional degrees than women
   b) women are largely discouraged from pursuing formal education
   c) there are more male role models than female
   d) more women major in liberal arts and the humanities

19. _____ has been considered a man's business in almost all societies through the world:
   a) Teaching
   b) Politics
   c) Computer programming
   d) Art

20. In Western society the traditional roles of females and males are not only substantially different but also:
   a) equal
   b) unequal
   c) segregated
   d) complementary

21. Sociologists assert the income gap between men and women is due to:
   a) women need less money than men, because they already receive support
   b) women want a happy family more than a good job
   c) men have more experience than women
   d) sexism and discrimination

22. The two types of sexual harassment are sexual comments and advances aimed directly at an individual, and:
   a) a physical attack by a man or a woman
   b) media stereotypes
   c) a hostile environment
   d) the double standard

192

23. According to the radical feminist approach, the greatest evil of American society is that it is a
_____ society.
   a) patriarchal
   b) matriarchal
   c) egalitarian
   d) sexist

24. Which of the following statements about women's political action is TRUE?
   a) The women's movement never really got organized until the 1930s.
   b) The women's movement developed separately from the civil rights movement.
   c) The modern feminist movement has scored remarkable successes.
   D) The nineteenth century women's movement won the right to vote.

25. Which of the following policies belongs more to radical feminism?
   a) a belief in women" legal rights
   b) control of the National Organization of Women
   c) the development of a women-centered culture
   d) better laws against sexual discrimination

26. The consensus among most social psychologists is that sexual inequality can be reduced by:
   a) political action
   b) changing gender roles
   c) making new laws
   d) genetic engineering

27. Which of the following is a central complaint put forward by the emerging men's movement?
   a) the perpetuation of negative stereotypes of men
   b) the superiority of men in some areas
   c) the idea of men as soft and gentle
   d) women bashing

28. Which of the following strategies for ending women's inequality comes from the conflict
perspective?
   a) a reduction in the gap between expectations and actual conditions
   b) organizing and using political power to gain equality
   c) changing the biosocial nature of women
   d) changing the content of the socialization process

29. All of the following are social changes needed to help women, EXCEPT for:
   a) government supported day care
   b) stronger enforcement of the laws
   c) quota programs for women
   d) tough sentences against rapists

30. Which perspective sees the problems of present-day gender roles as coming from economic
changes that upset traditional cultural patterns?
   a) conflict
   b) functionalist
   c) feminist
   d) interactionist

PROJECTS

PROJECT 10.1 Gender Role Socialization and Problems of Gender

Gender role socialization is the name of the process that explains how we acquire social expectations that are geared to each biological sex. Some feel that our gender roles are a result of our biological make-up, whereas most sociologists believe that while biology plays an important part, ultimately it is our social environment that creates the roles. As a result of social expectations regarding each biological sex, a number or gender-related issues have emerged. the objective of this project is to have you examine the many ways in which society encourages members of each sex to conform to a specific set of expectations and how these expectations are at the root of many gender-related social issues and problems.

Journal instructions:
1. Before beginning this project, read the section in any current introduction to sociology text book that discusses theories and agents of gender role socialization. Also, reread the section in chapter 10 of Coleman and Cressey's text about how gender socialization takes place. Then make a list of situations and examples in which gender role socialization might occur both for yourself and for children.

2. For an <u>entire week,</u> keep a journal in which your record as <u>thoroughly</u> as possible every instance of gender role socialization that you experience and that you observe other people experiencing. These include observations of interpersonal relationships (yours and others around you), family, friends, advertisements, school, media (television, radio, newspapers, magazines), and so on. Briefly describe each situation and event and discuss the underlying gender role message being sent. Pay particular attention to situations which involve gender role socialization among children. Every example is important. Be extensive in your note taking and observations.

3. At the end of the week, do a content analysis of your observations. That is, organize the types of socialization experiences that you recorded into categories (for example, everyday interaction, education, religion, family, media, and so on).

4. In your journal organize your observations in terms of how they might illustrate each of the gender role theories and/or agents of socialization that you read about in Coleman and Cressey's text and in the introductory textbook. You may use your examples more than one time.

5. Finally, go through each of the categories of socialization experiences you examined (#3 above). Think about and list in your journal any possible social problems or issues related to gender that may result from the types of gender role socialization that you observed throughout the week. Think carefully about this. If you can't think of specific problems or issues that you have witnessed, think about what possible problems or issues could develop for females and for males as a result of each type of gender role socialization

Option: essay
Using the above information, write an essay (around four to five pages, typed) in which you discuss the types of gender role socialization you observed (use your field journal) and social problems or issues related to gender that could develop as a result of these types of socialization.

PROJECT INSTRUCTIONS ARE CONTINUED ON THE FOLLOWING PAGE.

Option: bibliography
Use your library's and/or computer indexes (e.g.., *Social Science Index, Sociological Abstracts*, and so on) to develop a bibliography of ten articles from sociology journals and sociological web sites that deal with gender role socialization and gender-related social problems and/or issues. Type your bibliography using the format found in the journals or in your textbook.

Option: research paper
Complete the above journal and bibliographic instructions if you have not already done so. Write a paper (around seven to nine pages, typed) in which you:

1. Briefly discuss the process of how we acquire gender roles and review some theories of gender role socialization.

2. Discuss the way in which you collected the data for the journal observations.

3. Use information from five of the journal articles from the bibliography you developed and theories of gender role socialization to discuss the information you collected through your journal observations.

4. Discuss two or three problems related to gender that can be linked to gender role socialization.

5. Be sure to support your ideas with bibliographic material. Provide proper documentation throughout the paper and include a reference page.

PROJECT 10. 2 Gender Inequality in the Workplace

Even though people are developing more **androgynous gender roles**—that is, roles that exhibit both masculine and feminine traits—gender inequality in the workplace still exists. It exists primarily in the form of **gender segregation** and **gender stratification.** Men and women tend to be employed to do different types of work and for unequal pay. Besides the wage gap between men and women, other factors such as **the glass ceiling, mommy tracks, a split labor market,** and other help to perpetuate inequality in the work place. The **glass ceiling** refers to the barrier that enables women to glimpse the upper management positions, but not attain them because of male traditions, prejudices, and stereotypes of women. **Mommy tracks** refers to employment situations in which women who choose to integrate family responsibilities into their schedules may have to sacrifice professional advancement. There is also a **split labor market** for men and women. The **primary labor market** employs people who are on a career path that will likely advance them to higher-level positions. The **secondary labor market** contains jobs that contain little, if any, chance of professional advancement. The purpose of this project is to have you examine the extent to which gender segregation and stratification exist in the workplace and to consider why.

Journal instructions:
1. Identify a large corporation or other organization that employs many people, such as the college you attend, an insurance company, a hospital, or any large business for which you can obtain access of a list of types of employment and the names of the employees. The easiest choice for you will be the college that you attend.

2. Obtain a list of all of the types of employment that exist at the place of employment you selected (for example, secretaries, administrators, faculty members, groundskeepers, cafeteria workers, and so on). This can be obtained from the director of human resources or other public records, such as the college catalog. Once you obtain the list of types of employment, do the following:
   a) Read through the list of personnel and keep a list of each different type of employment or position at the organization you selected. If you selected your college, this probably will appear in the back of the college catalog.
   b) Count the number of men and the number of women in each employment position. Then, calculate the percentage of women and men that do each particular job. (For example, ninety five percent of the secretaries are female, five percent are men, and so on).
   c) Find out the number of members there are on the Board of Directors and what percentage are men and women.

3. After you have completed the above, interview someone who works in each of the positions you identified. Briefly describe, in your journal, what they do, the level of difficulty of their job, and the likelihood for professional advancement.

4. Rank the jobs in terms of what you think the salaries are, from the highest to the lowest. You do not have to know the actual salaries.

5. Based on all of the above data that you collected, divide the jobs into two lists: primary market and secondary market. What percentage of the employees in each market are female and what percentage are male?

PROJECT INSTRUCTIONS ARE CONTINUED ON THE FOLLOWING PAGE.

6. Interview two women and two men who work at the place of employment you identified. Be sure to assure them that their answers are strictly confidential and be sure to honor that commitment. Try to interview two people from the primary labor market and two from the secondary labor market. In your journal, write down their answers to the following questions:
   a) Do men and women in the primary labor market (mention the jobs you have in your primary market list) have the same chances for professional advancement?
   b) Are there any male traditions, stereotypes, or prejudices of women that still exist at this place of employment—either overtly or covertly—that impede the advancement of women there? If so, what are they?
   c) Are there any ways in which women are denied the same opportunities for advancement as men—again, either overtly or covertly?

Option: essay
Using the information that you collected in your journal above, write an essay (around five pages, typed) in which you discuss the extent to which gender segregation and gender stratification exists at the place of employment you studied. Do they exist? To what extent? Why? If you find that gender segregation and stratification exist, use the perspectives on gender discussed in Chapter 10 of your textbook to offer some possible explanations. Did you find any evidence in your observations or interviews that support any of the theories? If so, discuss.

Option: bibliography
Use your library's indexes to develop a bibliography of ten to fifteen articles from sociology journals or books written by sociologists that discuss gender segregation, gender stratification, primary and secondary labor markets, and gender inequality in the workplace. Additionally, identify two or three web sites that deal with gender inequality in the workplace. Type your bibliography using the bibliographic style found in the sociology journal or in your textbook.

Option: research paper
If you have not done so already, complete the above journal, essay and bibliography instructions. Write a paper, around seven to ten pages, in which you discuss gender inequality in the workplace, using the research you conducted as a case study. Integrate your research with sociological ideas found within at least five articles from your bibliography. Do the following:

1. Use ideas and information from around five of the articles in your bibliography to explain how different labor markets (primary and secondary) affect men and women differently.

2. Use information collected in your journal assignment to illustrate and discuss some of the ideas found in some of the articles in your bibliography.

3. Provide proper documentation of your references throughout the paper and include a reference page.

PROJECT 10.3 Gender Roles and Social Policy

Social policies surrounding women's (and some men's) rights are continually appearing in the news and in the political arena. One reason for this is that women's and men's changing roles in society, especially in the workplace and in the family, have led to the need for political representation that can help women achieve equality in the workplace and other areas of social life. Economic and political policies regarding family leave, child care, reproductive rights, sexual discrimination, sexual harassment, the Equal Rights Amendment, and others are some of the major issues that politicians concerned with gender equality have said need to be addressed. The objective of this project is to have you identify and examine the current social policies that are being considered, both nationally and locally, and the debates that surround them.

Journal instructions:
1. Look through back issues of national and local newspapers for the previous one to two years. Locate fifteen to twenty news articles, essays, letters to the editor, and so forth that address various policies related to women's issues. (See the introduction to this project for some ideas.) Try to get a representation of different policies and diverse viewpoints on these issues.

2. Keep a record of the news items (articles, essays, letters to the editor., etc.) in our journal. You may want to photocopy each and keep them in your journal, or summarize each, indicating the newspaper, date, and page.

3. List each of the policy issues and briefly summarize what the various positions (that is, views) regarding each one are. (For example, what are the various positions regarding the reproductive rights of women, national child care policies, family leave policies, comparable worth, and so on?)

4. Discuss the assumptions about gender roles that are contained with the various positions about the policy. For example, what are the assumptions and stereotypes about gender roles in a position that supports enough child care resources to allow both parents to work full-time outside the home? What are the assumptions and stereotypes about gender roles in a position that does not support enough child care resources to allow both parents to work full-time?

5. Select one of the above policy issues that you identified. Interview an activist (for example, a community leader, politician, clergy person, and so on) who supports the policy and one who opposes the policy. Ask the person to provide you with sold reasons for the position he or she takes. In addition, ask the person to explain his or her views about women's and men's respective roles in society, especially with regard to the family and work.

Option: essay
Write an essay (around five pages, typed) in which you summarize and discuss the major social policy debates today that involve gender. Your discussion should include a list of at least three or four important policy debates, the stereotypes about gender that are contained within each side of the debate, and the different positions that are being taken toward each policy proposal.

PROJECT INSTRUCTIONS ARE CONTINUED ON THE FOLLOWING PAGE.

Option: bibliography
Develop a bibliography of around ten to fifteen articles from popular periodicals and sociology journals and/or books written by sociologists about the policy you identified above (#5 in the journal instructions). Make sure that at least six of your articles are from the sociological literature. Be sure you obtain references that can provide you with at least three arguments for and three arguments against the policy. Type your bibliography following the format found in one of the sociology journals.

Option: research paper
Write a paper (around seven pages, typed) in which you present a policy debate for and against a particular issue that concerns women primarily. In your debate, be sure to include a discussion of the stereotypes and assumptions about gender roles that underlie each position in the debate. Use at least five sources from your bibliography (above), at least three of which must be articles from sociology journals and/or books written by sociologists. Be sure to provide proper documentation of your references and include a reference page.

PROJECT 10. 4 Using Sociological Perspectives to Examine Women's Issues and Men's Issues

It is becoming more and more evident that women and men face very different issues in society today. Some of these issues concern obtaining greater equality for women, some concern how men are dealing with this increased equality for women. There are others as well. Regardless of the issue, though, most deal with stereotypes and assumptions about women's and men's respective roles. The sociological perspectives each offer very different explanations about why these assumptions and stereotypes exist. Understanding the different explanations of these stereotypes and assumptions is very useful in helping us to understand what the issues are about and in helping to propose solutions to deal with them. The objective of this project is to have you identify some women's and men's issues and to explain them using the sociological perspectives.

Journal instructions:
1. Be an observer at three meetings of a "women's group" and three meetings of a "men's group." If you can not locate any meetings that are designed specifically to deal with women's or men's issues, identify some groups or organizations that are predominantly made up of women and some that are predominantly made up of men. You can probably find one women's and one men's group on your college campus or in your community.

2. In your journal, keep a list of the issues and topics that the women and men discuss at their respective meetings. Write down comments about the issues that they talk about that are gender-related issues. These could include problems dealing with everyday life, political issues, identity issues, and so on.

3. Interview one of two of the women and one or two of the men. Ask each what they feel some of the most important issues related to gender expectations today are and why. Ask them if there are any problems or issues that they face that are related to gender expectations.

4. Once you have conducted your observations and interviews, discuss each of the issues you identified from each of the functionalist, conflict, feminist, and interactionist perspectives. How would each perspective explain the origin of the issue, why the issue still exists, and how it might be overcome. Use your observations and interviews to illustrate the viewpoints of each perspective.

5. Finally, after you have completed the above, briefly discuss, in your journal, which sociological perspective you feel is the most useful and accurate in explaining the issue and in proposing a solution.

Option: essay
Write an essay (around five pages, typed) in which you use the three major sociological perspectives to discuss women's and men's issues and problems. Some things you could talk about in your essay include: What are some of the most important issues women and men face that are a result of gender stereotypes, prejudices, and discrimination? How did these issues develop? Are the types of issues that women and men face very different or are they similar? Who tends to suffer more from gender expectations? Again, be sure to use the sociological perspectives to discuss these, or other, ideas.

PROJECT INSTRUCTIONS ARE CONTINUED ON THE FOLLOWING PAGE.

Option: bibliography
Develop a bibliography of around ten to fifteen articles from sociology journals or books written by sociologists about issues and problems that men and women face as a result of gender. Type your bibliography following the format found in one of the sociology journals.

Option: research paper
Using information from your field journal, essay, and at least five items from your bibliography, write a paper (around seven pages, typed) in which you discuss women's and men's issues from the point of view of each of the three major sociological perspectives. Make sure that you integrate material from your observations, interviews, and bibliographic material. Be sure to document your sources properly throughout your paper and include a reference page.

CHAPTER 11

SEXUAL BEHAVIOR

CHAPTER OUTLINE

Human Sexuality

Contemporary Sexual Behavior
        Heterosexual Behavior
                A Historical Sketch
                A Sexual Revolution?
        Homosexual Behavior
                Origins
                The Gay and Lesbian Community

Sexual Behavior and Social Problems
        Discrimination Against Gays and Lesbians
        Adolescent Sex and Unwanted Pregnancy
        AIDS
        Child Molestation
        Prostitution
                The Social World of Prostitution
                Becoming a Prostitute
                Prostitution and the Law
        Pornography

Solving the Problems of Sexual Behavior
        Education and the Media
        The Legal System
        Tolerating Diversity

Sociological Perspectives on Sexual Behavior
        The Functionalist Perspective
        The Conflict Perspective
        The Feminist Perspective
        The Interactionist Perspective

CHAPTER LEARNING OBJECTIVES AND ESSAY QUESTIONS

After studying this chapter, you should be able to:

• Outline and discuss aspects of social problems related to sexuality.

• Describe the sociological perspective on human sexuality.

• Discuss the history and contemporary forms of sexual behavior, including homosexuality.

• Analyze some of the problems and issues regarding sexuality today.

• Outline and discuss some of the ways the government and parents are responding to the problems of sexual behavior.

• State, explain, and compare the four sociological perspectives on sexual behavior.

KEY POINTS FOR REVIEW

• Social forces shape human sexual behavior in many ways. For example, appropriateness, desirability, timing, location, and other factors related to sexual behavior are all the product of social forces. Anthropological studies have revealed a wide range of sexual customs and behaviors in cultures around the world. Almost every form of sexual behavior—including heterosexuality, homosexuality, pre-marital sex, incest, and others—is considered normal somewhere under some circumstances. The distinction between normal and deviant sex comes from society, not biology, and we learn what is appropriate within our society.

• The study of sexual behavior is difficult and confusing because many people are unwilling the describe their sexual behavior to scientists. Sex surveys, such as Kinsey's, are the best sources of data on sexual behavior. However, it is unlikely that respondents to sex surveys accurately represent the overall population. Nevertheless, the research does provide social scientists with some rough estimates regarding sexual practices.

• Most people have both homosexual and heterosexual urges at one time or another. The differences between homosexuals, bisexuals, and heterosexuals are a matter of degree.

• Contemporary Western sexual morality is rooted in the Judeo-Christian religious tradition after the fall of the Roman Empire. The repression of sexuality was reemphasized by the seventeenth century Puritans and shaped early American sexual beliefs and practices and were later reinforced during the nineteenth century Victorian era.

• Sexual attitudes and practices have changed since the Victorian era. A double standard—which traditionally allowed more liberal sexual behavior for males than females—has declined, but has not disappeared. Men still have much more sexual freedom than women. Sexual activity has increased within and outside of marriages. Sexual freedoms have increased due to cultural changes which include the decline of the influence of traditional religious morality, the increase of women's economic and political power, a cultural emphasis on individual freedom and self-determination, the increased use of erotic materials as entertainment and in the media, the development of more effective birth control techniques, and a basic redefinition of sexuality.

• Homosexuality is one of the most understood of all types of sexual behavior. Stereotypes of homosexuals—for example, that male homosexuals are all effeminate and that females are all masculine, and that homosexuals have different personality characteristics than heterosexuals—have proven to be untrue for most homosexuals.

• There is no conclusive proof about the causes of homosexuality. Some studies suggest that it is determined by biological factors. Classic psychoanalytic theory views homosexuality in males as the result of an excessively close relationship with the mother and a distant and rejecting father. Sociological theory sees it as the result of social conditions in which it is learned. For example, among adolescents the encouragement of marked gender differences, combined with the pressures of mate selection, may make association with the same sex less painful and embarrassing than association with the opposite sex. Further, the belief that one is either homosexual or heterosexual often causes individuals who engage in exploratory homosexual behavior to define themselves as homosexuals.

• There is considerable disagreement among social scientists about how common homosexuality actually is. It is likely that between one to four percent of American men are primarily or exclusively homosexual. There has been a growing trend among homosexuals during the last two decades to "come out of the closet." Gay and lesbian communities are now acknowledged as a part of urban life throughout North America. Such communities provide a supportive social environment that allows gays and lesbians to be themselves without fear of condemnation by the outside world.   Gays and lesbians share many common problems created by the prejudice against them, but their sexual attitudes reflect some of the same gender differences as heterosexual men and women.

• There is a great deal of confusion about the problems of sexual behavior and what to do about them because of society's deep uncertainty about sexuality. One problem is the blatant discrimination that gays and lesbians suffer. A reason for this is that the law does not protect the basic civil rights of homosexuals in most states. The law does not recognize homosexual marriages and, in many states, homosexuality is a crime. Homosexuals also are discriminated against in military service. Homosexuals have been organizing to end such discrimination, but have only been moderately successful in a few states.

• Another problem of sexuality is adolescent sex and unwanted pregnancy. While there is disagreement about the percentage of adolescents having sexual intercourse, there is agreement that young people are having sex at an earlier age than they did in the past. This poses a special problem since young people are often confused about how to deal with their own sexuality. The birth rate for unmarried American teens has skyrocketed in the last two decades. This is largely due to ignorance about sexual matters, especially contraceptive use.

• A third problem is sexually transmitted diseases, especially AIDS. Sexually transmitted diseases have always been part of most societies, but none have been as devastating as AIDS. Worldwide, heterosexual intercourse is the most common way AIDS is transmitted, but in the wealthy industrialized nations, AIDS is much more widespread among gay men. About one million persons are infected with AIDS in the US. In the US there is evidence that the epidemic has peaked among male homosexuals and is increasing among intravenous drug users and heterosexual women whose partners are intravenous drug users.

• A fourth problem of sexuality is child molestation. Fifty to eighty percent of child molestation's are committed by family friends, relatives, or acquaintances. Some claim that there

204

has been a big increase in child molestation in recent times, but there is no convincing evidence to support this. The apparent increase may be the result of a willingness of more people to acknowledge the problem and to talk about than before. There are many theories as to why people become child molesters. There is mounting evidence that child molesters often learned that behavior in their own childhood when they were the victims of sexual abuse.

• A fifth problem is prostitution. Prostitution has declined dramatically in the past half-century. Not all prostitute are women. Male prostitution is also common. Prostitution has a long history in North America. For a long time, it was illegal but carefully ignored by most police departments. Laws intended to solve the problems of prostitution have generally made the problem worse. The prohibition of prostitution and closing of houses of prostitution has led to an increase of streetwalkers and involvement by organized crime.

• Finally, pornography is seen by many as a social problem. However, there is much debate about what is and what is not pornography. The Supreme Court defines "obscene" any material that appeals to "prurient" interests, is contrary to community standards, and lacks all "redeeming social value." However, these criteria are impossible to apply objectively. Various studies conclude different things about the results of exposure to pornography. Generally, the scientific evidence shows that violent pornography promotes sexual violence, but materials showing non degrading sex and simple nudity do not promote illegal activities. A problem with thinking about pornography is that any type of restriction on the freedom of expression creates additional problems.

• There are approaches for dealing with problems of sexual behavior: improving education and preventive measures, advocating changes in the laws and the criminal-justice system, and learning to tolerate diversity In the first category, one proposal is that the media should run public service announcements for teenagers about the importance of birth control and safe sex practices, especially if it is going to continue to broadcast sexually titillating programs that are aimed at teenagers. A second proposal is to create more effective sex education programs in schools. In the second category, one proposal is to enforce laws more strictly in cases of clear cut sexual crimes such as incest, child molestation, and rape. The second proposal is to remove any unnecessary laws regarding private acts between consenting adults, thus reducing the burden on the criminal justice system and the rampant discrimination against homosexuals. Further, legalizing prostitution and submitting it to government regulation could reduce the spread of sexually transmitted disease. Finally, enact legislation that would protect the civil rights of gays and lesbians. Third, people need to recognize that contemporary culture contains a mishmash of contradictory attitudes, beliefs, and values about sexuality. It is unlikely that we will ever arrive at a consensus about such a personal area of our life. What we can do is recognize our diversity and accept the fact that in a democracy we need to be tolerant of others even if they do not share our opinion or attitude.

• The functionalist perspective views sexuality in terms of whether or not specific behaviors are functional or dysfunctional for society. For example, functionalists note that prostitution benefits society by creating jobs for people with few skills, provides a sexual outlet for people who are without one, and reduces the risk of hostile men who might use violence to satisfy their sexual desires. On the other hand, functionalists see premarital and extramarital sex as dysfunctional because it undermines the kinship system. In general, if a sexual practice undermines traditional social institutions more than it benefits them, functionalists oppose the practice.

205

• From the conflict perspective, problems of sexual behavior stem from conflicting ideas about sexual morality. Conflict theorists believe that actions to control sexual attitudes and behaviors are part of a larger effort by traditional groups to maintain their cultural dominance by controlling criminal law. They see the attempt to stamp out prostitution and homosexuality as the oppression of sexual minorities. Conflict theorists recommend that these sexual minorities organize and agitate for social change and that there would be fewer problems of sexuality if laws prohibiting sexual acts between consenting adults were repealed.

• Feminist theorists agree that all sexual behavior between consenting adults should be legalized. One of the main concerns of feminists, though not all feminists, is the violence that men commit against women in the form of pornography.

• The interactionist perspective is concerned about the effects of the constant use of sex to sell consumer goods and to boost television ratings, motion picture profits, and magazine sales. This erotic bombardment creates serious problems for many people who cannot live up to the demands for sexual attractiveness and instant fulfillment generated by the media. From the interactionist perspective, the solution to problems of sexuality lie in more effective sex education in the schools, therapy for those with sexual problems, greater availability of contraception, and greater responsibility on the part of the media.

• Other perspectives, such as the biosocial perspective, focus on the biological aspects of sexuality and their impact on social behavior. One area of focus is on the process of evolution and the biosocial argument is that men have a higher sex drive in order to increase their chances of passing their genes on to the next generation. Critics of this approach point out that without proper socialization, that type of behavior could actually be maladaptive to a species' survival.

NOTES:

KEY TERMS

The following key terms are found in your textbook on the page number indicated in parentheses. In the space provided, write a brief definition of the key term **in your own words**. Then **provide an example** of the term, such as a culture in which the practice takes place, or people that you might know whose behavior illustrates the term, a current event that illustrates the term, how a term could be used to shed light on or help solve a particular social problem, and so on. You could include examples from the news, books, movies, or anything else that will illustrate the term and help you remember it. Include any comments from your class discussions or textbook that might help you remember and understand these key terms. Use additional paper if necessary, but keep it with your study guide to help you review for exams.

sexual orientation (p. 346)

_____

_____

_____

_____

premarital intercourse (p. 350)

_____

_____

_____

_____

homosexuals (p.349)

_____

_____

_____

_____

bisexuals (p. 349)

_____

_____

_____

heterosexuals (p. 349)

_____

_____

_____

_____

double standard (p. 350)

_____

_____

_____

_____

gays (p. 351)

_____

_____

_____

_____

lesbians (p. 351)

_____

_____

_____

_____

sodomy (p. 356)

_____

_____

_____

_____

sexually transmitted diseases (p. 358)

_____

_____

_____

_____

child molestation (p. 361)

_____

_____

_____

_____

prostitution (p. 351)

_____

_____

_____

_____

pornography (p. 364)

_____

_____

_____

_____

call girls (p. 362)

_____

_____

_____

_____

madam (p. 362)

——

——

——

——

streetwalkers (p. 362)

——

——

——

——

street hustlers (p. 363)

——

——

——

——

bar hustlers (p. 363)

——

——

——

——

NOTES:

210

PRACTICE TEST

Multiple Choice

1. Anthropological studies in cultures around the world have discovered:
    a) a variety of heterosexual but few homosexual customs and behavior
    b) very few norms that regulate sexual behavior
    c) a narrow range of sexual customs and behavior
    d) a wide range of sexual customs and behavior

2. The distinction between normal and deviant sex comes from:
    a) society
    b) genetic codes
    c) religious beliefs
    d) political actions

3. Puritans condemned all sexual activities outside of marriage while the Polynesian people of the South Pacific have free sexual attitudes and practices. These examples support the position that:
    a) sexual customs and behavior vary greatly around the world
    b) sexual behavior is based on heredity
    c) the Polynesian people of the South Pacific are deviant
    d) sexuality in most societies is restricted by social customs

4. Which of the following is a reason why studying sexual behavior is difficult and confusing?
    a) Researchers are always evaluating their own sexual behavior.
    b) Researchers are members of religious groups who oppose sexual values.
    c) Researchers are deeply divided over sexual morality.
    d) Many people are unwilling to describe their sexual behavior to researchers.

5. Research has shown that the incest taboo:
    a) is found in all cultures
    b) is not a cultural universal
    c) is no longer needed
    d) bans sexual relationships between first cousins in all cultures

6. Which of the following groups demanded almost the complete repression of sexuality?
    a) the Roman empire
    b) the Puritans
    c) the Polynesians
    d) twentieth century Americans

7. Which of the following statements about the "double standard" is true?
    a) It is as strong as ever.
    b) It has largely disappeared
    c) It is weaker but still exists.
    d) It has evolved into a triple standard

8. Attempts to prove that homosexuality is caused by heredity have:
   a) discovered a solid link
   b) produced little conclusive evidence
   c) explain the universality of homosexuality in various cultures
   d) determined homosexuality is really disguised heterosexuality

9. Alfred Kinsey's data suggested that the first wave of sexual liberation in American society occurred in the:
   a) 1890s
   b) 1920s
   c) 1960s
   d) 1980s

10. The differences between homosexuality, bisexuality, and heterosexuality is:
    a) genetic programming
    b) a matter of deviance and normality
    c) a matter of degree
    d) a matter of taste

11. All of the following are types of methodological problems that make it difficult to measure the actual changes in sexual behavior, EXCEPT that:
    a) subjects of studies are often not representative of the overall population
    b) research projects have never had solid financial backing
    c) a vast number of respondents lie on questionnaires
    d) usually a large number of people refuse to respond to questions

12. Recent surveys of sexual activity within marriage discovered that married couples:
    a) rarely engage in oral sex
    b) rarely practice masturbation
    c) have experienced an increase in overall sexuality
    d) more often go to prostitutes

13. For sociologists, homosexuality is best explained by:
    a) religious teaching
    b) biological defects
    c) the conditions in which sexuality is learned
    d) the bond between the child and the mother

14. Many teenagers become pregnant because they:
    a) actively want to have a child
    b) are simply ignorant about sexual matters
    c) had their interest in sex kindled by sex education classes
    d) want to be popular with their classmates

15. All of the following are true about homosexuality and the law, EXCEPT that:
    a) homosexual acts are legal in most of the U.S.
    b) during the middle ages, homosexuals were commonly tortured to death
    c) homosexuals still suffer open legal discrimination
    d) the professions of the law, teaching, and medicine are still largely closed to homosexuals

212

16. Which of the following groups is most likely to be involved in child molestations?
    a) older teenagers who often baby-sit children
    b) therapists and teachers
    c) strangers
    d) family friends and relatives

17. The epidemic of AIDS among male homosexuals has:
    a) helped the gay liberation movement
    b) led to the extinction of homosexuality
    c) led to a new wave of hostility toward gays
    d) created more conversions to homosexuality

18. AIDS has created the biggest behavior changes among:
    a) homosexual women
    b) heterosexual women
    c) homosexual men
    d) heterosexual men

19. The Supreme Court's efforts to define what is obscene:
    a) have ended in failure
    b) have now clearly defined what is obscene
    c) have created widespread agreement among most Americans
    d) are no longer an issue of concern to the court

20. All of the following statements about prostitution are true, EXCEPT that:
    a) the demand for prostitution has decreased
    b) there is a status hierarchy among prostitutes
    c) prostitution is a major way AIDS is spread
    d) male prostitution is common

21. The three major TV networks:
    a) refuse to inform teenagers about sexuality
    b) promote sexuality through many TV shows
    c) do not allow paid advertising for most birth control devices
    d) do all of the above activities regarding sexuality

22. Many experts feel that sex crimes without victims:
    a) are more serious than sex crimes with victims
    b) should be decriminalized
    c) require psychotherapy rather than imprisonment
    d) actually do have victims

23. Which of the following statements is true?
    a) All pornography promotes violence
    b) Sexual violence inspires sexual performance
    c) Violent porn contributes to violent sex crimes
    d) Simple nudity promotes degrading sex

24. Which of the following innovations in school has had great success in cutting down on teenage pregnancy?
    a) health clinics on school campuses
    b) free distribution of condoms
    c) religious training
    d) comprehensive sex education

25. According to sociologists, all of the following are ways of responding to problems of sexual behavior, EXCEPT for:
    a) abstinence
    b) education and prevention
    c) increasing tolerance
    d) changing the laws

26. The criminal justice system has been criticized for:
    a) too strictly enforcing the laws against rape and pornography
    b) not enforcing the law strictly enough
    c) not having enough laws to effectively regulate sexual deviance
    d) actually encouraging sexual deviance

27. All of the following are ways that outlawing deviant behavior creates more problems than it solves, EXCEPT that these laws:
    a) help the community to define its moral codes and limits
    b) lead to attacks on some persons or groups who are politically unpopular
    c) create deviant subcultures
    d) prevent effective control and regulation of deviance

28. Biosocial theorists argue that the major determinant of sexual behavior is:
    a) social forces
    b) powerful groups imposing their morality on others
    c) the functional requirements of society
    d) evolution

29. Which sociological perspective argues that problems of sexual behavior are attempts by powerful groups to force their morality on others?
    a) functionalist
    b) biosocial
    c) conflict
    d) interactionist

30. Many functionalists feel that:
    a) violent pornography has little impact on sexual behavior
    b) prostitution and soft-core pornography are dysfunctional for society
    c) prostitution is actually function for society and should be legalized
    d) stricter laws regulating all pornography and prostitution are needed

214

PROJECTS

PROJECT 11.1 AIDS-Related Social Issues

AIDS is spreading at rates which continuously surpass previous projections. Over 300,000 Americans have been diagnosed with AIDS and over one million people have been infected with HIV. The World Health Organization (WHO) estimates the total cases of AIDS worldwide to be greater than 1.5 million, with eight to ten million people infected with HIV. The rapid spread of AIDS is a social problem that has led to a number of important related social issues, especially relevant to sex practices. For example: Should condoms be distributed upon request in schools? Should there be sex education in schools? If so, at what age (or grade) should sex education begin? Should "safer sex" education be a part of sex education programs? Should health-care practitioners (physicians, nurses, chiropractors, dentists, and so on) who have AIDS be allowed to continue to practice? Should health care-practitioners be required to treat AIDS sufferers? There are many other questions. The purpose of this project is to help you become aware of the social consequences of AIDS, especially as they relate to all of our family and personal lives.

Journal instructions:
1. Identify as many AIDS-related issues as you can that have occurred in the news over the past five years. You can probably do this effectively by looking through a sample of months in the various periodical and news indexes in your college library or local library (for example, *Reader's Guide to Periodical Literature, Social Science Index, New York Times Index, Newsbank,* and so on). Additionally, you can probably find numerous web sites that deal with AID-related issues. Obtain around twenty articles and two or three web sties that discuss a variety of the above issues or other issues related to AIDS.

2. Make a list of the issues for which you found articles, and list all the articles and web sites that pertain to each issue. Briefly summarize what each of the issues is about.

3. Use these issues to think about and discuss in your journal what the various consequences of AIDS may be for society. For example, what impact might early childhood sex education have on the types of relationships that people form at different stages in their life? How will the need to practice safer sex affect marriage rates and the ages at which people marry? How will the increasing rate of HIV and AIDS affect health insurance policies and the amount of money that families have to spend?   There are many other issues related to AIDS. Try not to take a position for or against a policy or an issue. Rather, try to think of all the possible consequences—positive and negative—that each issue raises.

Option: essay
Using the material that you compiled in your journal (above) write an essay (around three to five pages, typed) in which you discuss the social consequences of AIDS. Consider the impact on institutions such as marriage, the family, government, the economy, religion, education, health care, and others.

Option: research paper
Conduct further library research to find five or six articles from <u>sociology</u> journals and/or books written by sociologists that discuss the social consequences of AIDS. Write a paper (around five to seven pages, typed) in which you present an overview of the social consequences of AIDS from the point of view of sociologists and use the issues you identified in your work above to illustrate what these consequences might be. Be sure to provide proper documentation.

PROJECT 11.2 Observing Prejudice and Discrimination Against Gays and Lesbians

As Coleman and Cressey point out, no other group is discriminated against as much as homosexuals are. As you learned elsewhere in your text, discrimination often is the result of stereotypes and prejudice. The objective of this project is to have you observe stereotypes and prejudice toward homosexuals in everyday life, the extent to which discrimination exists, the degree to which the prejudice and stereotypes represent all homosexuals, and problems that exist as a result of these stereotypes.

1. For one week, keep an extensive journal in which you record examples of gay and lesbian stereotypes and prejudices that you observe, hear, witness, express personally, or feel. These can occur anywhere: interactions between friends, in your family, by teachers or students in or out of the classroom, on television programs, in advertisements, in newspapers, in magazines, on MTV, in the movies, and so on. Be sure to keep your journal with you at all times for one week so that you can record the stereotypes when you observe them.

2. In your journal, describe each of your observations of gay and lesbian stereotypes.

3. On what basis (for example, myth, personal experience, and so on) do you think each of these stereotypes was made?

4. Interview at least one (but preferably four or five) male and female homosexual. Discuss with them the stereotypes and prejudices that you observed. Record their answers in your journal: Ask them:
    a) To what extent do each of these stereotypes accurately represent them?
    b) To what extent do they feel that the stereotypes represent the majority of the homosexual population?
    c) Is there any basis for each of the stereotypes?
    c) Have they ever experienced any problems (especially discrimination) as a result of homosexual stereotypes? Explain.
    d) Have any of their homosexual friends ever experienced any problems as a result of homosexual stereotypes? Explain.

5. Look through issues of popular periodicals (newspapers, news magazines, and so on) for around the past year to identify social issues and problems faced by homosexuals that are directly related to prejudice and discrimination. Use your library's periodicals' indexes to do this. Find around five to ten articles that discuss these issues and problems and summarize them in your journal.

Option: essay
Write an essay (around four pages, typed) in which you discuss your stereotypes and discrimination toward homosexuals and the consequences for homosexuals. As part of your discussion, explore how each of the three sociological perspectives (functionalist, conflict, and social psychological) would explain or account for the existence of the stereotypes and discrimination you observed (in your journal, above). Use information from your field journal (above) as the basis for your essay.

INSTRUCTIONS FOR THIS PROJECT ARE CONTINUED ON THE FOLLOWING PAGE.

Option: bibliography
Develop a bibliography of ten to fifteen articles from sociology journals and/or books written by sociologists about social problems faced by homosexuals, currently and/or throughout history. Type your bibliography following the format found in one of the sociology journals.

Option: research paper
Write a paper (around seven pages, typed) in which you integrate material from your field journal, essay, and bibliography (at least five sources) to discuss prejudice, discrimination, and issues faced by homosexuals in contemporary American society and/or throughout the world. Be sure to cite your sources properly throughout your paper and include a reference page. *Suggestion:* If you have done a good job on your essay (above), you can develop your paper by integrating relevant material from your bibliography.

217

PROJECT 11. 3 Issues and Problems Related Sexual Behavior

Coleman and Cressey discuss a number of serious issues and problems that are related to sexual behavior. Some of these problems will have important consequences for society and for you. The objective of this project is to have you examine the extent to which the problems Coleman and Cressey mention exist in the world, the U.S., and in area where you live.

Journal instructions:

1. Re-read the section in chapter 11 about problems of sexual behavior and make a list of these in your journal.

2. Go through past issues of national and local newspapers and news magazines for around the past year and identify articles that pertain to issues and problems of sexual behavior. Look for articles that discuss problems mentioned by Coleman and Cressey and others as well. You do not have to go through every issue of every newspaper or magazine. You can use periodicals indexes (either in your library or through your computer) or you can take a systematic sample of time periods throughout the year—for example, Wednesday of each week, or the first Monday of each month, or everyday from the first week of every month, and so on—from which you can get back issues. In your journal, list each of the articles you find (along with the name of the periodical, date, pages, and author) and summarize briefly (a sentence or two) what the articles are about. Find at least thirty (30) articles. Additionally, locate at least three or four web sites that deal with problems of sexual behavior and summarize their contents.

3. Categorize the issues and problems (for example, AIDS, teen pregnancy, sex education, child molestation, rape, discrimination against homosexuals, prostitution, pornography, and so on).

4. Which issues and problems appear most often? The least often? Who is affected by each issue or problem? What are the consequences for society if the problem persists? As far as you can tell from the articles you identified, what steps are currently being taken to deal with each problem? Which sociological perspective (functionalism, conflict, social psychological) do you think underlies each of the solutions being taken to deal with the problem? Discuss these questions in your journal.

Option: essay
Write an essay (around four to five pages, typed) in which you use information from your field journal (above) to discuss what you think are the two or three most serious issues and problems related to sexual behavior that exist today. Use one or more of the sociological perspectives to discuss reasons and solutions to the problem.

Option: bibliography
Develop a bibliography of ten to fifteen articles from sociology journals and/or books written by sociologists about one of the issues or problems you identified above. Type your bibliography following the format found in one of the sociology journals.

Option: research paper
Write a paper (around seven pages, typed) in which you discuss one problem or issue of sexual behavior in contemporary society. Use information that you gathered in your field journal (above) at least five articles from your bibliography. The approach you take in your paper will be guided much by the types of articles in your bibliography and what you have discussed in your field journal. Be sure to document your sources properly.

PROJECT 11.4 Safe Sex Survey Among College Students Survey

Coleman and Cressey discuss a number important surveys of sexual behavior that have described the sexual practices of Americans throughout the years. While the surveys yield important information, there are some methodological difficulties entailed in doing them. One of these problems is in obtaining accurate information from people who are willing to participate in the survey. The objective of this project is twofold. First, you will obtain information about college students about an important problem of sexual behavior, failure to practice safe sex. Second, you will learn about some of the methodological difficulties entailed in doing survey research about sexual behavior.

Journal instructions:
1. Make a list of the safer sex practices of which your are currently aware. Discuss how likely you have been in the past,, are currently, or would be to engage in the safer sex practice. After each safer sex practice that you do not always follow (or have not, or are not likely to), discuss why.

2. In your journal, make a list of contraceptive techniques and after each discuss how likely you have been in the past, are currently, or would be to engage that type of contraception. After each, discuss why or why not.

3. After you have examined your own practices with regards to engaging in safer sex and using contraception, conduct a survey of students at your college. You can do this on your own or you may choose to work with others in the class who are doing this project. Obtain a sample of about one hundred students to participate in your survey. A random sample is best, but if that is not possible or practical, use a convenience sample that may be available (various classes, residence halls, meeting places such as the cafeteria, campus center, library, or others). You can design your own survey, or use the one on the following page. If you wish, you can modify the questionnaire on the following page to include additional questions, or you can modify it to conduct a survey on either safer sex practices or contraceptive use.

4. Summarize the results of your questionnaire responses. Then answer the following questions about sexual practices at your college:
    a) Would you say that people who are sexually active at your college generally practice safer sex?
    b) Of the people who do not always practice safer sex, what types of unsafe sexual activity are most common?
    c) Are there any differences in safer sex practices according to age, race, religion, gender and class?
    d) Would you say that people who are sexually active at your college generally use contraceptives?
    e) What types of contraceptives are used more often? Least often?
    f) Are there any differences in contraceptive use according to age, race, religion, gender, and class?

Option: essay
Write an essay (around five pages, typed) in which you use the results of the above survey to discuss safer sex and contraceptive practices among students at your college. Be sure to integrate comments made on the questionnaires.

INSTRUCTIONS FOR THIS PROJECT ARE CONTINUED ON THE FOLLOWING PAGE.

Option: bibliography
Develop a bibliography of around fifteen articles from sociology journals and/or books written by sociologists about sex practices of young adults and college students. Type your bibliography following the format found in one of the sociology journal.

Option: research paper
Use information from at least five items from your bibliography (above) and the results of your survey research to write a paper (around seven pages, typed) about safer sex practices and contraceptive use of young adults and college students. Here are some things you might discuss (but do not feel limited to these). Compare the results of what you found at your college with results of other surveys discussed in articles from your bibliography. Summarize the results of your survey. If you are adept at performing statistical analyses, you can examine the relationships between specific variables (for example, age and likelihood of using specific practices, gender and frequency of sexual activity, and so on). There are numerous approaches to take with this paper. Further, if you do this research conscientiously, you will have enough material to write papers in other courses related to this topic. Be sure to provide proper documentation of your sources throughout the paper and include a reference (works cited) page.

SAFE SEX SURVEY BEGINS ON THE FOLLOWING PAGE.

Safer Sex and Contraceptive Practices Among College Students Survey

This survey is being conducted for a class on Marriage and the Family. The purpose of this survey is to determine the extent to which college students practice safer sex and to find out which types of contraceptives they use when they are sexually active. Your answers will be kept strictly confidential and you will remain anonymous. Thank-you for your cooperation.

1. Age   _____16-18   _____19-21   _____21-23   _____24 and above

2. Race   _____

3. Religion   _____(if none, please say "none")

4. Gender   _____Male   _____Female

5. Class   _____Freshmen   _____Sophomore   _____Junior   _____Senior

6. Have you been sexually active (that is, have engaged in intercourse, oral sex, or other forms of intimate sexual activity with another person) within the past five years?
_____Yes   _____No

If you checked "yes," please answer the remainder of this questionnaire. If you checked "no," do not answer the remainder of the questionnaire and please wait patiently until the questionnaires are collected

7. When sexually active, how likely are you to:

	Always	Often	Sometimes	Never
• discuss safer sex practices with your partner?	____	____	____	____
• use a condom?	____	____	____	____
• use nonoxynol-9?	____	____	____	____
• avoid anal sex	____	____	____	____
• avoid multiple sex partners	____	____	____	____
• avoid casual sex	____	____	____	____
• avoid drug use	____	____	____	____
• require the partner to have an AIDS test	____	____	____	____

8. When sexually active, how likely are you (or your partner) to use the following methods of contraception?:

	Very likely	Somewhat likely	Not very likely	Never
• birth control pill	____	____	____	____
• IUD	____	____	____	____
• diaphragm	____	____	____	____
• condom	____	____	____	____
• spermicidal foam	____	____	____	____
• rhythm	____	____	____	____
• withdrawal	____	____	____	____
• surgical sterilization	____	____	____	____
• other methods (fill in)_____	____	____	____	____

9. If there are any safer sex practices that you do not <u>always</u> follow (items listed in question 7), please comment as to why not.

_____

_____

_____

_____

_____

10. Please comment on why you use the types of contraceptive devices that you indicated that you are likely or very likely to use.

_____

_____

_____

_____

CHAPTER 12

DRUG USE

CHAPTER OUTLINE

Drugs and Addiction
      Alcohol
      Tobacco
      Marijuana
      Opiates
      Psychedelics
      Sedative-Hypnotics
      Amphetamines
      Cocaine
      Steroids

Why Use Drugs?
      Biological Theories
      Behavioral Theory
      Personality Theories
      Interactionist Theory

Drug Control in North America

Solving the Drug Problem
      Prevention
      Treatment
      Legal Repression
      Increased Social Tolerance
            Legalization
            Decriminalization
            Maintenance
            The Dutch Approach

Sociological Perspectives on Drug Use
      The Functionalist Perspective
      The Conflict Perspective
      The Feminist Perspective
      The Interactionist Perspective

223

CHAPTER LEARNING OBJECTIVES AND ESSAY QUESTIONS

After studying this chapter, you should be able to:

• State why the social problem of drugs is so surrounded by myths and misinformation.

• Describe the basic characteristics of many types of drugs and explain why they promote addiction.

• Explain the biological, behavioral, personality, and interactionist theories of why people use drugs.

• Review the history of alcohol and drug use control efforts.

• Outline and discuss the several ways people and governments have responded to the drug problem.

• Compare and contrast four sociological perspectives on drug use.

KEY POINTS FOR REVIEW

• Drug use is surrounded by myths and misinformation. Here are some facts about drugs. Legal drugs, such as alcohol and nicotine (found in tobacco). can be just as dangerous as illicit drugs such as heroin, cocaine, or marijuana. Drug use is not confined to the dregs of society but, rather, drugs are a big business. Drug use has declined sharply since its peak in 1979. Legal drugs are used much more often than illicit ones. The drug problem is widespread and costly to society.

• Drug addiction is difficult to define precisely and has many definitions. Coleman and Cressey believe that the most useful definition of addiction is "the intense craving for a drug that develops after a period physical dependence." Two essential characteristics of an addictive drug are tolerance and withdrawal discomfort. Drug addiction is psychological as well as physiological. Drugs vary in their addictiveness ranging from highest to lowest in the following order—nicotine, heroin, cocaine, alcohol, caffeine, and marijuana. Cultural expectations surrounding drug use greatly affects how people react to specific drugs.

• Alcohol is an accepted part of American culture and plays an important part in social interactions from business deals, bonding rituals among friends, daily recreational activities, and so forth. This widespread acceptance means that it creates more problems than other drugs. Alcohol is a depressant. Prolonged heavy use of alcohol may lead to a number of health problems—such as cirrhosis of the liver, heart problems cancer—and addiction. Additionally, children of alcoholic mothers suffer from both physical and mental problems. An alcoholic is a person whose persistent drinking problem disrupts his or her life in ways such as interfering with the ability to hold a job, accomplish household tasks, participate in family and social affairs, and so on. There are more alcoholics in the US than users of all illicit drugs combined. One of the most serious problems of alcohol use is drunk driving. Drinking is a particular problem among college students with males still drinking the most, but the biggest increase in recent years is among females.

224

• One in four Americans over the age of 17 smokes cigarettes. The sales of tobacco, like those of alcohol, have been decreasing in recent years. Nicotine—the most addictive widespread drug—is found in tobacco. Nicotine is a stimulant. Tobacco smoking accounts for one in every five deaths in the US and is the number one cause of death. Cigarette smoking is related to cancer of the larynx, mouth, esophagus, and lungs, bronchitis, emphysema, ulcers, heart and circulatory disorders, and a reduction of the life span. Children of women who smoke have slower rates of physical and mental growth.

• The most widely used illegal drug is marijuana. About 1 in three Americans have tried marijuana, but only about 1 in 20 is a current user. The health hazards of marijuana are highly debatable. There are significant health hazards associated with the excessive use of marijuana—such as increased risk of cancer and other lung problems caused by inhaling smoke, and possible harm to unborn babies—but marijuana is less physically dangerous than tobacco and alcohol. The psychological effects of marijuana are strongly influenced by the social environment and the expectations of the users. Problems associated with marijuana are impaired reaction time and coordination.

• Opiates are a group of natural depressants—such as opium, codeine, morphine, and heroin—and synthetic depressants—such as and methadone—and are highly addictive. Opiate addiction causes serious health problems, but these problems come primarily from the way the drugs are used. The use of infected needles without proper sterilization is linked with the spread of hepatitis and AIDS. Death from overdose is also a common problem from opiate addiction. Opiate use is rare in the US, but the significant decrease in cost and increase in purity have led to fears that its use may increase significantly. Most heroin addicts in the US live in major cities.

• The physical effects of the most popular psychedelic drugs—such as LSD, mescaline, and MDMA(or "ecstasy")—are relatively minor. However, taken in large doses, they may lead to profound psychological changes and problems. The greatest dangers of psychedelic drugs are psychological rather than physical. The social environment has a significant effect on the outcome of a psychedelic "trip."

• Sedative-hypnotics—such as barbiturates and tranquilizers—depress the central nervous system. Medically, they are used for relaxation and sleep. They have similar effects as alcohol. They are addictive and are especially dangerous, often fatal, when combined with alcohol.

• Amphetamines are stimulants such as Benzedrine, Dexedrine, and Methedrine. Excessive use can produce a psychosis-like state similar to schizophrenia. Long-term use leads to physical deterioration such as significant loss of weight, hair, and teeth.

• Cocaine is a natural stimulant derived from coca leaves. Its effects are similar to amphetamines except that it does not last as long. The short life of its effects leads users to use it frequently. Heavy use can lead to personality changes, psychotic episodes, irritability, and depression. Physical problems include damage to nasal passages (since it is usually "snorted" or sniffed) and lung damage. It is highly addictive. Because of its high cost, many of its users are well-off financially. However, crack—a much less expensive and more powerful derivative of cocaine–is popular among the underclass.

• Steroids are synthetic drugs similar in structure to the male hormone testosterone. They are taken for building muscle and increasing athletic performance. Problems resulting from heavy steroid use include elevated cholesterol levels, high blood pressure, heart problems irritability, liver damage, sterility, atrophy of the testicles in males, the development of male characteristics (deeper voice, more body hair) in females. and the stunting of the growth in young users.

• There are numerous theories—biological, behavioral, personality, and interactionist—as to why we use drugs. Biological theories maintain that some people take drugs because they are genetically predisposed to do so. However, the results are inconclusive. It is unclear whether the biochemical composition that differentiates drug addicts is the cause or the result of their addiction. Further, there are significant differences in the use of drugs historically, geographically, and culturally, suggesting that drug use is learned and controlled by society. Behavioral theory suggests that drug use is learned through a process of conditioning and positive reinforcement. Some personality theories contend that some people weak personalities and low-self esteem turn to drugs to try to escape their problems. Critics of this view hold that drug users have as many personality characteristics as any other group of people and, therefore, this view does not explain why some turn to drugs and others do not. Interactionist theory sees drug use simply as one more behavior pattern that is learned from interaction with others in our culture. From this perspective, drug use is determined by individuals' attitudes toward drugs, the meaning drug use has for them, their overall world view, and their system of values—all of which are learned through social interaction.

• The US has a history of drug control efforts. The earliest controls, before 1700, came from religion and family. By the 19th century, state prohibition laws came into effect, ultimately resulting in the Eighteenth Amendment to the Constitution in 1919 which prohibited the manufacture, sale, and transportation of alcohol. This was repealed in 1933 by the Twenty-first Amendment. In 1937 the Marijuana Tax Act was passed by Congress which eventually led every state to prohibit marijuana. During the 1980s, American society began to focus on the problem of drug abuse and a "war on drugs" began.

• There have been numerous proposals for dealing with the drug problem. Many people believe that the best way is through prevention—specifically, discouraging young people from using drugs before they start. A second approach is through treatment of people who are already drug abusers. Treatments have included such techniques as individual psychotherapy, aversive therapy, group support (such as Alcoholics Anonymous), and therapeutic communities. A third approach is legal repression—prohibiting the manufacture and sale of illegal drugs. Alternative approaches to the drug problem focus on increased social tolerance, such as legalization, decriminalization, maintenance programs for addicts, or the Dutch Approach where soft drug use (marijuana) is illegal, yet tolerated, but penalties against hard drug use (heroin, cocaine) is strictly enforced and harshly penalized. The essence of the social tolerance approach is that the larger social problems that result from prohibiting drug use would be eliminated.

• Functionalist theory argues that the tremendous increase in drug use in industrial society is the result of people trying to escape from difficult and unpleasant circumstances such as poverty, worker alienation, and racism. Thus, the way to reduce drug abuse is to deal with the underlying social problems that leads to it. Other functionalists see the increase in drug use as the result of the weakening of the family and religious institutions that formerly kept antisocial behavior in check. For these theorists, the best way to deal with the drug problem is to strengthen these institutions.

• Conflict theorists maintain that the social problems underlying drug use, such as unemployment and poverty, stem from exploitation and injustice rather than from social disorganization. The solution these theorists offer is to attack exploitation rather than drug use itself. Other conflict theorists argue that drug use is normal and occurs in all societies around

226

the world. They feel it becomes a problem only when groups who oppose drugs try to use the power of the state to force their morality on everyone else. Their solution is to legalize prohibited drugs and stop jailing people who have not committed any other crime.

• The feminist perspective examines the link between gender role expectations and drug problems. Traditionally, men have had higher rates of drug use than women and women have had to conceal their behavior more. Thus the drug problem in women tends to be more hidden. Gender stereotypes have played a part in the types of drugs that physicians have prescribed to women. The use of prescription "medicines" to treat women for emotional problems has allowed women to avoid the definition of their behavior as drug use. On the other hand, men are likely to feel a stronger stigma in seeking help from physician for their emotional problems and often turn to heavy drinking as a solution. Feminists recommend that those trying to solve drug problems recognize the differences between the genders regarding this issue.

• The interactionist perspective focuses on how people learn to become drug users and on the ways in which society defines drugs and drug use.

NOTES:

227

KEY TERMS

The following key terms are found in your textbook on the page number indicated in parentheses. In the space provided, write a brief definition of the key term **in your own words**. Then **provide an example** of the term, such as a culture in which the practice takes place, or people that you might know whose behavior illustrates the term, a current event that illustrates the term, how a term could be used to shed light on or help solve a particular social problem, and so on. You could include examples from the news, books, movies, or anything else that will illustrate the term and help you remember it. Include any comments from your class discussions or textbook that might help you remember and understand these key terms. Use additional paper if necessary, but keep it with your study guide to help you review for exams.

addiction (p. 382)

_____

_____

_____

_____

tolerance (p. 382)

_____

_____

_____

_____

withdrawal (p. 382)

_____

_____

_____

_____

depressant (p. 383)

_____

_____

_____

alcoholic (p. 384)

_____

_____

_____

_____

stimulant (p. 391)

_____

_____

_____

_____

decriminalization (p. 404)

_____

_____

_____

_____

passive smoking (p. 386)

_____

_____

_____

_____

opiates (p. 388)

_____

_____

_____

_____

sedative-hynotics (p. 391)

_____

_____

_____

_____

individual psychotherapy (p. 401)

_____

_____

_____

_____

aversive therapy (p. 401)

_____

_____

_____

_____

drug maintenance (p. 405)

_____

_____

_____

_____

NOTES:

PRACTICE TEST

Multiple Choice

1. Which of the following is NOT a myth surrounding the issue of drugs?
   a) We are in the midst of a rising "drug epidemic."
   b) The only dangerous drugs are the illegal substances like cocaine.
   c) Drug use is confined to a few ragged deviants on the margin of society.
   d) Drugs are a big business.

2. Drugs, like alcohol, that slow down the activity of the central nervous system are:
   a) stimulants
   b) addictive drugs
   c) depressants
   d) tranquilizers

3. All of the following are reasons why young people smoke, EXCEPT for:
   a) youthful rebelliousness
   b) addiction
   c) a link created by advertising between smoking and maturity
   d) a predisposition toward smoking

4. An intense craving for a drug that develops after a period of physical dependence is called:
   a) tolerance
   b) intense dependency
   c) addiction
   d) compulsion

5. People whose drinking problem disrupts their lives are defined as:
   a) moderate drinkers
   b) heavy drinkers
   c) alcoholics
   d) abstainers

6. The effects of WHICH of the following drugs are largely determined by the social environment?
   a) marijuana
   b) cocaine
   c) alcohol
   d) tobacco

7. Withdrawal is defined as:
   a) an epidemic that is created when many people use drugs
   b) sickness users experience when they stop using drugs
   c) an immunity to the effects of a drug
   d) an intense craving for a drug

8. Drugs, like nicotine, that raise blood pressure and speed up the heart rate are called:
   a) depressants
   b) opiates
   c) stimulants
   d) psychedelics

9. The greatest danger of psychedelic drugs are:
   a) physical
   b) economic
   c) social
   d) psychological

10. Synthetic derivatives of the male hormone testosterone are called:
   a) steroids
   b) sperm
   c) amphetamines
   d) crack

11. Sociologists that argue that the use of illegal drugs is culturally learned are likely following which of the following perspectives?
   a) biological
   b) personality
   c) behavioral
   d) interactionist

12. Surveys of young people and the general public indicate that cocaine use has:
   a) increased dramatically over the last ten years
   b) plummeted in the last five years
   c) risen among rich users but declined in poor areas
   d) always been an underclass drug

13. All of the following are types of sedative-hypnotic drugs, EXCEPT for:
   a) barbiturates
   b) Quaaludes
   c) Valium
   d) amphetamines

14. Which of the following statements about the biological basis of drug use is the most accurate?
   a) The large number of persons who are drug addicts are genetically predisposed to use them.
   b) Although there apparently is a genetic predisposition toward drug use among certain individuals, it is still learned behavior.
   c) Little research has actually been done on the link between genetics and drug use.
   d) Biological factors do not explain most types of drug use.

15. By the nineteenth century, Americans had established two different drinking patterns, which were rural, middle class abstainers and:
    a) big city, immigrant alcohol users
    b) rural, working class abstainers
    c) frontier farmers who abstained from alcohol use
    d) rural, immigrant farmers who used alcohol moderately

16. The major criticism of personality theories of drug use is that they:
    a) are too predictive of addiction
    b) do not take biological facts into account
    c) are little more than a reflection of popular stereotypes
    d) are unable to predict who might become a drug addict

17. Most of the new drugs that have become popular among recreational users in the twentieth century were:
    a) imported from the orient
    b) discovered accidentally from plants growing in the wild
    c) created in the labs of amateur scientists
    d) produced by the pharmaceutical corporations

18. One reason why groups like American Indians have high rates of alcoholism is because:
    a) of a genetic predisposition
    b) of an absence of norms regulating alcohol use
    c) they are the target of liquor industry ads
    d) of America's overall approval of drinking

19. The government's "war on drugs" in the 1980s involved all of the following EXCEPT that it:
    a) focused on tougher drug law enforcement
    b) actually was responsible for a decline in drug use
    c) was the biggest drug campaign ever
    d) led to the overflowing of prisons

20. The most successful drug treatment programs involve:
    a) individual psychotherapy
    b) aversive techniques
    c) therapeutic communities
    d) group support

21. All of the following are consequences of outlawing a drug, EXCEPT for:
    a) running up costs of repression that society cannot afford
    b) totally stamping out its use
    c) the widespread corruption of public officials
    d) the substitution of one dangerous substance for another

22. Which of the following acts in NOT part of the DUTCH approach to drugs?
    a) the tolerance of soft drugs
    b) tough enforcement efforts aimed at dealers of hard drugs
    c) increasing the numbers of persons using drugs
    d) decriminalization of all users

23. The most common response of American society to a drug seen as a problem has been:
    a) developing self-help programs
    b) making it a crime
    c) taking it off the market
    d) making it into a political issue

24. A way to deal with the drug problem that involves supplying addicts with a drug while still prohibiting it among the public at large is called:
    a) maintenance
    b) decriminalization
    c) legalization
    d) repression

25. All of the following are reasons why preventive drug programs fail, EXCEPT that:
    a) attempts to scare young often are seen as untrue
    b) they pursue an unrealistic goal of total prevention
    c) only a few schools have actually tried to use them
    d) they actually entice students to try drugs

26. One criticism of therapeutic communities is that they:
    a) involve using drugs in small amounts
    b) only appeal to those who can accept their ideology and discipline
    c) rely too heavily on long-term psychotherapy
    d) only employ ex-drug addicts

27. All of the following are benefits that could come from an increased social tolerance for drug use, EXCEPT for:
    a) reducing organized crime
    b) de stigmatizing drug users
    c) eliminating the need for addict crime
    d) eliminating most drug use

28. According to the functionalist perspective, drug use is a means of escaping from unpleasant social conditions that have arisen as society has:
    a) become disorganized
    b) tolerated rugs more
    c) become more unequal
    d) labeled addicts as deviants

29. Some conflict theorists consider drug use to be normal behavior and argue the problem lies in the state's attempts:
    a) to corner the market
    b) substitute other drugs
    c) repress it
    d) legalize it

234

— 30. Which of the following ways to deal with the drug problem is most favored by social psychologists?
   a) treatment programs
   b) government repression
   c) maintenance programs
   d) legalization

NOTES:

PROJECTS

PROJECT 12.1 Curtailing Drug Abuse: Internal Control, External Control, or Both?

Coleman and Cressey discuss numerous approaches to responding to the problem of drug and alcohol abuse. Approaches widely vary including such things as prevention, treatment, legal repression, or legalization. Some of the approaches they mention focus on internal control (for example, group support, education, therapy, and others) and some focus on external control (for example, legal repression). The objective of this project is to have you examine which types of controls are more effective and to apply your conclusions to examine the issue of legalization of all drugs.

Journal instructions:
1. Attend a meeting of a support group for drug abusers (for example, Alcoholics Anonymous).

2. Keep a detailed journal in which you record your observations of the meeting. Here are some things to look for during you observation:
    a) How is the meeting organized?
    b) How are newcomers socialized into the group?
    c) How are members encouraged to deal with their substance abuse problem?
    d) What methods does the group use to help substance abusers?

3. Interview one of the members of the group or someone you know that is (or was) a member of such a support group. Ask them the above questions. In addition, ask them:
    a) Did the fact particular drugs were illegal prevent you from using them?
    b) What eventually led you to seek help from the support group?

4. Interview a drug counselor or psychotherapist about techniques they use to help people overcome their drug problems. Additionally, ask them what their views are on legalization and if they feel that would help people deal with their problems better? Record their views in your journal.

5. After you complete your observations and interviews, discuss in your journal the extent to which each type of technique offered by Coleman and Cressey was effective in helping curtail the people you observed.

Option: essay
After completing the above field journal, write an essay (around five pages, typed) in which you discuss what you think the government's role should be in helping to curtail drug abuse. Base your decision upon:
    a) the conclusions you reached in your journal about the effectiveness of the different approaches you examined and observed;
    b) the three sociological perspectives on drug abuse (functionalism, conflict theory, and the social psychological theories).

INSTRUCTIONS FOR THIS PROJECT ARE CONTINUED ON THE FOLLOWING PAGE.

Option: bibliography
Develop a bibliography of ten to fifteen articles from various sources (sociology journals, newspapers and magazines, commentary magazines, books, and so on) that can provide you with arguments for and against the legalization of controlled drugs. Make sure that your bibliography has a <u>balance</u> of articles from sociology journals and popular periodicals, and make sure that it contains a balance of views for and against legalization. Type your bibliography following the format found in one of the sociology journals.

Option: research paper
Using material from your field journal, essay, and bibliography (at least five sources, at least two of which must be articles or books by sociologists), write a paper (around seven to eight pages, typed) in which you:

a) Explain and introduce what the issue of legalization is about.

b) Carefully present <u>strong</u> arguments for <u>and</u> against drug legalization.

c) Write a conclusion to your paper in which you use sociological perspectives about drug use and your research to elaborate <u>your</u> position for or against legalization. It is imperative that your position be based upon your research findings and application of sociological perspectives.

d) Document your sources throughout your paper and include a reference page.

PROJECT 12.2 Applying the Sociological Perspectives to Issues and Problems of Drugs

Is there a drug problem today? What is the cause of it? Why are some drugs legal and others not? Why are some people arrested for using drugs that are not harmful, while some others are permitted to use drugs that are harmful? It seems that there are many myths about drug use today, and how to solve the "drug problems." Often, society reacts to a problem with a broad generalization and, as a result, misinterprets the real problem or how to solve it. Sociological perspectives can be a useful way of helping to gain an additional, hopefully clearer, perspective on some problems. The objective of this project is to have you examine some of the major drug issues and problems today from the point of view of the sociological perspectives

Journal instructions:
1. Search your library's indexes—or computerized bibliographic indexes—for articles about issues and problems related to drugs that have appeared in newspapers and news magazines during the past two to three years. List all of these in your journal. Be sure to copy the bibliographic information (that is, newspaper or magazine, date, pages, author, etc.) along with the title of the article. Your list is likely to be extensive.

2. Without reading the articles, develop some different categories that you can place each of the articles in. For example, drug-related crimes, drug arrests, drug rehabilitation, drug cartels, and so on. Develop as many categories as necessary, but remember that your goal is to condense all of the articles into these categories. You probably will arrive at around ten categories, but create more if necessary. Write these in your journal.

3. In your journal, write a brief paragraph about what each of the categories includes or is about.

4. Discuss how each of the three major sociological perspectives (functionalism, conflict theory, and the social psychological perspectives) would approach or explore each of the categories. What types of questions would each focus on? What explanations would each offer? What kinds of solutions would each pose? What important insights does each perspective offer about each of the issues? Which perspective is the most relevant or useful, from your point of view, for explaining and dealing with each issue?

Option: essay
Locate and read two or three articles from newspapers or news magazines for each of the categories that you created, above. Write an essay titled, "Drug Use in America: Popular Views and Sociological Perspectives," "Myths and Realities on Drug Use in America," or a similar topic. Your objective in the essay is to compare the views about drugs that appear in the news with sociological interpretations. In some cases, the views presented in the news may be similar to those offered by some of the sociological perspectives. In some cases, they may be very different. If they are similar, which sociological perspectives are they most similar to? When they are different, discuss how. And so on. Feel free to address any issue that you feel is important and interesting. Conclude your essay with a discussion about how accurately the news reflects the realities of drug use. Your essay should be around five pages (typed). Integrate material from the articles you read to illustrate your ideas.

INSTRUCTIONS FOR THIS PROJECT ARE CONTINUED ON THE FOLLOWING PAGE.

Option: bibliography
Develop a bibliography of ten to fifteen articles from sociology journals and/or books written by sociologists about one or two of the categories related to drug issues that you developed in your journal, above. Type your bibliography following the format found in one of the sociology journals.

Option: research paper
Write a paper (around 7 to 10 pages, typed) in which you compare popular views on drug issues/problems with sociological views. Use material that you developed in your journal and essay activities (above) and at least five items from your bibliography sociology articles and/or books. *Suggestion: Use your essay as a first draft of this paper instead of starting all over. Go back and integrate material from your sociological bibliography.* Be sure to document your sources properly throughout your paper and include a reference page.

CHAPTER 13

CRIME AND VIOLENCE

CHAPTER OUTLINE

OUTLINE CONTINUED ON NEXT PAGE

Sociological Perspectives on Crime and Delinquency
    The Functionalist Perspective
    The Conflict Perspective
    The Feminist Perspective
    The Interactionist Perspective

242

CHAPTER LEARNING OBJECTIVES AND ESSAY QUESTIONS

After studying this chapter, you should be able to:

• Explain why the fears of crime and violence do not correspond with the facts about the current crime rate.

• Describe the nature of several different types of crime and violence, including murder, rape, and syndicated crime.

• State and explain how sociologists try to measure crime and violence, and the problems of establishing the amount of crime that takes place.

• Analyze the causes of crime and violence, including biological, personality, and sociological theories.

• Discuss how American society has tried to deal with crime through the police and prisons.

• Describe how American society has tried to respond to the problems of crime and violence.

• Outline and discuss four sociological perspectives on crime and violence.

KEY POINTS FOR REVIEW

• While crime and violence are real problems in American society, the average citizen is poorly informed about the nature of the crime problem. The public is often mislead by sensationalistic news reporting looking to sell newspapers or win TV ratings, and the claims of politicians who use fears of crime on behalf of promoting their own programs.

• An act, no matter how indecent or immoral, is not a crime unless the criminal law has listed it as such. Further, there is a large difference between what the criminal law says and what the police and courts actually do. Because there are so many different behaviors that are considered crimes, there is an extensive classification system of crimes. The most serious offenses are felonies and the less important ones are misdemeanors. For statistical purposes, crimes are usually classified as offenses against persons (violent crime), crimes against property (property crime), and crimes against public decency and order (victimless crime).

• Homicide, manslaughter, assault, and rape are some violent crimes. Murder is illegal homicide (killing) with "malice." Manslaughter is illegal homicide without malice (such as killing someone while driving intoxicated). Assault is when one person attacks another with the intention of hurting or killing the victim. Most assaults and murders occur between relatives or friends, occur by someone who is under the influence of alcohol, and are committed by and against men.

• Forcible rape is defined as sexual intercourse forced upon a person without consent. Statutory rape is sexual intercourse between an adult and someone below the legally defined age of consent. There are two patterns of forcible rape: that which arises between friends or acquaintances ("date rape") and that which occurs between strangers. It is extremely difficult to measure the incidence of rape accurately.

243

• Property crime occurs nearly ten times more often than violent crime. Five types of property crime include theft (taking the property of another)—the most common property crime—robbery (theft by force), and burglary (unlawful entry into a structure with the intent to commit a felony), fraud (using trickery and deception to obtain someone's property), and arson (the intentional burning of property, often for purposes of insurance fraud). Offenders range from occasional criminals to professional criminals.

• Syndicated crime (often referred to as "organized crime") involves criminals who work together in large groups and often resemble legitimate businesses. The principal source of income for syndicated criminals is selling goods and services to the public, such as drugs, prostitution, gambling, loan sharking, and so forth. At the outset, new criminal syndicates are usually run by a small group of violent toughs operating in a small area. If successful, they may grow and may even operate a number of legitimate businesses along with their criminal operations. An increasing problem is the growing links that are being created between criminal syndicates operating in different parts of the world.

• White-collar crime is any crime committed by a person of respectability in the course of his or her occupation. Two types of white-collar crime include organizational crimes (committed by people who act n behalf of the organization for which they work) and occupational crimes (committed solely to advance one's personal interests). White-collar crimes cost more money and more lives than all other types of crimes put together. Yet, numerous studies have shown that those charged with white-collar crimes are less likely to be prosecuted and convicted than those charged with comparable "street crimes."

• Juvenile delinquents are those who break laws pertaining to the behavior of juveniles. Juvenile delinquency has been studied more careful than any other category of crime. Juveniles have special problems apart from adult criminals. The influence of the family is greater. Children are much more likely to become delinquent if one of their parents is a criminal, if they are from a poor home, and if they are from a single-parent family. A unique problem of juvenile offenders stems from the nature of adolescence in industrial societies which place difficult demands on young people and keeps them in an extended in-between period of adolescence and adulthood. Finally, juvenile gangs are becoming increasingly problematic.

• Measuring crime is difficult because criminals are often unwilling to talk about their activities and the general public's knowledge about their own victimization is often inaccurate. Criminologists use four principal means to measure crime: the Uniform Crime Reports (crimes reported to the police), National Crime Victimization Surveys (surveys of a random sample of Americans about how they were victimized during a given year), arrest statistics (information about the characteristics of those who have been arrested), and self-report studies (reports based on a sample of the population asked to anonymously report on the crimes they themselves may have committed).

• While the Uniform Crime Reports show a steady increase in crime since the end of World War II, the National Crime Victimization Survey shows a slow, steady decline. This discrepancy may be due to flaws in the Uniform Crime Reports, such as police departments intentionally exaggerating increases in crime in order to justify requests for more money and personnel.

• Criminologists have found that age, gender, and geographic area have an important influence on the incidence of crime. In the US there are 4 times as many men as women arrested, but the crime rate for women has been growing faster than for men. The biggest increases have been in

244

the nonviolent property crimes. Teenagers and young adults have the highest crime rate. The highest crime rates are found in inner-city slums and decreases as one moves out from the central city to the wealthier residential areas. Most studies reveal that there are higher crime rates among the poor and minorities.

• The US has the highest murder rate, and other violent crimes, of any industrialized nation.

• There are numerous explanations about the causes of crime. According to early classical theory, people who commit crimes choose to do so after weighing the options. This rational explanation, while flawed, is still highly popular. Challenges to classical theory come from biological theories, personality theories, and sociological theories.

• Biological theories maintain that criminals are biologically different than "normal" people. Many studies have demonstrated biological differences that criminals have, however there is very little conclusive evidence that specific biological traits cause criminal behavior, or society's reaction to people with certain traits may lead them to commit crime. Further, it is unclear whether or not some of the traits that biological theorists feel are related to crime are the cause of criminal behavior or the result of being incarcerated, or learned in some other social environment such as the family.

• Personality theories maintain personality traits lie at the root of criminal behavior. However, since many non-criminals have the same "sociopathic" traits as criminals, it is very unclear whether people break the law because they are sociopaths, or they become labeled sociopaths once they break the law..

• There are numerous sociological theories of crime and violence. They either focus on the reasons an individual commits criminal acts or they examine the larger social forces that determine the overall rates of crime and violence. Differential association theory says people become criminals because they are exposed to more people with attitudes and definitions that are favorable to a certain type of crime than are opposed to it. Another related theory holds that crime and violence are learned from contact with deviant subcultures that support criminality. Labeling theory examines the process by which people are branded as criminals and the effects such labeling as on them. Some sociologists say that people are naturally inclined to break the law and focus, rather, on why people do not break the law. Control theory answers this question by saying that non criminals are constrained by society—by internal or external social control mechanisms—and thus are prevented from breaking the law. Other theories focus on social structure. Strain theory maintains that crime is produced by the strain in societies that tell people that wealth is available to all yet at the same restricts some people's access to the means for achieving wealth. Finally, critical theory argues that it is the capitalist economic system that is the root cause of our crime problem by encouraging the exploitation of one group by another and by promoting the selfish quest for personal gain.

• The criminal-justice process reflects a conflict between the need to prevent crime and the need to protect the rights of individuals. Societies, thus, range from police states, where there is total control of individuals, to societies where individuals run wild. Police have become the symbols of the system of justice, however, only a small part of the work done by a police department is directly concerned with fighting crime. After an arrest, an individual must go through the court system. Only about one in ten defendants in the federal courts in the US actually has a trial. Most defendants make a deal through a process known as plea-bargaining. Once a person is convicted of a crime, he or she goes through the corrections system, usually prisons. The goals of the prison system are retribution (to get even), deterrence (to make others afraid to commit

245

similar crimes), incapacitation (to protect the public from the criminal), and rehabilitation of the criminal. The number of Americans in prison has tripled in the last fifteen years.

• There are a variety of proposals to deal with crime and violence. One is to increase the level of punishment, such as extended prison terms. A second approach is to focus primarily on violent crime. A third proposal is to attack the roots of crime through social intervention.

• The functionalist perspective focuses on crime rates rather than individual criminal behavior. Functionalists hold that a certain amount of crime is inevitable because it makes a contribution to social order. It provides a sense of solidarity for non-criminals, provides an escape valve from the pressures of excessive conformity, and reinforces society's values about appropriate and inappropriate behavior. Functionalists argue that high crime rates have been caused by the hectic pace of social change in the twentieth century and the social disorganization it created. Old traditions have been broken down, yet new ones have not yet emerged. To deal with such problems, functionalists call for greater social integration, a return to traditional values, and support for traditional institutions such as the family and religion. Further, they feel that crime can be stemmed by making the criminal justice system more efficient.

• Conflict theory emphasizes the fact that both crime and the laws that define it are products of a struggle for power. Conflict theorists argue that a few powerful groups control the legislative process and that these groups outlaw behavior that threatens their interests. They also see class and ethnic exploitation as a basic cause of many different kinds of crime. Further, they say that the greed and competitiveness that are part of capitalist culture encourage crime. Conflict theorists feel that violence has always been one of the principal means of enforcing male dominance. Thus, as social changes have eroded male dominance, males have resorted to violence to "keep women in their place." Conflict theorists believe that crime will disappear only if inequality and exploitation are eliminated. This can occur through more equal treatment of the police and courts to ethnic groups and minorities and more attention given to white-collar crime.

• The feminist perspective is concerned with the role that violence plays in the explitation of women and it concludes that violence has always been one of the principal means of establishing and enforcing male dominance. As industrialization and techonological advances have eroded male privelege in society, violence against women has become an increasingly important tool in keeping wome "in their place." Women are also perpetrators of crime. While the crime rate for women is well below that of men, it is increasing much more rapidly. As women have gained in financial responsibilities, their crime rates have gone up. Feminists feel that the criminal justice system should crack down harder on spouse abuse and other kinds of violence that men perpetrate against women.

• The interactionist perspective focuses more on the causes of crime than the other perspectives. From their view, criminal behavior is learned in interaction with others, especially within one's primary groups. The interactionist solution to crime is that if crime is learned, then it can be unlearned. Such education can take place through the media and through taking measures to avoid the contagion of youngsters by confirmed criminals as sometimes happens in juvenile halls and prisons.

KEY TERMS

The following key terms are found in your textbook on the page number indicated in parentheses. In the space provided, write a brief definition of the key term **in your own words**. Then **provide an example** of the term, such as a culture in which the practice takes place, or people that you might know whose behavior illustrates the term, a current event that illustrates the term, how a term could be used to shed light on or help solve a particular social problem, and so on. You could include examples from the news, books, movies, or anything else that will illustrate the term and help you remember it. Include any comments from your class discussions or textbook that might help you remember and understand these key terms. Use additional paper if necessary, but keep it with your study guide to help you review for exams.

violence (p. 414)

_____

_____

_____

_____

crime (p. 414)

_____

_____

_____

_____

felony (p. 415)

_____

_____

_____

_____

misdemeanor (p. 415)

_____

_____

violent crime (p. 415)

_____

_____

_____

_____

property crime (p. 415)

_____

_____

_____

_____

victimless crime (p. 415)

_____

_____

_____

_____

murder (p. 415)

_____

_____

_____

_____

homicide (p. 415)

_____

_____

_____

_____

manslaughter (p. 415)

_____

_____

_____

_____

assault (p. 415)

_____

_____

_____

_____

forcible rape (p. 416)

_____

_____

_____

_____

statutory rape (p. 416)

_____

_____

_____

_____

theft (p. 418)

_____

_____

_____

_____

robbery (p. 418)

----

burglary (p. 418)

----

fraud (p. 418)

----

arson (p. 419)

----

syndicated crime (p. 420)

----

white-collar crime (p. 421)

_____

_____

_____

_____

organizational crimes (p. 421)

_____

_____

_____

_____

occupational crimes (p. 421)

_____

_____

_____

_____

juvenile delinquent (p. 423)

_____

_____

_____

_____

status offenses (p. 423)

_____

_____

_____

_____

Uniform Crime Reports (p. 425)

_____

_____

_____

_____

National Crime Victimization Survey (p. 425)

_____

_____

_____

_____

self-report study (p. 425)

_____

_____

_____

_____

classical theory (p. 430)

_____

_____

_____

_____

positive school (p. 430)

_____

_____

_____

_____

sociopathic personality (p. 432)

_____

_____

_____

_____

differential association (p. 432)

_____

_____

_____

_____

deviant subcultures (p. 433)

_____

_____

_____

_____

labeling theory (p. 433)

_____

_____

_____

_____

control theory (p. 434)

_____

_____

_____

_____

strain theory (p. 434)

_____

_____

_____

_____

anomie (p. 435)

_____

_____

_____

_____

critical theory (p. 435)

_____

_____

_____

_____

crime-control model (p. 435)

_____

_____

_____

_____

due-process model (p. 435)

_____

_____

_____

_____

police brutality (p. 436)

_____

_____

_____

_____

bail (p. 436)

_____

_____

_____

_____

plea bargaining (p. 437)

_____

_____

_____

_____

retribution (p. 437)

_____

_____

_____

_____

deterrence (p. 437)

_____

_____

_____

_____

255

incapacitation (p. 437)

_____

_____

_____

_____

rehabilitation (p. 437)

_____

_____

_____

_____

probation (p. 438)

_____

_____

_____

_____

NOTES:

PRACTICE TEST

Multiple Choice

1. All of the following statements about the current crime scene are true, EXCEPT that:
   a) crime is spreading to the suburbs
   b) the crime rate has been increasing dramatically
   c) man persons are so terrorized by crime that they are afraid to leave their houses
   d) the great cities of North America have high crime rates

2. Which of the following is not a form of violence, based on the definition provided by Coleman and Cressey?
   a) spanking a child
   b) thermonuclear war
   c) felonies
   d) terrorism

3. An act that is intended to cause physical pain, injury, or death to another is called:
   a) an act of violence
   b) a crime
   c) a felony
   d) an assault

4. Which of the following is NOT a type of crime?
   a) use of illicit drugs
   b) murder
   c) an immoral act
   d) rape

5. Legally, the most serious offenses are:
   a) misdemeanors
   b) laws
   c) crimes
   d) felonies

6. A violation of the criminal law is called:
   a) violence
   b) a misdemeanor
   c) a felony
   d) a crime

7. Which of the following is the definition of manslaughter?
   a) The killing of any human being.
   b) The killing of an enemy during wartime.
   c) The unlawful killing of another without malice or forethought.
   d) The unlawful killing of another with malice or forethought.

8. Sexual intercourse between an adult and someone below the legally defined age of consent is called:
   a) statutory rape
   b) date rape
   c) forcible rape
   d) illegal intercourse

9. Which of the following is the most frequent type of property crime?
   a) robbery
   b) theft
   c) burglary
   d) fraud

10. Which of the following statements about juvenile delinquency is NOT true?
    a) Juvenile delinquency is the least sociologically studied area of delinquency.
    b) A substantial portion of all juvenile delinquents have never violated the adult law.
    c) The concept of juvenile delinquency was created in the late nineteenth century)
    d) Violations of the juvenile law that are not against the adult law are called status offenses.

11. Which of the following countries has the highest rate of reported murders?
    a) Russia
    b) the United States
    c) Canada
    d) Italy

12. Which of the following types of crime costs more money and more lives than all other types of crime put together?
    a) murder
    b) robbery
    c) syndicated (organized) crime
    d) white-collar crime

13. All of the following are variables that Coleman and Cressey list as major influences on the incidence of crime, EXCEPT for:
    a) age
    b) race
    c) gender
    d) geographical area

14. Psychologists and psychiatrists define the inability to form close social relationship and lack of moral feelings as the _____ personality.
    a) criminogenic
    b) deviant
    c) sociopathic
    d) psychopathic

15. Most defendants in the court system:
    a) make bail
    b) plea bargain
    c) go to trial
    d) are never formally arrested

258

16. The Cosa Nostra, the Yakuza of Japan, ad the South American cocaine cartels are all examples of:
    a) syndicated crime
    b) organized burglary rings
    c) drug cartels
    d) white-collar crime

17. Data from the National Crime Survey indicate that crime has actually:
    a) been declining
    b) been increasing
    c) never occurred some of the time
    d) stayed about the same for over ten years

18. Which of the following is a reason why the biological theories of crime are inaccurate?
    a) They focus too much on personality types.
    b) The definition of what is criminal and what is not is constantly changing.
    c) Biological factors really have nothing to do with crime.
    d) Humans are too biologically diverse to link crime with genetics.

19. The two models of criminal justice are the crime control model and the _____ model.
    a) biogenic
    b) social justice
    c) due process
    d) efficiency

20. Which of the following is NOT sociological approach to understanding crime?
    a) labeling
    b) differential association
    c) sociopathic personality
    d) control

21. All of the following are purposes of prison, EXCEPT for:
    a) retribution
    b) incapacitation
    c) rehabilitation
    d) justification

22. Which of the following is a problem created by increasing punishment of criminal offenders?
    a) self-righteousness
    b) more intense labeling
    c) a loss of a sense of compassion
    d) the enormous cost of punishment

23. Which of the following is probably responsible for the recent decline in the crime rate?
    a) an aging population
    b) getting tough
    c) social justice
    d) personal enlightenment

259

24. All of the following are ways of responding to the problems of violence and crime, EXCEPT for:
    a) focusing on violence
    b) increasing punishment
    c) tackling the roots of crime
    d) abolishing crime

25. Which of the following would be the most efficient procedure for getting at the roots of crime?
    a) social intervention
    b) tougher punishment
    c) dropping laws
    d) increasing the number of parole officers

26. The police spend most of in _____ activities.
    a) arrest
    b) detective
    c) violent
    d) peace-keeping

27. The aspect of crime that is the greatest threat to the public and needs the most attention is:
    a) violence
    b) drugs
    c) syndicated crime
    d) the protection of rights

28. Sociologists who study how the rapid industrialization of America during the twentieth century is associated with an increasing crime rate are probably using WHICH perspective on crime and violence?
    a) labeling
    b) conflict
    c) functionalist
    d) interactionist

29. Sociologists who would recommend integrating offenders into primary groups that discourage criminal behavior are most likely using WHICH perspective?
    a) functionalist
    b) interactionist
    c) conflict
    d) feminist

30. Sociologists who explain crime as a result of the exploitation and inequality of the poor probably hold WHICH perspective?
    a) functionalist
    b) conflict
    c) interactionist
    d) feminist

260

PROJECTS

PROJECT 13.1 Applying the Explanations of Crime and Violence

As with most areas of social life, popular explanations of crime and violence often are erroneous, misleading, or incomplete. As you have read in chapter 13, there are a variety of explanations for crime and violence (various biological, personality, and sociological theories). The objective of this project is to examine the acts of crime and violence that are currently occurring from the viewpoint of varying sociological, and other scientific, perspectives.

Journal instructions:
1. For an entire week, record in your field journal all articles about crime and violence that appear in a local and a national daily newspaper. (If you do not have at least ten items, then look in newspapers from previous weeks.) List the headline (or title), author, newspaper, date, pages, and a brief summary of the article.

2. Re-read the sections in chapter 13 about explanations of and sociological perspectives on crime and violence. Briefly summarize these in your journal.

3. For each criminal or violent act you listed, identify at least three possible explanations (at least two of which must be sociological) that could be used to examine and explain the act. Besides identifying the applicable theories, discuss how the theories you selected could explain the act.

Option: essay
1. Arrange all of the acts of crime and violence that you recorded in your journal into types—for example, murder, theft, sexual crimes, and so on.

2. Using your field journal notes for supporting material, write an essay (around five pages, typed) in which you discuss which theories and explanations of crime and violence are the most useful for understanding each of the different types of crime and violence you categorized. For example, which theories or explanations are most useful for explaining sexual crimes? Which ones are most useful for explaining syndicated crimes? And so forth.

Option: bibliography
Using your library's (or computerized) indexes, develop a bibliography of ten to fifteen articles from sociology journals and/or books written by sociologists about one of the types of criminal or violent acts you identified above. Type your bibliography following the format found in one of the sociology journals.

Option: research paper
Write a paper (around six to eight pages) in which you use at least four items from your bibliography to explain the current newspaper examples of the criminal or violent act that you selected (above). Possible things you can discuss in your paper are: What are the differences between the news accounts and the sociological explanations of the crime? Do the news accounts rely on any scientific theories (biological, personality, sociological)? What variables are used in the sociology articles to help explain the act of crime or violence you selected? What statistics or facts are relevant to explaining the act? And so on. Do not feel limited to these questions. Be sure to document your sources throughout your paper.

CHAPTER 14

URBANIZATION

CHAPTER OUTLINE

Understanding Human Communities
    The Cities
    The Suburbs
    Small Towns and Rural Areas
    Growth, Competition, and Dominance

Problems of Urbanization
    Crisis on the Farm
    The Decline of the Central City
    Local Government
    Housing
    Inefficient Transportation
    Ethnic Segregation
    Urban Problems in Less Developed Countries

Solving the Problems of Urbanization
    Creating Community
    Urban Renewal
    Controlling Urban Growth
    Improving the Cities of Less Developed Countries

Sociological Perspectives on Urbanization
    The Functionalist Perspective
    The Conflict Perspective
    The Feminist Perspective
    The Interactionist Perspective

CHAPTER LEARNING OBJECTIVES AND ESSAY QUESTIONS

After studying this chapter, you should be able to:

• Define the key concepts of urbanization and megalopolis, and understand how urbanization has swept the world.

• Describe the nature of cities and their impact on human behavior.

• Trace the development of the suburbs and explain why they are criticized.

• Explain how people live in rural areas.

• Describe and discuss the many problems of urbanization as rural areas and central cities decline.

• Discuss how society responds to problems of urbanization through reorganizing government and controlling urban growth.

• Discuss and compare four perspectives on urban growth.

KEY POINTS FOR REVIEW

• Urbanization has had a significant and far-reaching impact on societies during the last two hundred years. The origins of the city can be found at the beginning of recorded history, but it was not until the industrial revolution sent waves of immigrants to the cities in search of new jobs and opportunities that the first urban societies emerged.

• Because huge urban areas often have little overall political or economic integration, the U.S. Bureau of the Census uses the concept of the metropolitan statistical area (SMSA)—which includes a central population center and the surrounding communities that are dependent on it—as its measure to describe urban life.

• While urban growth in Third World countries has yet to be as massive as in industrialized countries, these cities are now growing almost twice as fast as those in the industrialized countries.

• Civilizations have always been centered in cities, and cities are still dominant in our social life. Large newspapers and broadcasting companies, which set our tastes and define our world, are usually based in cities. Cities spawn and attract actors, artists, writers, and other intellectual innovators who set the cultural styles of our age. Immigrants usually move to cities when they first come to a country. Despite the benefits of cities, there are also many problems that result from urban life including traffic congestion, crime, pollution, and many others.

• One of the most fascinating topics that sociologists study about city life is the way that people who live in the city see their world. Some, like the German sociologist Georg Simmel, say that the overload of stimuli in the city causes people to become indifferent to their surroundings. This can offer them more personal freedom, yet may also leave them feeling isolated and alone. In 1938, Louis Wirth wrote a now-famous essay—"Urbanism as a Way of Life—in which he concluded that diversity is one of the most important features of city life. People are highly specialized in their work and know each other only in superficial and impersonal ways. The city, thus, is a complex mass of people living together, performing their specialized tasks, without deep emotional ties. People come to accept their differences from each other and their isolation. Others, such as Herbert Gans, say that Wirth overlooked the many city dwellers who have a strong sense of community such as the affluent and the "ethnic villagers" who live in tightly knit ethnic neighborhoods. Gans concluded that social class and age a greater effect on urban lifestyles than does city living itself.

• Until the industrial revolution, most of the world's people lived in rural villages. This is still true in the less developed nations today. Villages are very homogeneous places with the villagers sharing the same set of values and traditions, and remaining largely isolated from world affairs. The benefits of living in rural areas include stronger feelings of group identity, less deviant behavior, and less crime. Disadvantages include lack of anonymity and less personal freedom, innovation, and individuality.

• In the past two decades, conflict theorists have begun emphasizing the importance of competition in shaping the patterns of development. Rural residents are no longer as isolated as they once were and now have to compete on the wider economic market. The decline of farming as an occupation has also led to changes in rural life. People in rural areas are continuing to migrate to cities in search of opportunities, as they always have, but now many are moving to small and medium sized cities and suburbs rather than larger cities.

• More Americans now live in suburbs than in cities or rural areas. While the first suburbs can be traced to the 1760s, the fastest growth took place in the two decades following World War II. The congestion , crime, pollution and decay of the cities pushed people out while the spaciousness, good schools, personal safety, and a pleasant environment at a price the middle class could afford. In addition the three things necessary for the growth of suburbs were in place: automobiles, highways, and private homes. Americans now have a love-hate relationship with the suburbs. They value it as a refuge from the troubles of the big city, but dislike the lack of individuality and blandness that often accompanies suburbs.

• Urbanization has brought a range of problems. Farmers have been particularly hard-hit by the process of urbanization. Big corporate farms have flourished, but many family farms have ended in bankruptcy and foreclosure. Big corporate farms have the financial resources to withstand hard times (due to nature's unpredictability), but many family farmers do not. As a result, corporate farms have been able to buy up prime land at bargain prices. The family farm cannot compete with large, corporate farms. This has left many rural residents with lower average income, poorer health care, and less education than people in the city. Further, the migration of people away from rural areas has eroded their tax base. As young adults move out, rural areas are left with a disproportionately large population of children and elderly.

• The flight to the suburbs has eroded the power of the central city. A shrinking tax base has led to the inability of big-city governments to sufficiently repair their crumbling infrastructures (roads, sewers, water systems, and so on). Additionally, the loss of the middle class in cities has also meant the loss of political power. While some urban neighborhoods have flourished in spite of this, many others have deteriorated in pockets of intense poverty. As a result, many young men have turned to the illicit economy to find jobs in prostitution, gambling, extortion, and, especially, illegal drugs.

265

• The departure of many people of the city to the suburbs has created a major financial bind for many city governments, leaving a large percentage of poor people with services that cannot be paid for. Thus, the power of local urban political institutions has steadily declined. Besides lack of a strong tax base, local city governments are also best by a variety of other problems ranging from graft, corruption, and a wasteful duplication of services.

• A stunning increase in the cost of buying a private home has been a major contributor to the growing division between the haves and the have-nots. Additionally, there is a critical shortage of low-cost housing for people whose incomes fall below the middle class. While the number of poor people has been increasing, the supply of affordable housing has been decreasing. One cause for the decline in low-cost housing is gentrification; the refurbishing of old, low-cost neighborhoods to accommodate more wealthy people. A second cause—similar to private gentrification—is government-sponsored local community redevelopment which, again, has neglected the housing needs of the poor.

• Inefficient transportation is another problem that has resulted from urbanization. An over-dependence on private automobiles has led to extreme traffic congestion, pollution, and not enough public transportation. The lack of public transportation has been further propelled by the automobile, tire, and petroleum industries that benefit more from a reliance on private transportation. A lack of sufficient public transportation makes it difficult for the poor and the elderly to get to work and to carry out necessary daily activities.

• Ethnic segregation is another problem in cities in industrialized nations. The isolation of immigrants and minorities in ethnic communities cuts them off from many economic opportunities and makes them easy victims of exploitation.

• Less developed countries face additional urban problems. They have higher urban populations, tend to cluster in a single huge city and have more rapid urbanization which can compound the problems associated with social change. They have extremely high poverty rates, little fire or police protection, lack of sufficient clean water and sanitation, high spread of disease, and enormous housing problem.

• There are many proposals as to how to deal with the problems of urbanization. These include revitalizing local governments to give them more economic and political power, developing urban renewal programs to create more housing and economic opportunities, and controlling urban growth. The primary obstacle to each of these proposals is economic. Proposals to deal with problems of cities in less developed countries include constructing more residential dwellings, improving transportation, sewage, and water lines, creating more job opportunities, and slowing down the speed or urbanization.

• From the functionalist perspective, the rapid urbanization of North America has disrupted traditional institutions including the family, economics, education, politics, and religion. The old patterns that were functional for rural living were abandoned too rapidly without integrating new ones. The rapid flight to the suburbs disrupted the natural process of reaching a new stability, thus throwing urban life into chaos. Functionalists argue that we must slow the pace of social change in order to allow metropolitan areas adjust to new conditions and reach a stable balance among the major social institutions. They feel this can be achieved by placing restrictions on immigration to the cities, creating large-scale development programs that create new economic opportunities in rural areas, creating more centralized metropolitan governments, and developing community-building programs (such as neighborhood watch).

266

• From the conflict perspective, the problems of urbanization are the result of the struggles between competing interest groups, especially rural landowners and urban industrialists. Once the power shifted to the urban industrialists, rural life suffered. When the wealthy and powerful moved from the cities to the suburbs, the balance of power shifted again leaving the cities with an increasing number of poor and powerless. Conflict theorists believe the solution to urban problems lies in political organization and action. People in city slums and poor rural areas must band together and demand fairer treatment.

• The feminist persepective has focuses on the ways in which the process of urbanization has affected women. there have been some contradictory results. On the one hand, urbanization has freed many women from the traditional constraints in rural communities, thus giving women new opportunities. On the other hand, the breakdown of the traditional community had led top increases in crime and violence directed against women and has made childrearing a more difficult task. Feminists feel that there should be new efforts to build community and a sense of mutual responsibility in urban neighborhoods.

• The interactionist perspective has focused on the effects of urbanization on individuals' attitudes and feelings. While city life may have its advantages, many interactionists have concluded that the sense of community and identity present in small-town living has important psychological advantages over the cold impersonality of the city. Thus, interactionists propose ways to bring some of the benefits of the small town back into urban life and to create a greater sense of community.

NOTES:

KEY TERMS

The following key terms are found in your textbook on the page number indicated in parentheses. In the space provided, write a brief definition of the key term **in your own words**. Then **provide an example** of the term, such as a culture in which the practice takes place, or people that you might know whose behavior illustrates the term, a current event that illustrates the term, how a term could be used to shed light on or help solve a particular social problem, and so on. You could include examples from the news, books, movies, or anything else that will illustrate the term and help you remember it. Include any comments from your class discussions or textbook that might help you remember and understand these key terms. Use additional paper if necessary, but keep it with your study guide to help you review for exams.

urbanization (p. 456)

_____

_____

_____

_____

megalopolis (p. 456)

_____

_____

_____

_____

meetropolitan statistical area (MSA) (p. 456)

_____

_____

_____

_____

suburb (p. 459)

_____

_____

_____

highway lobby (p. 459)

_____

_____

_____

_____

infrastructure (p. 464)

_____

_____

_____

_____

villages (p. 460

_____

_____

_____

_____

gentrification (p. 467)

_____

_____

_____

_____

community (p. 472)

_____

_____

_____

_____

political decentralization (p. 472)

_____

_____

_____

_____

urban renewal (p. 473)

_____

_____

_____

_____

enterprise zone (p. 473)

_____

_____

_____

_____

NOTES:

PRACTICE TEST

Multiple Choice

1. The shift from rural to urban living is called:
    a) suburbanization
    b) city growth
    c) gentrification
    d) urbanization

2. Throughout history, civilization has always been centered in:
    a) cities
    b) the countryside
    c) megalopolises
    d) the nation-state

3. The part of an urban area that lies outside the central city is called the:
    a) metropolis
    b) suburbs
    c) rural zone
    d) farming area

4. A large area is which several cities are fused together is called a(n):
    a) metropolitan area
    b) urban area
    c) megalopolis
    d) metropolitan statistical area

5. Louis Wirth felt that the psychological impact of urban life led to:
    a) the height of civilized living
    b) superficial and impersonal relationships
    c) strong, local communities
    d) a way of life that promoted intense, personal relationships

6. All of the following were elements of suburban expansion that the federal government helped provide, EXCEPT for:
    a) the building of highways
    b) the development of automobiles
    c) housing subsidies
    d) distinctive cultural values

7. A metropolitan statistical area is:
    a) a central population center and its surrounding community
    b) areas where cities fuse together
    c) an area of cultural homogeneity
    d) a measure of the degree of urbanization

271

8. Herbert Gans argued that Wirth's analysis of the city was wrong because he discovered:
    a) high levels of social mobility
    b) wider amounts of urban insecurity
    c) a t of homogeneous, tightly knit, ethnic villages
    d) the impact of television

9. Which of the following most accurately describes today's suburbs?
    a) set of similar bedroom communities
    b) a checkerboard of widely divergent communities
    c) an endless expanse of crackerbox houses that are very similar
    d) Lilly-white, middle class neighborhoods

10. One of the advantages of living in a rural community is:
    a) a lack of social space
    b) too much individuality
    c) an emphasis on role playing
    d) knowing one another as people

11. All of the following are reasons for the decline of the city, EXCEPT for the:
    a) decline in urban values
    b) crumbling of the infrastructure
    c) movement of business out of the city
    d) leaving of inner cities with a disproportionate share of the poor

12. The refurbishing of old neighborhoods to accommodate more wealthy persons is called:
    a) urbanization
    b) gentrification
    c) urban renewal
    d) suburbanization

13. Which of the following factors helped lead to the transformation of rural areas?
    a) a sharp reduction of farming as an occupation
    b) a set of distinctive cultural values
    c) highways that linked suburbs to the central cities
    d) a dramatic increase of computing as an occupation

14. All of the following are reasons for the crisis of the family farmer, EXCEPT for:
    a) the volatility of farming
    b) a lack of financial resources
    c) agribusiness
    d) a decline of the work ethic

15. Which of the following are problems of local government that contribute to the urban crisis?
    a) corruption and scandals
    b) a confusing network of fragmented local governments
    c) little control over their own affairs
    d) all of the above contributed to the crisis

16. Rural settlements:
    a) are making a dramatic resurgence, especially in the Third World
    b) sill dominate farm areas
    c) are largely things of the past in the industrialized nations
    d) are largely things of the past throughout the entire world

17. Which of the following types of persons are hit hardest by the process of urbanization?
    a) farmers
    b) tribal warriors
    c) suburbanites
    d) the urban poor

18. Urban "dead zones" are places that are:
    a) left vacant by suburban migration
    b) ruled by street criminals and gang violence
    c) zoned for high pollution businesses
    d) politically neutral areas of cities

19. Traffic congestion is so band in some urban areas that _____ results.
    a) a move to bicycles
    b) intense pollution
    c) gridlock
    d) a move to an alternative transportation system

20. Creation of larger governmental units:
    a0 could create another useless level of government
    b0 old provide services more rationally
    c) would create a stronger sense of local area identity
    d) would help counter the power of the federal government

21. Uncontrolled urban growth leads to all of the following problems, EXCEPT for:
    a) urban sprawl
    b) destruction of the natural environment
    c) a reduction of poverty
    d) a decline in the quality of life

22. Separate ethnic neighborhoods become a problem for cities when:
    a) persons are forced to live in them
    b) one neighborhood is more diverse than another
    c) neighborhoods lead to political fragmentation
    d) one group comes to dislike another

23. Housing, business, and other kinds of rebuilding in cities is usually called:
    a) redevelopment
    b) urban renewal
    c0 spiritual regeneration
    d) poor people's removal

273

24. Which of the following groups most strongly opposes control of urban growth?
    a) home owners
    b) environmentalists
    c) government agencies
    d) developers

25. In the Third World, urbanization:
    a) is much slower
    b) is out of control
    c) has many fewer problems
    d) opposes government policy

26. Most government programs for the cities, such as loans and enterprise zones:
    a) disrupt ethnic villagers' social life
    b) have little impact on the poor
    c) are geared to help the poor
    d) help the rich and the middle-class

27. All of the following are ways to help the cities of the Third World, except for:
    a) improving the overall economic foundation
    b) slowing down the speed of urbanization
    c) installing democratic governments
    d) control of population growth

28. Sociologists who recommend decentralizing metropolitan areas into small unites so that people will have the opportunity to live in genuine communities an neighborhoods are most likely using the _____ perspective.
    a) conflict
    b) interactionist
    c) functionalist
    d) feminist

29. Conflict theorists see the problems of urbanization as resulting from:
    a) social disorganization
    b) a lack of genuine neighborhoods and communities
    c) competition between interest groups
    d) modernization

30. The belief that rapid urbanization leads to rapid disorganization and the subsequent rise in the rates of crime, suicide, and mental illness is a view held by the _____ perspective.
    a) conflict
    b) interactionist
    c) functional
    d) modernization

274

PROJECTS

PROJECT 14.1 How Urbanization Affects Our Lives

As you read in chapter 14, the experience of the city affects our lives. Two American sociologists Louis Wirth and Herbert Gans took different views on the impact the city has on us. Positive or negative, city life is a reality. German sociologist Georg Simmel also expressed his views on the unique impact that the city has on us. It is interesting that these sociologists have contrasting views on the city. The objective of this project is to examine your own experience of the community where you live using a sociological perspective and to see if you agree more with Wirth, Gans, Simmel, or all three.

Journal instructions:
1. Spend half a day in a busy section of big city near you by yourself. Visit as many different places as you can: a post office, a restaurant, stores, a hospital, doctor's office, public park, public transportation, and so on. Your objective is to become as immersed as possible in the city as you can during that period. Keep your journal with you and record your observations of how you feel throughout the half-day. Additionally, keep a record of things you observe that you think are typical of life in a big city. Finally, make a list of things that you see are problems of living in big cities.

2. Spend a half a day in a suburban area near you and follow the above instructions.

3. Spend a half a day in a rural area near you and follow the above instructions.

4. Using your journal notes, summarize and discuss what you think the advantages and disadvantages of living in a big city, a rural area, and the suburbs.

5. Use each of the three sociological perspectives on urbanization to explain the problems of city, rural, and suburban life. Which perspectives do you think make the most sense, in terms of what you observed?

Option: essay
Write an essay (around 3 to 5 pages, typed) in which you discuss how cities, rural areas, and suburban areas shape our individual experience and security. Incorporate as many examples from you journal observations into your essay as you can.

Option: bibliography
Develop a bibliography of 10 to 15 articles from sociology journals and/or books written by sociologists that deal with the experience of living in cities, rural areas, and/or suburbs. Type your bibliography following the format found in one of the sociology journals.

Option: research paper
Write a paper (around 5 to 7 pages, typed) in which you compare the experience of city, rural, and suburban life. Integrate theories, findings, and ideas from at least 5 items from your bibliography with material that you developed in your journal and essay above. Be sure to cite your sources throughout you paper and include a reference page.

PROJECT 14. 2 Assessing Urban Issues, Problems, and Needs

There are numerous issues and problems faced by urban areas throughout the world: poverty, unemployment, crime, pollution, waste disposal, water purity, transportation, housing, population congestion, and so on. Rural and suburban areas may face some of these problems also, but usually not to the extent that urban areas dol. In order to deal with issues and help solve problems, it is important first to be able to determine what they are and if it is possible to solve them. Sociological perspectives can be useful tools in helping to examine and solve such problems. The objective of this project is to have you examine some urban issues and problems that affect a city near you.

Journal instructions:
1. Select an urban area near where you live. Identify, and discuss in your journal, what you think are the five most important problems and issues that that area has had to deal with the last few years. In order to find this information out, you should:
> a) Do a content analysis of articles, news stories, essay, letters to the editor, and other news items about urban issues and problems that have appeared in the area newspaper during the past few years.
> b) Interview people from law enforcement, social service, and community service agencies to obtain data about crime, poverty, unemployment, drug abuse, homelessness, or other problems and issues.
> c) Talk with people who live and work in the area to find out what they think some of the most important issues and problems are.
> d) Interview a city government official or city planner to find out some of the most important issues and problems that the city government has had to deal with during the past few years. Ask the person you interview what is being done, either by the city or by private organizations, to help deal with these issues and problems. also, find out if there are any public or private resources with which to deal with these issues and problems.

2. In your journal, examine each of the problems and/or issues you identified from the point of view of each of the three sociological perspectives on urbanization. How would each explain each of the problems and/or issues? What types of solutions would each propose? Be sure to use evidence that you collected in your discussion.

Option: essay
Pretend that you have been hired as a consultant by the urban area you studied above in order to determine what some of the major issues an problems are, what types of resources are available to deal with them, and what you would recommend to help solve the problems. Present your ideas in an essay (around four pages, typed based upon the information you collected (above), ideas found within chapter 15, and insights provided by each of the three sociological perspectives on urbanization.

Option: bibliography
Select one of the problems or issues you identified above. Develop a bibliography of around ten to fifteen articles from sociology journals and/or books written by sociologists about that particular problem or issue. Type your bibliography following the format found in one of the sociology journals.

PROJECT INSTRUCTIONS ARE CONTINUED ON THE FOLLOWING PAGE.

Option: research paper
Using your material you developed in your journal and essay (above) and at least five items from your bibliography (above), write a paper (around five to seven pages, typed) in which you discuss a specific problem faced by urban areas. In addition, discuss ways to address the problem, using sociological ideas. Be sure to cite your sources properly throughout your paper and include a reference page.

CHAPTER 15

POPULATION

CHAPTER OUTLINE

Why the Explosive Growth?
        Growth Rates
        The Demographic Transition

The Impact of Population Growth
        The Less Developed Countries
        The Industrialized Nations

Migration
        Leaving the Third World
        The Impact on Industrialized Nations

Solving the Population Problem
        Feeding the Hungry
        Controlling Population Growth
            Social Change
            Birth Control

Sociological Perspectives on Population
        The Functionalist Perspective
        The Conflict Perspective
        The Feminist Perspective
        The Interactionist Perspective

CHAPTER LEARNING OBJECTIVES AND ESSAY QUESTIONS

After studying this chapter, you should be able to:

• Outline and discuss the extent and dangers of world population growth.

• Define several terms that describe population processes and state reasons for discuss the reasons for explosive population growth.

• Analyze the impact of population growth on America and the Third World.

• Outline and discuss ways of combating population growth and feeding the world's people.

• State and compare the different sociological perspectives on population.

KEY POINTS FOR REVIEW

• There are twice as many people in the world—over 5.6 billion—than there were 40 years ago. This rate of growth is likely to continue. Many scientists believe that the earth cannot support such rapid growth. The crucial task facing the human race is to ensure that the population explosion is curbed by rational programs of population control and not by famines or wars.

• Demographers study the causes and effects of the changes in human population. One thing that affects a nation's population growth is immigration and emigration. The world's population is determined by birthrates and death rates. The age composition of a population must be examined to determine whether its growth rate is unusually high or low. The cause of the population explosion is the decrease in death rates—which began in the second half of the eighteenth century in Western Europe—and not an increase in birthrates (which have actually declined).

• According to the theory of demographic transition, there are three distinct stages of population growth. In the first stage, both birth and death rates are high and population growth is moderate. In the second stage, the process of industrialization begins, and technological improvements bring a sharp decline in death rates, with birthrates declining more slowly. In the third stage, birthrates drop down far enough to balance death rates, and the population stabilizes. The theory implies that the Third World nations—now in the second stage—will stabilize once they become industrialized. Critics of this theory, however, point out that the theory was based upon population changes that occurred during the industrialization of the Western countries, with situations quite different than the Third World nations.

• One of the first people to recognize the dangers of unrestricted population growth was Thomas Malthus. He warned that food supplies increase arithmetically, but uncontrolled populations increase geometrically. While Malthus underestimated the world's capacity to produce food, many demographers fear that as the world's supply of fossil fuel is used up he will be proven right.

• The biggest problem that results from uncontrolled population growth in Third World countries is lack of enough food, followed by mass poverty and environmental degradation. Even though most people are able to get enough food to survive, 10 to 25 percent of the world's population suffers from chronic hunger or malnutrition. Poor diet in childhood leads to physical and mental impairment as adults. The tiny plots of family land typical of the Third World can support only a limited number of people; hence, many young people migrate to cities adding to the flood of unskilled and uneducated immigrants in urban centers. In turn, because of lack of opportunities, many live in slums or shantytowns in homes that lack running water, sewerage, and electricity. Because the population is growing so fast in Third World countries, poverty is another major problem. Finally, the rapid growth rates have created a disproportionate number of children with much fewer working-age adults.

• Population growth creates similar problems for agricultural and industrialized nations, but the difference is in scale. Although the industrialized nations have the economic resources to provide food, shelter, and clothing for an expanding population, they do not always do it. Birthrates are highest among the poorest people, who are least able to support their children and win government support. An additional problem faced in industrialized nations is the impending shortage of energy and raw materials. It is difficult to measure precisely the effects of population growth in industrialized nations, but it is quite clear that the cost enacted from disrupting nature is—and will continue to be—very high.

• Another significant development in world population are the waves of immigration that affect every country. The flow of people from overpopulated rural villages to the urban slums of the Third World and the migration of refugees from famine and war-torn countries to neighboring countries have created areas of extremely poor living conditions. In addition, many Third World people are migrating to the industrialized nations. The impact this immigration has on the industrialized nations is a very controversial issue. In the past, immigrants provided a valuable pool of cheap labor for the industrialized nations and were seen as an economic asset. However, now many see immigrants as taking away some jobs from native born citizens and holding down the overall wages paid for low-skilled work.

• There have been numerous recommendations offered to deal with the problems of overpopulation. The first is to find more efficient ways to feed the hungry. Suggestions for this include: inventing new methods for growing more food, improving agricultural production with more mechanization (in industrialized countries); using intermediate technology (machines that are less sophisticated than those in industrialized countries but more effective than traditional reliance on human and animal power) in Third World countries; reorganizing the agricultural economy through land reform (taking land from the rich landlords and redistributing it to the peasants who actually do the work); cultivating more land, utilizing the sea more efficiently; and wasting less.

• The most urgent task is to gain control of the world's explosive population growth. Many political leaders who are interested in controlling population focus their efforts on industrialization, believing that attitudes toward the family and reproduction will change as the economy. However, it is not likely that this will occur quickly enough or to the extent that many leaders expect. More direct population controls, therefore, are suggested. This can occur through family planning counseling, bonuses for couples with few children and penalties for those with many, mandatory restrictions, incentive programs, and sex education programs.

• From the functionalist perspective, population growth can perform several functions including more security during natural disasters, stronger defense against foreign aggressors, a larger workforce, and more consumer items. Its dysfunctions can include things such as serious environmental damage and a shortage of natural resources, intense competition for jobs, unemployment, overcrowding, the spread of disease, and a decline in the standard of living.

281

Functionalists maintain that the population problem will be solved only when the dysfunctional attitudes, values, and institutions that promote excessive birthrates are changed.

• From the conflict perspective, the population crisis is a direct result of European colonialism and the growth of a world economy that is divided between rich industrialized nations and poor agricultural ones. Additionally, it sees the forces that oppose population control as a reflection of a conflict between the interests of the masses and those of leaders and ruling elites. Overpopulation is harmful to most people, but it is an economic an political asset to the ruling class. Conflict theorists see the causes of malnutrition and hunger as a problem of distribution , not production. From the conflict theorist point of view, the solution lies in redistributing the world's food so that everyone is adequately fed.

• Feminists have examined how social restrictions placed on women have played a critical role in the population problem. The cultures with the highest birth rates are those that deny women equal access to education and jobs. The feminist response to the population crisis is to give the women of the developing nations more rights and more freedoms and provide women with birth control technology, economic assistance, and the emotional support necessary to help them create a more powerful independent role for themselves.

• The interactionist perspective looks at the problem of overpopulation as the result of the way traditional cultures define the world and their attitudes and beliefs about childrearing and family life. From this perspective, learned traditional attitudes about the family, work, and the roles of men and women must change before birth control measures can be effective. These attitudinal changes must interact with shifting economic, social, and political conditions leading to concrete economic and social improvements.

NOTES:

KEY TERMS

The following key terms are found in your textbook on the page number indicated in parentheses. In the space provided, write a brief definition of the key term **in your own words**. Then **provide an example** of the term, such as a culture in which the practice takes place, or people that you might know whose behavior illustrates the term, a current event that illustrates the term, how a term could be used to shed light on or help solve a particular social problem, and so on. You could include examples from the news, books, movies, or anything else that will illustrate the term and help you remember it. Include any comments from your class discussions or textbook that might help you remember and understand these key terms. Use additional paper if necessary, but keep it with your study guide to help you review for exams.

demography (p.487)

_____

_____

_____

_____

birthrates (p. 488)

_____

_____

_____

_____

death rates (p. 488)

_____

_____

_____

_____

growth rate (p. 488)

_____

_____

_____

total fertility rate (p. 489)

_____

_____

_____

_____

replacement rate (p. 489)

_____

_____

_____

_____

demographic transition (p. 489)

_____

_____

_____

_____

green revolution (p.499)

_____

_____

_____

_____

intermediate technology (p. 499)

_____

_____

_____

_____

land reform (p.500)

NOTES:

PRACTICE TEST

Multiple Choice

1. Which of the following statements accurately describes how much the world population is actually increasing?
   a) We have almost reached a stable world population growth.
   b) There are twice as many people today as there were forty years ago.
   c) There are twice as many people today as there were eighty years ago.
   d) The world's population will double in the next ten years.

2. The study of the causes and effects of changes in the human population is the study of:
   a) sociology
   b) urbanization
   c) birth rates
   d) demography

3. Most of the world's population will be born:
   a) pretty evenly around the world
   b) in China and the Philippines
   c) in the developed countries
   d) in the underdeveloped countries in Africa, Asia, and Latin America

4. The growth rate is determined by subtracting the death rate from the birth rate, and:
   a) dividing by 1000
   b) adjusting for migration
   c) adding projections for the future
   d) adjusting for internal population movements

5. The real cause of the population explosions the:
   a) decrease in the death rate
   b) increase in the birth rate
   c) overall growth rate
   d) lack of contraceptive technology

6. The most immediate population crisis today is in:
   a) Africa
   b) the Philippines
   c) Latin America
   d) Asia

7. The birth rate is:
   a) the number of babies born in a year
   b) the number of babies born in a year divided by the total population
   c) the number of babies born in a year divided by 1000
   d) the number of births minus the number of deaths

8. All of the following are stages of the demographic transition, EXCEPT for:
   a) high birth rates and high death rates
   b) high death rates and low birth rates
   c) low death rates and high birth rates
   d) low birth rates and low death rates

9. The number of children a woman is likely to have in her lifetime is called:
   a) the crude birth rate
   b) fertility
   c) fecundity
   d) the growth rate

10. Industrialization brings down birthrates because it:
    a) changes the structure of the family
    b) improves medical care and disease control
    c) changes the components of culture
    d) alters the death rate

11. The main problem created by overpopulation the agricultural countries of the Third World is:
    a) poor distribution of food
    b) too little foreign aid
    c) periodic famines
    d) a tendency to horde

12. Population growth has greatly accelerated the process of:
    a) government bureaucracy
    b) energy creation
    c) industrial development
    d) environmental destruction

13. According to the theory of demographic transition, the Third World is in the _____ stage of transition.
    a) first
    b) second
    c) third
    d) fourth

14. All of the following are problems in the Third World crated by the population explosion, EXCEPT for:
    a) lack o proper nutrition for infants and mothers
    b) disruption of traditional village life
    c) new forms of political and economic life
    d) the age composition of the population

15. The age composition of the Third World countries contributes to the population explosion because:
    a) the massive number of people are young
    b) the massive numbers of people are old
    c) not enough old people are available to fully care for infants
    d) too few people are available to work

16. All of the following are reasons why the Green Revolution has failed, EXCEPT that it requires:
    a) added fertilizer that poor countries cannot afford
    b) expensive petroleum products
    c) forcing peasants off traditional lands
    d) more land than is currently available

17. Thomas Malthus, in his famous essay on population, argued that overpopulation was inevitable because food supplies increased arithmetically while population increased:
    a) twice every forty years
    b) haphazardly
    c) geometrically
    d) linearly

18. The current pattern of population growth in the industrialized nations is:
    a) at zero population growth level
    b) increasing the level of social inequality
    c) too low to sustain America's population
    d) greater than the Third World nations

19. One American baby will use more resources in its lifetime than _____ Asian babies.
    a) five
    b) ten
    c) fifteen
    d) thirty

20. E. G. Schumacher's recommendation to use human and animal labor rather than advanced machines is now called the strategy of _____ technology.
    a) intermediate
    b) advanced
    c) primitive
    d) anti-

21. One way to cut down on the waste of food is to:
    a) raise more lean animals
    b) kill more rats
    c) adopt vegetarian diets
    d) move families closer to the sources of food

22. The creation of new strains of wheat and rice that yield more food per acre is called:
    a) genetic evolution
    b) the Green Revolution
    c) the ultimate solution to the world's food problem
    d) intermediate technology

23. One way to reorganize the agricultural economy that gets individual farmers to grow more food is:
    a) land reform
    b) communism
    c) lowering the birth rate
    d) use more fertilizer

288

24. The most urgent task facing the human race today is:
    a) nuclear war
    b) technological lag
    c) gaining control over the world's population
    d) land reform

25. Attempting to cultivate more land will not help feed the world's hungry because:
    a) most good land is already in use
    b) most good land is unreachable by modern machines
    c) most countries do not have the technology to cultivate more crops
    d) the world's hungry are not able to consume additional food

26. One way some political leaders favor to change attitudes and thereby control population is through:
    a) abstinence
    b) family planning
    c) industrialization
    d) infanticide

27. Most family planning programs in the Third World have failed for all of the following reasons EXCEPT that:
    a) most traditional cultures believe more children means a stronger family
    b) most family planning programs are poorly organized
    c) many religions oppose family planning
    d) the gender role revolution has actually promoted a higher birth rate

28. According to the feminist perspective on population, a major cause of out-of-control population growth has been due to
    a) social restrictions placed on women
    b) providing too much food to the rich
    c) disorganization
    d) the wrong attitudes toward children

29. Functionalists note that as death rates have dropped, attitudes encouraging fertility have become:
    a) functional
    b) dysfunctional
    c) nationalistic
    d) traditional

30. Sociologists that believe that the food shortage is caused by a distribution system that gives too much food to the wealthy and too little to the poor likely follow the _____ perspective.
    a) functinalist
    b) conflict
    c) interactionist
    d) feminist

PROJECTS

PROJECT 15.1 Population Problems Related to Fertility, Mortality, and Migration

Fertility is a measure of the rate at which people are born. Mortality is a measure of the rate at which people die. Migration is the movement of people into or out of a geographical area. these factors can have significant impact upon the welfare andtypes of problems that societies face.

Journal instructions:
1. Look through newspapers and news magazines for the past year to identify five to ten issues and problems (such as starvation, overpopulation, spread of disease, unemployment, and so on) in various countries throughout the world that are the result of a country's fertility, mortality, or migration rates.

2. In your journal, describe these issues and problems and briefly discuss what each of the countries is doing to try to cope with them. That is, what policies have they undertaken or are they considering that might help them deal with these issues or problems.

3. In your journal, discuss each of the issues and problems that you identified from point of view of each of the three sociological perspectives on population. What does each see as the source of the problem or issue? How does each suggest that the problem or issue be handled?

Option: essay
Write an essay (around four pages, typed) in which you summarize and discuss the problems related to births, deaths, and migration that you identified. Additionally, include a discussion about how each of the sociological perspectives on population would explain and solve the problem. Finally, discuss which perspective you think provides the most useful explanation and solution, and why.

Option: bibliography
Select one of the countries that you discussed in your journal and essay (above). Develop a bibliography of ten to fifteen articles from sociology journals and/or books written by sociologists that discusses the causes and effects of demographic changes in that country. If you cannot find enough articles about a specific country, then find articles on the causes and effects of demographic changes in general. Type you bibliography following the format found in one of the sociology journals.

Option: research paper
Select one of the countries that you discussed in your journal (the one that you did your bibliography about is preferable) that faces problems or issues related to mortality, fertility, or migration. Write a paper (around five to seven pages, typed) in which you discuss how birth rates, death rates, and migration have affected that country's issues and problems now and in the past, and the types of policies that have been enacted to deal with these issues and problems. Use at least five items from your bibliography. Incorporate material from your journal and essay (above). Be sure to provide proper documentation throughout your paper and include a reference page.

PROJECT 15. 2 How Population Trends Affect Your Life

A *population pyramid* is a graphic representation of how many males and females from each age category there are in a particular country. Population pyramids enable us to see what percentage of people are of each age and gender at a given time. the percentage of the population that is your age can have important effects on many areas of your life: mate selection, educational opportunities, cost of education, job opportunities, cost of housing, and many others. The objective of this project is to have you identify and examine the problems and issues related to your age that people from your age group will face during your lives.

Journal instructions:
1. Locate a population pyramid of the United States that includes your age group. Many introductory sociology texts have examples of them. In addition, you can find on in the Population Reference Bureau's *Statistical Abstract of the United States,* 1991, p. 16, or other current statistical abstracts. These are readily available on web sites.

2. Find the year in which you were born on the pyramid. Look at the percentage of people of your age and of each gender in comparison to people older and younger than you. In your journal, list and discuss all the ways in which the size and composition of people in your age group might affect your opportunities and lifestyles (for example, educational, housing, marital, cost of living, and others) and speculate as to the types of problems and issues you may face throughout your life as a result of being in your position in the pyramid. Discuss this in your journal.

3. After you complete the above, compare your age and gender group with your parents' and grandparents' groups and how their opportunities and lifestyles, problems and issues, wee affected by population characteristics. Discuss this in your journal.

Option: essay
Write a paper (around five pages, typed) in which you use examples from your journal to discuss the impact of population trends on life experiences.

Option: bibliography
Select two or three of the issues or problems that may arise as a result of your position in the population pyramid. (See your journal, above). Develop a bibliography of ten articles from popular periodicals (newspapers, magazines, and so on) and ten articles from sociology journals and/or books written by sociologists about the problems or issues you identified. Type your bibliography following the format found in one of the sociology journals.

Option: research paper
Write a paper (around seven pages, typed) in which you discuss two or three particular problems or issues that you will face as a result of your position in the population pyramid. Support your views with at least three articles from popular periodicals and at least three from sociological periodicals. You can use items from your bibliography (above). Be sure to document your sources throughout your paper and include a reference page.

CHAPTER 16

THE ENVIRONMENT

CHAPTER OUTLINE

CHAPTER LEARNING OBJECTIVES AND ESSAY QUESTIONS

After studying this chapter, you should be able to:

• State and discuss the views of the environment that humans through history have held.

• Define and illustrate the concept of ecology.

• Describe how humans have created air and water pollution and have deteriorated the land.

• State and discuss how vital resources like coal and minerals are rapidly dwindling.

• Analyze the origins of the environmental crisis.

• Describe the several ways American society has responded to the environmental crisis.

• State and compare four sociological perspectives on the environment.

KEY POINTS FOR REVIEW

• For centuries, people have taken the environment for granted, assuming that it is boundless. only recently have people begun to realize its fragility as our natural resources are becoming depleted and pollution is increasing.

• The science of ecology shows us that humans are not superior beings above animals and plants, but part of a complex network of living things. Life on this planet exists within a delicate balance in a thin biosphere of soil and water composed of many ecosystems that require energy for their survival. Virtually all energy comes from the sun and proceeds through many transformations in a food chain before in decomposes and is naturally recycled.

• Early hunting and gathering people interfered very little with the ecosystem's natural processes. With developments in technology, the invention of agriculture, and the development of cities, the earth's ecological balance began to become disrupted. Forests were cut down, rivers, re-channeled, and human waste was improperly disposed of. The process intensified with industrialization, and the rate of destruction, pollution, and energy depletion accelerated.

• Air pollution is rapidly becoming a global problem. The greatest source of air pollution in North America is transportation. Coal, oil, and natural gas used for heating and electricity, pollutants emitted from factories, and burning trash are also major contributors. Carbon monoxide, hydrocarbons, oxides of sulfur and nitrogen, ozone, tiny particles of soot, ashes, and other industrial by-products increasingly pollute the air. The effects on the natural environment include temperature inversion, photochemical smog, acid rain, and the greenhouse effect. These things affect human, animal, and plant life. Increases in skin cancer, eye problems, lung problems, suppression of the immune system, harm to animals, and a decrease in crop yields are only a few of the problems created by air pollution. Changes in weather patterns have already been noted and will eventually have catastrophic effects on both the natural environment and on our social and economic lives.

• Water pollution is another significant problem. Organic wastes are important water pollutants. In small quantities, they are quickly broken down by bacteria, but too much organic waste can disrupt this process, leading to the death of fish and other forms of marine life. Water pollutants come in the form of human waste, chemical fertilizers, industrial poisons and chemicals, pesticides, oil spills, and others. In 1994 the Environmental Protection Agency (EPA) concluded that one of every three rivers in America were not in good condition and the situation in coastal waters is worse. Marine life is dying at an unprecedented rate. Recently, it has been found that even our drinking water is becoming contaminated. The Natural Resources Defense Council found, in 1994, that 20 percent of America's drinking water is not adequately treated for toxic chemicals, bacteria, parasites, and other pollutants.

• An environmental problem faced especially by Third World nations is the deterioration of land. The world's forests are shrinking at an alarming rate, while the desert wastelands grow. Natural forces, such as periodic droughts, certainly play an important part of the problem of desertification, but much of the damage is being done by humans. Overgrazing by livestock, poor irrigation techniques that poison the soil, heavily mechanized agricultural techniques, the disposal of huge quantities of industrial waste, the destruction of land by mining companies and, of course, deforestation by humans to get lumber and fuel are major reasons for the problem.

• Toxic wastes, including chemicals and radiation, contribute to the problem of environmental pollution. The United States is the largest producer of toxic wastes—between 264 and 509 million tons a year—but it is a worldwide problem. Radiation is a problem that is extremely frightening because we still know relatively little about its long-term effects. The treat of nuclear war is the largest fear, but radioactive wastes generate by nuclear plants are deadly pollutants and fill the environment regardless of whether or not there is a war.

• One of the most serious consequences of our assault on the natural environment has been a sharp reduction in biodiversity. Extinctions are occurring—and increasing—at an alarming rate.

• The earth's resources are limited. We are just beginning to realize that there are only limited amounts of oil, coal, and uranium. The world's supply of oil and minerals cannot possibly support all the world's people in the style to which the wealthy nations have become accustomed. Most of our current energy comes from non-renewable resources. One example of which we have become painfully aware is oil. In the 1970s the world experienced its first great energy crisis as crises in the mid-east disrupted the flow of oil to the rest of the world. Some experts predict the world's supply of oil will be used up within 100 years. Other non-renewable sources of energy, such as coal, are also rapidly being depleted. Worldwide consumption of non-renewable resources has grown at a staggering pace. Sources of renewable energy are being explored—such as hydroelectric power, geothermal energy, and solar energy—that will have to be adopted eventually if the world is to maintain its current rate of energy usage.

• There are a variety of causes of the environmental crisis. Our magnificent technological advances that have made life so much more comfortable have also brought havoc to the biosphere. Technology in itself, though, is not to blame. The real culprit is exploitative technology which is designed to produce the greatest immediate rewards without regard to the long-term consequences to the environment. This has been occurring for thousands of years ranging from unsound farming techniques to damage resulting from industrialization to the destruction of the ozone layer from nuclear radiation. A second cause of the environmental crisis is unregulated population growth. A third reason lies in our culturally-based attitudes toward nature and humanity's place in it. Our culture tends to see nature as a wilderness to be conquered and subdued by human effort. Many other cultures—such as Native Americans and the Aborigines of Australia—see nature as sacred and to be respected.

• Responding to the environmental crisis is difficult because many measures can retard the economy. The ultimate solution, for now, is sacrifice. People must change their life styles in such a way that energy consumption will be reduced. A second response to the environment crisis can be found in political action. Environmentally destructive patterns of behavior both among consumers and producers needs to be changed through government efforts such as education and global involvement. Third, an energy conservation plan that helps stretch our natural resources must be adopted. Fourth, new non-exploitative technology and renewable sources of energy need to be developed. And fifth, there must be limits to the unlimited population growth that the world is currently experiencing.

• From the functionalist perspective, today's environmental problems are seen as latent dysfunctions of industrialization. The technological and economic changes that have helped to create modern industrial society threw the environment out of balance and created our current problems. The solution, according to some functionalists, is to reduce the dysfunctions of the industrial economy through more efficient pollution control and through new technological improvements that are more efficient and less destructive. Other functionalists disagree and feel that the solution must lie in changing our system of values and reorganizing society so that it is not so environmentally destructive.

• From the conflict perspective, exploitation of the environment is another result of an economic structure that depends on the exploitation of the poor by the rich and on an ever-increasing exploitation of the natural environment. One solution, according to conflict theorists, is to make firms pay for the environmental damage they cause. Additionally, they feel that we must create a new kind of world system based on equality and respect for the dignity of all people, and reduce our emphasis on profits at the expense of humanity.

• From the feminist perspective, the roots of our environmental crisis are found in the same patriarchal culture that has oppressed women. "Eco-feminists" see a contradiction between the feminine values of cooperation, nurturance, and mutual support and the masculine values of power and achievement. This cultural attitude has led to an exploitative relationship with the environment. To feminists, the solution to environmental problems lies in a fundamental shift in the values and perspectives our culture holds.

• From the interactionist perspective, learned attitudes and values are at the root of the environmental crisis. Most of us evaluate the world in individualistic terms and do whatever seems to satisfy our own needs. Since such attitudes are learned, interactionists feel that the best way to deal with environmental problems is through education. People must learn respect and reverence toward the natural environment.

296

KEY TERMS

The following key terms are found in your textbook on the page number indicated in parentheses. In the space provided, write a brief definition of the key term **in your own words**. Then **provide an example** of the term, such as a culture in which the practice takes place, or people that you might know whose behavior illustrates the term, a current event that illustrates the term, how a term could be used to shed light on or help solve a particular social problem, and so on. You could include examples from the news, books, movies, or anything else that will illustrate the term and help you remember it. Include any comments from your class discussions or textbook that might help you remember and understand these key terms. Use additional paper if necessary, but keep it with your study guide to help you review for exams.

ecology (p. 514)

_____

_____

_____

_____

biosphere (p. 514)

_____

_____

_____

_____

ecosystems (p. 514)

_____

_____

_____

_____

photo-synthesis (p. 514)

_____

_____

_____

food chain (p. 515)

_____

_____

_____

_____

temperature inversion (p. 516)

_____

_____

_____

_____

photo-chemical smog (p. 516)

_____

_____

_____

_____

acid rain (p. 516)

_____

_____

_____

_____

greenhouse effect (p. 518)

_____

_____

_____

_____

organic wastes (p. 519)

_____

_____

_____

_____

desertification (p. 522)

_____

_____

_____

_____

deforestation (p. 521)

_____

_____

_____

_____

meltdowns (p. 524)

_____

_____

_____

_____

strip mining (p. 522)

_____

_____

_____

_____

breeder reactors (p. 525)

_____

_____

_____

_____

nonrenewable resource (p. 528)

_____

_____

_____

_____

renewable resource (p. 528)

_____

_____

_____

_____

hydroelectric power (p. 530)

_____

_____

_____

_____

geothermal energy (p. 530)

_____

_____

_____

_____

solar energy (p. 530)

_____

_____

_____

_____

exploitative technology (p. 531)

_____

_____

_____

_____

neo-Malthusians (p. 534)

_____

_____

_____

_____

cornucopians (p. 534)

_____

_____

_____

_____

tragedy of the commons (p. 543)

_____

_____

_____

_____

PRACTICE TEST

Multiple Choice

1. Western culture views human creatures as:
   a) separate from the natural environment
   b) part of the natural order
   c) subservient to the natural order
   d) objects of divine intervention

2. The single greatest source of air pollution in North America comes from:
   a) animal methane
   b) transportation
   c) heating plants
   d) garbage dumps

3. Self-sufficient communities of organisms living in an interdependent relationship with one another are called:
   a) ecosystems
   b) biospheres
   c) food chains
   d) life zones

4. The buildup of gases from the burning of various fuels is changing the composition of the atmosphere. This is known as:
   a) temperature inversion
   b) the greenhouse effect
   c) acid rain
   d) ecological disaster

5. The food produced by green plants usually goes through many transformations before it is eaten by humans. this process is called:
   a) ecological transformation
   b) photosynthesis
   c) nutritional progress
   d) the food chain

6. All of the following are substances that pollute the water, EXCEPT for:
   a) industrial waste
   b) organic waste
   c) automobile exhausts
   d) chemical fertilizers

7. The shortage of energy and raw materials has led to new methods for obtaining them. Which of the following is an example of a new method that is environmentally undesirable?
   a) land restoration
   b) strip mining
   c) well-drilling
   d) advanced culling

8. Which of the following is an example of renewable energy?
   a) oil
   b) coal
   c) solar energy
   d) natural gas

9. The transformation of productive land into sand because of over-use is called:
   a) ecological damage
   b) exploitative technology
   c) desertification
   d) deforestation

10. All of the following are dangers that nuclear energy poses for people, EXCEPT for:
    a) crime and terrorism
    b) meltdowns
    c) leakage of radiation
    d) generational mutations

11. Unlike most energy, dwindling supplies of minerals can be:
    a) replaced by mining the oceans
    b) eventually discovered in Antarctica and other remote places of the world
    c) recycled
    d) renewed

12. Drinking water today:
    a) contains cholera and typhoid germs
    b) is pure and endless
    c) is entirely polluted
    d) is increasingly chemically polluted

13. The Environmental protection Agency estimates that _____ percent of hazardous waste is disposed of improperly.
    a) 70
    b) 80
    c) 90
    d) 100

14. The poorest one-third of the human population depends on _____ for energy.
    a) coal
    b) wood
    c) oil
    d) hydroelectric power

15. Technology that is designed to produce the greatest immediate rewards without regard to the long-term consequences to the environment is called _____ technology.
    a) traditional
    b) undeveloped
    c) modern
    d) exploitative

16. Which of the following types of scientists fear that, without a change in attitudes and behavior, the work is headed for an ecological disaster?
    a) the neo-Malthusians
    b) the cornucopians
    c) the neo-Darwinists
    d) the environmentalists

17. One way out of the environmental protection-unemployment cycle is:
    a) better technology
    b) a sacrifice of life-style
    c) new discoveries of energy
    d) more unemployment

18. All of the following are ways to conserve scarce resources, EXCEPT for:
    a) recycling
    b) closed water systems
    c) energy conservation
    d) slower life-styles

19. Which of the following is not a type of exploitative technology?
    a) unplanned agricultural development
    b) industrialization
    c) nuclear power plants
    d) low energy machines

20. Which of the following attitudes toward nature is more typical of tribal cultures?
    a) Nature is something to subdue and exploit,
    b) Human beings are a part of nature.
    c) The ideal of the future is based on a utopian past.
    d) Materialism and individualism are the core cultural values.

21. One reason why the environmental movement faces tough obstacles is:
    a) a lack of a clear vision
    b) members are polluters themselves
    c) well-funded lobbyists and other oppose change
    d) their methods are too radical

22. Which of the following is the most promising new technology that could help solve energy problems?
    a) semi-conductors
    b) garbage recycling
    c) hydroelectricity
    d) solar power

23. Which of the following types of energy is NOT renewable?
    a) hydroelectric power
    b) solar energy
    c) geothermal energy
    d) nuclear energy

24. Traditional believes in economic expansion and progress has blinded people to:
    a) the damage caused by reckless growth
    b) the need to develop new technology
    c) the need to recycle more waste
    d) the role of politics in saving the environment

25. Which modern ideal is now seen as the greatest barrier to responsible environmentalism?
    a) a belief in materialism
    b) religious idealism
    c) the Green movement
    d) manifest destiny

26. The two most important steps to be taken to preserve the natural environment are a stronger educational campaign to spread awareness of the environmental crisis and:
    a) more new technology to more efficient use of the world's resources
    b) a widespread, comprehensive campaign of recycling
    c) a movement to save the rain forest
    d) political and social action to bring about change

27. The world would be more peaceful and secure if people of the industrialized nations learned to accept:
    a) more charitable giving
    b) new forms of technology
    c) a lower standard of living
    d) more recycling

28. Sociologists who study how children learn to be willing to waste energy, throw garbage on the street, use plastic materials and drive a monstrous car are most likely using the _____ perspective.
    a) interactionist
    b) conflict
    c) feminist
    d) functional

29. For conflict theorists, exploitation of the environment is part of:
    a) a larger pattern of social exploitation
    b) a latent dysfunction of industrialization
    c) attitudes and values that emphasize individuality
    d) a natural progression of technology

30. Functionalists see environmental problems as _____ of the industrial revolution.
    a) exploitative outcomes
    b) improper attitudes
    c) latent dysfunctions
    d) manifest functions

PROJECTS

PROJECT 16.1 Should Government Enforce Stricter Environmental Protection Measures?

The environment has become one of the most controversial political topics of the decade. Political positions about the environment are varied. Some feel that stricter policies should be enforced that would regulate consumer and industrial behavior; others feel that regulation is unnecessary and will hurt the economy. this is not an issue that concerns just the United States, but concerns all countries around the world. The objective of this project is to have you examine the extent to which environmental problems affect all of us, and to discuss whether or not the government should play a greater role in dealing with such problems.

Journal instructions:
1. Using your library's and/or computerized bibliographic indexes, find newspaper or magazine articles about ten different environmental issues, problems, or policy debates that have appeared in the news within the past few years. Additionally, locate three or four web sites that deal with debates about environmental issues. Discuss each of these in your journal.

2. In your journal, categorize these issues or problems in terms of types. Develop whatever categories you think will work to help you do this (for example, industrial pollution, consumer pollution, water pollution, and so on). then, discuss what you see as the main reasons for each type of environmental problem.

3. Use the three sociological perspectives on the environment to discuss reasons for each of the problems/issues you identified and how each perspective might solve each. Discuss these in your journal.

Option: essay
Write an essay (around four pages, typed) in which you discuss what you feel are the three most significant environmental problems faced by nations of the world today. Discuss why these problems exist, from the point of view of the sociological perspectives.

Option: bibliography
Develop a bibliography of fifteen to twenty articles from sociology journals, commentary magazines, newsmagazines, and newspapers that discuss whether or not strict environmental protection measures should be enacted and enforced by the government. Additionally, identify three or four web sites that address issues related to environmental protection. Be sure that your bibliography contains a balance of articles from sociology journals and popular periodicals, and contains a balance of articles and web sites supporting and opposing stricter environmental protection measures. Type your bibliography following the format found in one of the sociology journals.

Option: research paper
Write a paper (around five to seven pages, typed) in which you:
      a) Introduce the debate about environmental protection and provide some examples of
      measures that have been suggested by various political groups.

PROJECT INSTRUCTIONS ARE CONTINUED ON THE FOLLOWING PAGE.

b) Present <u>balanced</u> arguments for <u>and</u> against stricter environmental protection measures.

c) Take a position for <u>or</u> against stricter environmental protection measures. In taking your position, use material from your library research <u>and</u> the sociological perspectives on the environment (functionalism, conflict theory, the social psychological perspectives) that might be relevant to your argument.
d) Use material from at least five items from your bibliography. Be sure to provide proper documentation throughout your paper and include a reference page.

NOTES:

CHAPTER 17

THE GLOBAL DIVIDE: PROBLEMS OF INTERNATIONAL INEQUALITY

CHAPTER OUTLINE

Global Inequality
      Wealth and Poverty
      Health and Nutrition
      Education
      Women and Children
      Social Structure

Explaining the Global Divide
      Modernization Theory
      World System Theory
      Evaluation

Responding to the Problems of the Less Developed Countries
      The Industrialized Nations
            Dropping Trade Barriers
            Forgiving Debt
            Foreign Aid
            Being Good Neighbors
      The Less Developed Nations
            Population Control
            Economic Development
            Political Reform

Sociological Perspectives on the Global Divide
      The Functionalist Perspective
      The Conflict Perspective
      The Feminist Perspective
      The Interactionist Perspective

CHAPTER LEARNING OBJECTIVES AND ESSAY QUESTIONS

After studying this chapter, you should be able to:

• State and explain the central question posed by the great global divide.

• Describe the extent of global inequality, especially in terms of wealth and income, health, and education.

• Analyze two theories that try to explain the origin of the global divide.

• Explain the ways of responding to the problems of the Third World.

• Compare four sociological perspectives on the global divide.

KEY POINTS FOR REVIEW

• Since the media covers only the most dramatic and desperate problems, many people have a distorted concept of what life in a poor country is really like, and only a few have much of an idea about the causes of global poverty or what to do about it.

• One way of making sense of global inequality is to think of the nations of the world as making up a kind of international class system. The countries of the industrialized world—such as the United States, the Western European countries, Canada, Japan, Australia, and others—are like the "upper class" and the less developed or Third World countries—including many Latin American, African, and Asian countries—are like the "lower class." Some in-between nations–such as South Korea, Taiwan, and Mexico—have characteristics of both kinds of societies and are like the "middle class."

• There are significant monetary differences between the industrialized nations and the Third World countries. However, the differences go far beyond money. It is difficult to measure a country's wealth in terms of money since the value of a country's currency fluctuates significantly. Further, different nations accumulate wealth in different ways. Much of a country's wealth is manifested in its physical assets such as roads, bridges, power plants, sewers, canals, housing, factories, clothing, sanitation and so on.

• One of the most fundamental problems in the poor nations is the absence of economic opportunities for their young people. This is often a result of rapid population growth and a weak educational system. Because of a lack of work in the rural areas, many young people migrate to the cities in search of work.

• Third World countries suffer inequality of health and nutrition. A baby born in the Third World is at least five times more likely to die in its first year of life than a baby born in a wealthy nation. People who live in industrialized countries live twelve years longer than people in poor nations. Many of these differences are the result of economic conditions, especially poor sanitation and lack of clean drinking water. Disease is plentiful and doctors are scarce. There is also a lack of sufficient food in poor countries. The problem is compounded with the lack of refrigeration in many areas, leading to spoiled food and disease.

310

• In industrialized nations, less than 1 percent of the population is illiterate compared with around 30% in some Third World countries, and most in others. The system of universal education and the mass media in wealthy nations are sources of solidarity for their citizens, leading to shared values and attitudes.

• Although women suffer from prejudice and discrimination in every nation, the problems are far more sever in the less developed nations. Traditional agricultural societies have a high degree of gender inequality. This is manifested in female infanticide when resources are scare and more educational and economic opportunities for males. In many parts of the world, women are second class citizens and largely controlled by men. Husbands have a legal right to control their wives and family property is often passed down to the sons. By contrast, the industrialized nations have made great progress toward the goal of equality for women.

• Children in Third World countries also suffer from disproportionate inequality. They have higher mortality rates and suffer greater poverty than children in industrialized countries.

• Underlying the disparities in the quality of life between industrialized and Third World countries are fundamental differences in their social structures, especially with regard to their class systems, political institutions, and economic institutions. Jobs in Third World countries include farming, exploiting any available natural resources (petroleum, timber, copper, uranium, and so on), and low-wage unskilled jobs in industries owned by multi-national corporations.

• The industrialized and the Third World countries each have a relatively small upper class that commands a disproportionate share of the wealth and power. However, the industrialized nations also have a large middle class with the skills to keep the technological economy going. The middle class in Third World countries is much smaller and weaker.

• Industrialized countries tend to have stable democratic governments whereas Third World countries are much more likely to be ruled by a dictator or a small group of bureaucratic elites who are not elected by the public. Governments in less developed nations, whether they are dictatorships or democracies, tend to be weaker and more unstable than in wealthy nations.

• Present-day global inequality can be largely explained by the industrial revolution and the capitalist economic system that made it possible. As far back as the fifteenth century, though, the development of trade, commerce, and manufacturing that took place in Western Europe enabled some nations to develop a much higher standard of living and a significant accumulation of wealth while other nations stagnated. Contemporary global inequality stems from the fact that some nations have undergone a full process of industrialization while others have not. Modernization theory and world system theory are two explanations of why some nations have fully industrialized while others have not.

• Modernization theory is a functionalist approach that sees industrialization as part of a process of social evolution they called modernization. According to this view, modernization is the result of the build-up of the numerous improvements in the structure and function of social institutions, namely, technological innovations and capital accumulation. This leads to changes in the organization of society. Institutions become more specialized and more efficient, rather than having the extended family try to fulfill all of the functions—for example, religious, educational, health care, and so on—that are necessary for a society to survive and prosper. According to W. W. Rostow, nations that industrialize go through three different stages—the "traditional" stage, the "take-off" stage, and the "drive for technological maturity" stage—but not

311

necessarily at the same pace. Reasons for different rates of progress in the process of modernization include differences in work ethics—such as the Protestant work ethic in Western Europe—political climate, religious attitudes, education, the hold that traditionalism has over a country, and the extent to which an elite may control the market place.

• World system theory is a conflict approach that argues that industrialization does not take place in isolated individual nations, but within a complex web of international economic and political relationships known as the world system. The world system consists of a core of the rich and powerful industrialized nations surrounded by a periphery of poor nations, which is exploited by the core for its natural resources and cheap labor. A semiperiphery of growing countries lies in-between the core and the periphery which is somewhat dominated by the core, but in turn dominates the periphery. The core is often led by a dominant nation—a hegemonic power—that is stronger economically, militarily, and politically than the other core nations. According to world systems theory, the cause of poverty in the peripheral nations is that the core nations have forced them into a position of economic and political dependence. Critics of this theory argue that it sees only the bad side of capitalism and it fails to point out that the standard of living in the poor countries has actually been helped through advances in the industrialized nations.

• As with other social problems, there are proposals on how to solve the global crisis. However, they fall into two broad categories: how industrialized nations can help the less developed nations and how less developed nations can help themselves. There are a number of suggestions as to how industrialized nations can help. These include dropping trade barriers to allow the poorer nations to market their products more freely, forgiving huge debts that poor nations have accumulated by borrowing money from the wealthy nations, providing foreign aid to poor countries, and being good neighbors to countries in need. There are also a number of suggestions as to how the less developed nations can help themselves. These include controlling their rate of population growth, developing means to develop their economy, and reforming their political systems. Each of the proposals for the wealthy and less wealthy nations has its advantages and disadvantages.

• From the functionalist perspective, social disorganization is at the root of the global crisis. There is growing cultural lag as people cling to traditional institutional attitudes—regarding the family, religion, the economy, education, health care, politics, and so on—that no longer make sense in a rapidly changing economic system. Functionalists recommend, therefore, that governments find ways—especially through education—to speed up the process of helping people change their attitudes so that they can conform with Western-style nations.

• Conflict theorists explain the global crisis as the result of international exploitation of the weaker countries by the stronger countries. The solution, according to conflict theorists, is to find ways to end the economic exploitation that has victimized the less powerful countries.

• The feminist perspective focuses on the poor women of the Third World. Feminists see the poor women of the third World as the most exploited of the exploited. third World women are denied the most basic human rights to control their own lives. Feminists advocate the kind of female oriented development projects that have proven to improve the status of women and to be effective techniques to stimulate the economy.

• The interactionist perspective on global inequality has focused primarily on the psychological consequences of modernization. The sense of security and belonging that is found in traditional, close-knit villages is becoming disrupted by modernization. As a result, people must face a social environment where few of the old rules seem to apply. Besides agreeing with the recommendations offered by both the functionalist and conflict theorists, interactionists make two additional suggestions. First, the governments of the less developed nations should try to improve the rural economy so that people can remain in their villages and avoid the psychological changes connected with modernization. Second, Third World leaders must develop ways to strengthen family and community institutions.

NOTES:

KEY TERMS

The following key terms are found in your textbook on the page number indicated in parentheses. In the space provided, write a brief definition of the key term **in your own words**. Then **provide an example** of the term, such as a culture in which the practice takes place, or people that you might know whose behavior illustrates the term, a current event that illustrates the term, how a term could be used to shed light on or help solve a particular social problem, and so on. You could include examples from the news, books, movies, or anything else that will illustrate the term and help you remember it. Include any comments from your class discussions or textbook that might help you remember and understand these key terms. Use additional paper if necessary, but keep it with your study guide to help you review for exams.

less developed countries (p. 549)

_____

_____

_____

_____

Third World (p. 549)

_____

_____

_____

_____

Sub-Saharan Africa (p. 550)

_____

_____

_____

_____

modernization (p. 560)

_____

_____

_____

urban subsistence economy (p. 552)

_____

_____

_____

_____

industrial revolution (p. 559)

_____

_____

_____

_____

ethnocentrism (p. 560)

_____

_____

_____

_____

capital accumulation (p. 560)

_____

_____

_____

_____

world system (p. 561)

_____

_____

_____

_____

core (p. 562)

----

periphery (p. 562)

----

semiperiphery (p. 562)

----

hegemonic power (p. 562)

NOTES:

316

PRACTICE TEST

Multiple Choice

1. The countries in the "lower class" of nations that are concentrated in the southern two-thirds of the planet are called the:
   a) Third World
   b) Fourth World
   c) underdeveloped countries
   d) dark continents

2. A baby born in the Third World is at least _____ times more likely to die in its first year of live than a baby born in a wealthy nation.
   a) two
   b) three
   c) five
   d) ten

3. One of the values of a universal education like that in rich countries is that it helps to:
   a) fight illiteracy
   b) preserve ethnic and language heritage's
   c) legitimize inequality
   d) serve as a kind of social cement

4. All of the following are types of wealth accumulated by industrialized countries that give them advantages over Third World countries, EXCEPT for:
   a) sanitation systems
   b) roads and bridges
   c) buildings
   d) land

5. The main cause of high infant and death rates in Third World countries is:
   a) human biological factors
   b) economic conditions
   c) poor cultural habits
   d) fatalistic religions

6. Which of the following is more typical of the class system of a poor nation than a wealthy nation?
   a) a relatively small upper class
   b) a large, vibrant middle class
   c) a small, weak middle class
   d) a large number of poor people

7. Which of the following is a fundamental problem of the Third World?
   a) an absence of economic opportunity for the young
   b) too slow population growth
   c) a lack of natural resources
   d) a refusal to leave traditional villages and customs

317

8. It is estimated that from 10 to 20 percent of the world's people suffer from:
   a) unemployment
   b) chronic malnutrition
   c) acute starvation
   d) cholera

9. The most obvious difference in government between industrialized and Third World countries is that industrialized nations have:
   a) more bureaucracy
   b) more dictatorial governments
   c) stable democratic governments
   d) fragile democratic governments

10. Functionalist theories feel that industrialization is part of a process of social evolution called:
    a) world theory
    b) natural selection
    c) differentiation
    d) modernization

11. Today's global inequalities clearly stem from the fact that some nations:
    a) have over-industrialized and used up their natural resources
    b) have not fully industrialized
    c) cannot fully industrialize
    d) have clearly chosen not to industrialize

12. The industrial revolution and the capitalist economic system did all of the following, EXCEPT:
    a) stimulated many technological advances
    b) colonial domination of Third World countries
    c) great class equalities
    d) a higher standard of living

13. According to modernization theorists, Third World countries lag behind because of:
    a) poverty
    b) traditionalism
    c) education
    d) religion

14. According to the world system theory, Third World poverty is due to:
    a) traditionalism
    b) political and economic exploitation
    c) disorganization
    d) evolution

15. According to a new perspective, the best way to see individual countries is not in an isolated way but within a web of international economic and political relationships. This view is known as:
    a) world systems theory
    b) modernization systems theory
    c) Eurocentric domination theory
    d) traditional economic theory

318

16. To understand the problems of the world today, we need to look at:
    a) the lack of capital, low educational levels and weak governments of poor countries
    b) exploitation of the poor nations by the rich countries
    c) both internal conditions of poor countries and the world economic system
    d) none of the above

17. All of the following are ways that the developed countries could help the undeveloped ones, EXCEPT for:
    a) dropping trade barriers
    b) forgiving debts
    c) promoting birth control policies
    d) providing foreign aides

18. The main cause of the debt crisis of Third World nations is:
    a) the oil crisis of the early 1970s
    b) exploitation of countries by the West
    c) a disorganized social structure
    d) psychological disorientation produced by change

19. Third World countries need to limit population growth because too many people hinders economic growth and:
    a) traditional religious values no longer apply
    b) there are environmental limits to growth
    c) interferes with a more equal distribution of wealth
    d) developing countries need to copy the West's preferences for small families

20. Which of the following statements about American foreign aid programs is true?
    a) It amounts to over four percent of America's Gross National Product.
    b) It is the largest amount of all industrialized countries.
    c) It usually goes to the world's neediest countries.
    d) It often goes to local elites rather than the poor.

21. One major reason why third World nations themselves do not more fully pursue economic development is:
    a) a lack of technology
    b) a lack of inspiration
    c) the role of elites who benefit from the current system
    d) revolutionary political movements

22. Many world system theorists feel the best thing core nations could do to help the peripheral countries is to:
    a) provide more military aid
    b) teach peripheral countries new ways to behave
    c) provide more foreign aid
    d) simply leave them alone

23. All of the following are overall strategies nations committed to reform might follow, EXCEPT for:
    a) encouraging foreign investments
    b) retaining a nationalist approach to development
    c) copying the industrialized nations
    d) abandon all traditional standards and lifestyles

24. According to the world system theory, the core nations are surrounded by a much larger number of poor nations called the _____ nations.
    a) secondary core
    b) semi-periphery
    c) periphery
    s) Third World

25. Which of the following often helps third World nations develop the unity needed begin the drive toward industrialization?
    a) a democratic vote
    b) foreign aid
    c) new technology
    d) a revolution

26. The key to industrial development in the Third World is probably:
    a) capital
    b) motivation
    c) land
    d) natural resources

27. All of the following are possible strategies Third World countries could follow to responsibly improve their economies, EXCEPT for:
    a) rural development
    b) use of inexpensive technology and local labor
    c) build modern factories
    d) allow foreign companies to partially run the economy

28. Which of the following proposals for helping the Third World belongs to followers of the conflict perspective?
    a) creation of stable governments in the Third World
    b) minimizing psychological stress of the transition to industrialization
    c) a joining of poor and working-class people around the world to create a more just international order
    d) working to keep a country's family and community institutions strong

29. Which of the following theories about world economic development is based on functionalist theory?
    a) modernization theory
    b) world system's theory
    c) world conflict theory
    d) developmental theory

30. If you believe that Third world leaders need to work to keep their country's family and community institutions strong to minimize the anxiety of economic transition, you are following the _____ perspective.
   a) conflict
   b) world systems
   c) interactionist
   d) functional

NOTES:

PROJECTS

PROJECT 17.1 Exploring Theories of Modernization in Underdeveloped Countries

While much of the sociological study of social change examines the changes that have occurred and continue to occur in the modernized, industrial nations of the world, Coleman and Cressey point out the importance of understanding how underdeveloped nations are changing. The way they change significantly affects their ability to achieve economic and political equality with the industrialized world. The objective of this project is to have you examine and apply the two major theories of social change: modernization theory and world systems theory.

Journal instructions:
1. In your journal, summarize, in your own words, the views of modernization theory and of world systems theory.

2. Identify one Third World nation that has been undergoing changes during the last ten years. Find articles that have appeared in newspapers and magazines during the last ten years (at least one article per year) that discuss some of the changes that have occurred in the country you identified.

3. Summarize the types of changes, issues, problems, solutions, and prospects that are discussed by the articles you found.

4. Find examples from your summaries that can be used to illustrate modernization theory and/or world systems theory of change in that country.

Option: essay
Using material that you gathered and compiled in your journal (above), write an essay (around four pages, typed) in which you use modernization theory and/or world systems theory to discuss the ways in which the country you selected has changed over the last decade.

Option: bibliography
Develop a bibliography of ten to fifteen articles from sociology journals and/or books written by sociologists that discuss changes in underdeveloped nations. Type your bibliography following the format found in one of the sociology journals.

Option: research paper
Write a paper (around five to seven pages) in which you do the following:
    a) introduce the topic of change that has been occurring in the Third World nation you selected;
    b) discuss some of the changes that have occurred in that country during the past ten years;
    c) use ideas from at least five items from your bibliography (above to help you explain some of the changes that have occurred;
    d) discuss the changes in that country in terms of modernization or world systems theory, depending upon which one you have found most support for and is most applicable;
    e) provide proper documentation throughout your paper and include a reference page.

PROJECT 17.2 Should the United States Provide Economic Assistance to Other Nations?

One of the suggestions mentioned by
Coleman and Cressey for increasing global equality is for the wealthier, industrialized nations to
provide economic support to the less equal nations. Foreign aid is a very controversial issue.
The objective of this project is to have you examine this issue from sociological points of view
and in contrast to the more popular notions about foreign aid.

Journal instructions:
1. In recent years, there has been much debate about whether or not to provide aid to other
countries. Identify one such country. (The former Soviet Union is an excellent example, but
you can select others if you wish.) Using your library's or computerized indexes, find at least
ten articles from the newspapers, newsmagazines, or commentary magazines that have discussed
the issue of whether or not the U.S. should supply aid to the country you identified. Be sure to
find about an equal number of articles that support providing aid and those that oppose aid. An
excellent place to begin your search would be in the *CQ Researcher* (formerly the *Editorial
Research Reports* of the *Congressional Digest*). In that you are likely to find a debate about this
issue and an annotated bibliography of articles about it.

2. In your journal, summarize the views taken by each of the articles you found.

3. In your journal, discuss how each of the sociological perspectives (functionalism, conflict
theory, and the social psychological theories) might approach the issue of providing aid to
foreign countries.

Option: essay
Using the material you compiled in your journal (above), write an essay (around four pages,
typed) discussing the pros and cons of providing aid to foreign countries. Be sure to provide a
balanced discussion weighing both the pros and cons.

Option: bibliography
Develop a bibliography of ten to fifteen articles from sociology journals and/or books written by
sociologists that examine the issue of aid to foreign nations, international inequality, Third World
inequality, and so on. Type your bibliography following the format found in one of the
sociology journals.

Option: research paper
Write a paper (around six pages, typed) in which you:
    a) Introduce the issue of economic aid to a Third World, developing, or other nation that
    may require assistance from the U.S.
    b) Discuss three reasons why the U.S. should provide economic assistance.
    c) Discuss three reasons why the U.S. should not provide economic assistance.
    d) Use sociological perspectives on international inequality to develop your own position
    on this issue. Be sure that you support your position using sociological information
    and/or perspectives.
    e) Make sure that you use at least four items from your bibliography.
    f) Provide proper documentation throughout your paper and include a reference page.

CHAPTER 18

WARFARE: REVOLUTIONARY, ETHNIC, AND INTERNATIONAL CONFLICT

CHAPTER OUTLINE

The Nature of War

The Escalation of Military Violence

The Consequences of War

Terrorism

The Causes of Warfare
     Revolutionary Warfare
          Exploitation and Oppression
          Relative Deprivation
          Institutions and Resources
          Ethnic and Regional Conflicts
     International Warfare
          Militarism
          Nationalism and ideology
          Economic and Political Gain
          International Political Organization

Solving the Problems of War and International Conflict
     Deterrence
     Arms and Disarmament
     Social Justice
     Encouraging Global Cooperation

The Prospects for Tomorrow: War and Peace in the Twenty-first Century

Sociological Perspectives on Warfare and International Conflict
     The Functionalist Perspective
     The Conflict Perspective
     The Feminist Perspective
     The Interactionist Perspective

CHAPTER LEARNING OBJECTIVES AND ESSAY QUESTIONS

After studying this chapter, you should be able to:

• State and discuss why the harsh realities of the nuclear age still remain.

• Explain the nature and types of war.

• Trace and discuss how military violence has expanded throughout history and remains a serious threat today.

• Analyze the several consequences of war, including its impact on economic and human life.

• Outline and discuss the nature, types, and extent of terrorism.

• Explain the causes of different types of war.

• State and discuss some of the ways government and citizens have worked to prevent war and international conflict.

• Discuss the prospects for peace.

• State, discuss, and compare four sociological perspectives on war and international conflict.

KEY POINTS FOR REVIEW

• Regardless of the world leader's proclamations that they have no aggressive intentions, all nations maintain military forces and claim the right to use them if the interests of their nations require it. The threat of war is real.

• The difference between war and peace is a matter of degree. War is defined as a protracted military conflict between two or more organized groups.

• Wars have occurred all throughout history. Modern warfare, starting with Napoleon, has been marked by a steady escalation of violence, usually in an all-out national effort to kill or subdue enemy civilians and soldiers. The nature of war has changed over the years from being fought mainly by professional soldiers and privileged elites to average citizens, often against their own will. The techniques of war have intensified and become more efficient, originally being fought face to face and now being fought from a great distance. The threat of nuclear war has helped to head-off a full-scale global conflict, but the possibility remains that someday an all-out nuclear war could develop. The threat of nuclear war becomes especially strong with increasing nuclear proliferation. The nuclear power plants and technical know-ho that the United States and other industrialized powers have sold to nations around the world have made it far easier for those nations to make nuclear bombs, thus increasing the possibility of nuclear war.

• War has serious consequences. The loss of human lives and war victims (maimed and crippled, widows and widowers, grieving parents, orphans, and others) and astronomical economic expenditures and losses are the most obvious. Some economists, though argue that military outlays for defense—in peacetime and during war—actually create jobs and stimulate the economy. This may be true, but others argue that there are more beneficial ways of stimulating the economy. One of the most feared consequences of war today is the impact of widespread radiation that can occur as the result of nuclear war. Besides the catastrophic effect on humans, the environment would suffer severe destruction as the result of a nuclear winter.

• Terrorism is another threat to peace. Terrorism usually involves violence used for political ends and often aimed at a non-military population. However, the definition of terrorism is not precise and sometimes difficult to differentiate from war. There are two general types of terrorism: revolutionary—used by groups trying to bring about major political changes in a country—and repressive—used by groups trying to protect an existing political order.

• There are numerous causes of warfare. Sociologists do not believe that it is part of human nature, nor do they believe it is the result of aggressive tendencies that lead to war. Nor do they believe that it is the result of sole individuals, such as Hitler, although such individuals can play a key part. Rather, it is the result of social conditions. Different social conditions explain different types of warfare.

• Revolutionary warfare has a variety of explanations. Some of the earliest theories—formulated by Karl Marx and Friedrich Engels—see revolutionary warfare occurring as the result of the exploitation and oppression of lower class workers. A related view is that it is not the absolute conditions of poverty that lead to revolution, but the experience of relative-deprivation (the differences between what people have and what they think they should have) that can lead to revolution. A third explanation is that the imbalances in the social institutions of a society, often created as a country modernizes its economy, may lead people to become more involved in politics faster than traditional institutions can accommodate, thus leading to revolution. Fourth, revolutions may occur when the people perceive that the government is not doing an adequate job and is run by elites trying to further their own interests. Finally, class divisions, geographic differences, and ethnic differences can lead to rebellious groups taking a stand against a government.

• The causes of revolutionary and international wars are usually quite different, but sometimes the internal conditions conducive to a revolution may also contribute to an international war. Militarism is one specific factor that contributes to international wars. This includes both the glorification and institutionalization of war. This means that war is portrayed as heroic and that there are significant arms that have been developed for war. A second factor that can lead to international war is the a feeling of nationalism or devotion to one's nation. Nationalism is an ideology that can stimulate violent confrontations. The third factor leading to war is economic and political gain. Most wars are fought to achieve some kind of gain. The fourth, and perhaps most basic, cause of international war is the way in which the world is politically organized. The planet is divided into nearly a hundred sovereign states that have their own military forces and a belief in their right to use them to protect or advance their national interests.

• There are a number of suggestions as to how to prevent wars and international conflicts. Military and political leaders often feel that the best way is through deterrence; that is, being so strong militarily that any potential adversaries will be afraid to attack. Advocates of arms control argue that the best way to prevent war is not by becoming strong militarily, but by an elimination or reduction in weapons by all nations. A third approach to preventing wars, especially revolutionary violence, is to change the conditions of inequality that cause the resentment of groups who would be prone to engaging in a revolution. Finally, many believe that the best way to prevent wars is to build the economic, political, and cultural foundations that would encourage global cooperation.

• Functionalist theory sees warfare and international conflict as an inevitable result of the world's political disorganization. Because of a high degree of international disorganization, war may actually be functional for settling major disputes. Additionally, functionalists say that warfare may provide short-term psychological and political benefits to individual nations, and may function to keep a weak, divided society together for a time. Functionalists see revolutionary warfare as the result of national systems failing to work smoothly and becoming dysfunctional. The best way to head of revolutionary conflict, from this view, is to implement gradual reforms designed to help a nation achieve a balance between its various social institutions.

• Conflict theorists see international war as the result of a vicious struggle for worldwide dominance and the economic rewards it brings. From this view, the best way to eliminate warfare and international conflict is to eliminate economic and political oppression.

• Feminist theorists are interested in why men are so much more warlike than women. Most feminists lay the blame on male gender role socialization. This socialization leads men in positions of political power to resort to violence sooner than they should. Feminists propose two solutions to the problem of political violence. First, they feel that women should band together to use their collective power to change the priorities and attitudes of world governments. Second, they feel that the socialization processes should change so that males are not encouraged to be warlike.

• The interactionist perspective sees the roots of war in the process of socialization and the way we are taught to see ourselves and the world around us.As we are growing up we are socialized to identify with a particular ethnic group and to develop disdain for others. We are taught to identify enemies as evil and winning with glory and righteousness. Interactionists also feel that growing up in cultures that place great importance on honor and pride are likely to learn that warlike policies are beneficial. In order to reduce warfare, according to interactionists, we must emphasize cultural characteristics that favor peaceful resolution of differences and applaud the ideals of non-violence over violence.

NOTES:

328

KEY TERMS

The following key terms are found in your textbook on the page number indicated in parentheses. In the space provided, write a brief definition of the key term **in your own words**. Then **provide an example** of the term, such as a culture in which the practice takes place, or people that you might know whose behavior illustrates the term, a current event that illustrates the term, how a term could be used to shed light on or help solve a particular social problem, and so on. You could include examples from the news, books, movies, or anything else that will illustrate the term and help you remember it. Include any comments from your class discussions or textbook that might help you remember and understand these key terms. Use additional paper if necessary, but keep it with your study guide to help you review for exams.

war (p. 580)

_____

_____

_____

_____

international wars (p. 581)

_____

_____

_____

_____

revolutionary wars (p. 581)

_____

_____

_____

_____

nuclear proliferation (p. 582)

_____

_____

_____

nuclear winter (p. 585)

_____

_____

_____

_____

terrorism (p. 585)

_____

_____

_____

_____

revolutionary terrorism (p. 586)

_____

_____

_____

_____

repressive terrorism (p. 586)

_____

_____

_____

_____

relative deprivation theory (p. 589)

_____

_____

_____

_____

330

militarism (p. 590)

_____

_____

_____

_____

nationalism (p. 591)

_____

_____

_____

_____

imperialism (p. 591)

_____

_____

_____

_____

deterrence (p. 593)

_____

_____

_____

_____

mutual assured destruction (p. 593)

_____

_____

_____

_____

disarmament (p. 594)

_____

_____

_____

_____

legitimacy (p. 596)

_____

_____

_____

_____

Universal Declaration of Human Rights (p. 596)

_____

_____

_____

_____

political economy (p. 602)

_____

_____

_____

_____

PRACTICE TEST

Multiple Choice

1. One reason why war can occur despite international peace efforts is because:
   a) countries maintain large armies and claim the right to use them
   b) the world realizes that some warfare is functional for the countries involved
   c) humans are instinctively aggressive and will always engage in war
   d) wealthy nations will always want to exploit the weaker ones

2. Throughout human history:
   a) conflict was inevitable and there were fewer wars
   b) constant warfare between nations has been the most typical
   c) war was the rule and peace the exception
   d) peace was the rule and war the exception

3. In the last two centuries, wars have killed _____ million people.
   a) 50
   b) 100
   c) 150
   d) 300

4. The two general types of terrorism are revolutionary terrorism and _____ terrorism.
   a) liberation
   b) spontaneous
   c) national
   d) repressive

5. A protracted military conflict between two or more organized groups is the definition of:
   a) war
   b) terrorism
   c) national tensions
   d) revolutionary conflict

6. Modern warfare has been marked by a:
   a) greater regulation of armed conflicts
   b) steady rise in threats but less armed conflicts
   c) a steady escalation of violence
   d) strong peace movement

7. Which of the following is not a true illustration of the economic costs of war?
   a) one new bomber could hire 250,000 teachers.
   b) Fourteen jet bombers would provide free lunches to 14,000,000 students.
   c) One tank would build 1000 classrooms in a Third World country.
   d) One year of military spending would eradicate all of the world's illnesses.

8. The kind of terrorism used by groups trying to bring about major political changes in a particular country is called _____ terrorism.
   a) international
   b) revolutionary
   c) exploitive
   d) national

9. Karl Marx and Friederich Engels believed that the injustices of capitalism would produce:
   a) nuclear terrorism
   b) a more equal society
   c) worldwide revolution
   d) relative deprivation

10. Sociologists make a simple division between international wars and _____ wars.
    a) national
    b) revolutionary
    c) local
    d) nuclear

11. The spread of atomic weapons to more and more nations around the world is called:
    a) international terrorism
    b) nuclear armament
    c) nuclear proliferation
    d) nuclearization

12. Which of the following would be the ultimate outcome of a nuclear war?
    a) a nuclear winter
    b) 100,000 deaths
    c) contamination of the land
    d) volcanic eruptions

13. Which of the following acts do governments most fear terrorists will ultimately carry out?
    a) high-jack planes
    b) foment riots
    c) develop new political parties
    d) build up steal nuclear weapons

14. Revolutions are sometimes caused by differences between what people have and:
    a) what other people have
    b) what they feel they should have
    c) what the world has
    d) how much they are allowed to have

15. In many ways, the most basic cause of international war is the way in which:
    a) imperialism has ruled the world
    b) most revolutions have succeeded historically
    c) the world is politically organized
    d) nations profit from war

16. Actual arms control agreements are more likely to be reached when the actual threat of war:
    a) is beginning to build
    b) has led to military confrontation
    c) is at its highest
    d) is at its lowest

17. All of the following are ingredients of global cooperation, EXCEPT for:
    a) cultural exchanges
    b) international guidance and control
    c) giving the UN more power
    d) establishing one, supreme military power

18. All of the following are causes of international warfare, EXCEPT for:
    a) relative deprivation
    b) militarism
    c) imperialism
    d) nationalism

19. Which of the following strategies to prevent war is most favored by military and political leaders?
    a) arms control
    b) deterrence
    c) social justice
    d) international cooperation

20. When conditions of social injustice prevail, a country might become involved in a
    _____ war.
    a) nuclear
    b) violent
    c) international
    d) revolutionary

21. According to the optimistic view of international relations, all of the following will take place, EXCEPT for:
    a) more support for the United nations
    b) disarmament
    c) a reduction of political tensions
    d) more support for international law

22. Which of the following would sociologists agree is NOT an explanation for war?
    a) inborn human aggressiveness
    b) militarism
    c) nationalism
    d) economic gain

23. Which of the following is NOT a political cause of revolutions?
    a) poorly run governments
    b) economic gain
    c) a government run by special interest groups
    d) class conflicts

24. Which of the following statements about preventing war and international conflict is most likely to be TRUE?
    a) International conflict can be entirely eliminated with enough hard work.
    b) War cannot be altogether eliminated.
    c) Nuclear war is inevitable.
    d) A major war could break out somewhere in the world within a month.

25. The consent of the government based on their beliefs that a government is just and fair is called:
    a) legitimation
    b) social justice
    c) class equality
    d) international government

26. With the crumbling of Soviet power:
    a) tensions between the U.S. and the Soviet Union have increased
    b) the U.S. has turned to confrontations with other countries
    c) the cold war has come to an end
    d) world peace has been established

27. According to the pessimistic view of the future of world conflict:
    a) the U.S. will go it alone
    b) stockpiles of nuclear weapons will fall into the hands of hostile governments
    c) overpopulation in the lands of the Third World will lead to military dictators
    d) all of the above will take place

28. Sociologists who feel that the only sure way to prevent wars is to emphasize nonviolent cultural traits that favor the peaceful resolution of differences are most likely to subscribe to the _____ perspective.
    a) functional
    b) conflict
    c) feminist
    d) interactionist

29. Conflict theorists feel that the world system is far from disorganized, but is well organized for:
    a) economic exploitation
    b) international cooperation
    c) new peace initiatives
    d) a new world culture

30. For functionalists, warfare and international conflict are inevitable because of:
    a) powerful nations exploiting the weaker nations
    b) international political disorganization
    c) individual aggressive tendencies
    d) warlike cultural traits

PROJECTS

PROJECT 18.1 Is the United States a Warrior Culture?

Coleman and Cressey suggest that one of the reasons for war is that people live within cultures that value war, or "warrior cultures." Is this true of the United States? The objective of this project is to have to examine the extent to which the U.S. is a "warrior culture" and, if it is, how it socializes its citizens to conform to this aspect of the culture.

Journal instructions:
1. For one week, keep a journal of everything you observe that may contribute to U.S. citizens having values, beliefs, and norms that support a "warrior culture." Read newspapers, listen to politicians, read television listings, movie reviews, listen to national anthems and patriotic music, and so on.

2. Look through past issues of newspapers and magazines published during a recent military involvement of the U.S. A good example would be the war with Iraq in the early 1990s. Locate and read around five to ten essays, letters to editors, editorials, and other commentaries that appeared in major national newspapers and local newspapers. Look for information that supports the notion that the U.S. may be a "warrior culture." Record your observations in your journal.

Option: essay
Write an essay (around three to five pages, typed) in which you discuss whether or not the United States is a "warrior culture." Use evidence from your journal to support your views.

Option: bibliography
Use your library's *Social Science Indexes* and/or the *Sociological Abstracts* to develop a bibliography of ten to fifteen articles from sociology journals and/or books written by sociologists about the sociology of war. Type your bibliography following the format found in one of the sociology journals

Option: research paper
Write a paper (around seven pages, typed) in which you discuss and compare different nations that have a "warrior culture." Some things you might discuss are: how people are socialized into a warrior culture, who benefits from a warrior culture, the extent to which nations with warrior cultures are more likely to engage in war, and others. Be sure to document your sources properly throughout the paper and include a reference page.

PROJECT 18.2 The Causes of War, Conflicts, and Terrorism

Sociologists have provided a number of reasons as to why armed conflicts exist. Not all armed conflicts are caused by the same reasons. The objective of this project is to have you examine the causes of some of the armed conflicts that have existed within the U.S., between the U.S. and other countries, and between other countries using sociological explanations.

Journal instructions:
1. Re-read the section in chapter 18 that discuss the causes of warfare. Briefly summarize these in your journal.

2. Identify one revolutionary and one international war that has occurred during your lifetime. These may have involved the U.S., but do not necessarily have to.

3. Look through past newspapers and magazines and/or history books to find information about the causes of and events leading to of the wars you identified. Try to identify causes that correspond with the causes discussed in your textbook. List and discuss these in your journal.

4. Use each of the three sociological perspectives on war to examine the two wars you identified. How would each explain why the war occurred? How would each suggest that the war could have been avoided?

Option: essay
Write an essay (around three to five pages, typed) in which you discuss the causes of the two wars you identified (above) using sociological explanations. Include a discussion as to how the wars might have been avoided.

Option: bibliography
Develop a bibliography of ten to fifteen articles from sociology journals and/or books written by sociologists about the causes of warfare. The sociology of war is a rapidly growing area in sociology. Some places to look for your articles are the *Social Science Index* and the *Sociological Abstracts*. Type your bibliography following the format found in one of the sociology journals.

Option: research paper
Using at least five items from your bibliography (above) and information you compiled in your journal and essay (above), write a paper (around seven pages, typed) in which you discuss the causes of the two wars you identified and how the wars might have been averted. Be sure to use and fully integrate the sociological perspectives and other sociological concepts and ideas found within chapter 18 in your discussion. Provide proper documentation of your sources throughout the paper and include a reference page.

ANSWER KEY TO PRACTICE TESTS

Chapter 1
1. b	6. b	11. d	16. a	21. b	26. c
2. b	7. b	12. b	17. a	22. d	27. c
3. c	8. d	13. d	18. d	23. b	28. b
4. a	9. d	14. c	19. b	24. a	29. a
5. c	10. c	15. c	20. b	25. b	30. d

Chapter 2
1. c	6. a	11. b	16. b	21. d	26. b
2. d	7. b	12. c	17. a	22. a	27. d
3. c	8. c	13. d	18. d	23. a	28. c
4. b	9. c	14. b	19. a	24. a	29. a
5. c	10. c	15. c	20. a	25. b	30. b

Chapter 3
1. c	6. d	11. c	16. d	21. c	26. b
2. c	7. d	12. d	17. c	22. d	27. b
3. a	8. b	13. b	18. d	23. c	28. b
4. c	9. d	14. b	19. a	24. b	29. d
5. a	10. a	15. a	20. b	25. a	30. a

Chapter 4
1. c	6. b	11. a	16. b	21. b	26. c
2. c	7. d	12. b	17. c	22. c	27. d
3. b	8. a	13. d	18. b	23. b	28. a
4. a	9. c	14. b	19. b	24. a	29. d
5. b	10. d	15. d	20. a	25. d	30. b

Chapter 5
1. b	6. d	11. a	16. b	21. d	26. d
2. c	7. a	12. d	17. d	22. a	27. c
3. a	8. b	13. a	18. a	23. b	28. d
4. c	9. c	14. c	19. c	24. b	29. a
5. c	10. d	15. c	20. d	25. c	30. b

Chapter 6
1. b	6. c	11. a	16. d	21. b	26. d
2. c	7. a	12. d	17. d	22. d	27. a
3. c	8. d	13. a	18. c	23. a	28. a
4. d	9. b	14. c	19. d	24. c	29. d
5. c	10. c	15. b	20. a	25. b	30. c

Chapter 7

1. c	6. a	11. c	16. d	21. b	26. b
2. b	7. d	12. d	17. b	22. c	27. c
3. a	8. a	13. d	18. d	23. a	28. b
4. d	9. a	14. a	19. c	24. d	29. c
5. c	10. b	15. c	20. c	25. d	30. b

Chapter 8

1. c	6. a	11. d	16. a	21. c	26. d
2. b	7. b	12. d	17. c	22. b	27. d
3. b	8. b	13. c	18. b	23. c	28. c
4. d	9. a	14. d	19. c	24. a	29. c
5. a	10. c	15. d	20. a	25. d	30. d

Chapter 9

1. a	6. a	11. d	16. b	21. b	26.b
2. b	7. b	12. b	17. a	22. a	27. c
3. d	8. c	13. d	18. c	23. a	28. b
4. c	9. c	14. a	19. a	24. d	29. d
5. c	10. b	15. c	20. a	25. a	30. b

Chapter 10

1. b	6. c	11. d	16. a	21. d	26. b
2. a	7. d	12. c	17. d	22. c	27. a
3. c	8. a	13. d	18. b	23. a	28. b
4. a	9. c	14. c	19. b	24. c	29. c
5. d	10. a	15. b	20. b	25. c	30. b

Chapter 11

1. d	6. b	11. d	16. d	21. d	26. b
2. a	7. c	12. c	17. c	22. b	27. a
3. a	8. b	13. c	18. c	23. c	28. d
4. d	9. b	14. b	19. c	24. d	29. c
5. b	10. c	15. a	20. c	25. a	30. c

Chapter 12

1. d	6. a	11. d	16. c	21. b	26. b
2. c	7. b	12. b	17. d	22. c	27. d
3. d	8. c	13. d	18. b	23. b	28. a
4. c	9. d	14. b	19. b	24. a	29. c
5. c	10. a	15. a	20. d	25. c	30. a

Chapter 13

1. b	6. d	11. b	16. a	21. d	26. d
2. c	7. c	12. d	17. a	22. d	27. a
3. d	8. a	13. b	18. b	23. a	28. c
4. c	9. b	14. c	19. c	24. d	29. c
5. d	10. a	15. b	20. c	25. a	30. b

Chapter 14

1. d	6. d	11. a	16. c	21. c	26. d
2. a	7. a	12. b	17. a	22. a	27. c
3. d	8. c	13. a	18. b	23. b	28. b
4. c	9. b	14. d	19. c	24. d	29. c
5. b	10. d	15. d	20. b	25. b	30. c

Chapter 15

1. b	6. d	11. c	16. d	21. c	26. c
2. d	7. b	12. d	17. c	22. b	27. d
3. d	8. b	13. b	18. b	23. a	28. a
4. b	9. d	14. c	19. d	24. c	29. b
5. a	10. a	15. a	20. a	25. a	30. b

Chapter 16

1. a	6. c	11. a	16. a	21. c	26. d
2. b	7. b	12. d	17. a	22. d	27. c
3. a	8. c	13. d	18. b	23. d	28. a
4. b	9. c	14. b	19. d	24. a	29. a
5. d	10. d	15. d	20. b	25. a	30. c

Chapter 17

1. a	6. c	11. b	16. c	21. c	26. a
2. c	7. a	12. c	17. c	22. d	27. d
3. d	8. b	13. b	18. a	23. d	28. c
4. c	9. c	14. b	19. b	24. c	29. a
5. b	10. d	15. a	20. d	25. d	30. c

Chapter 18

1. a	6. c	11. c	16. d	21. b	26. c
2. c	7. d	12. a	17. d	22. a	27. d
3. c	8. b	13. d	18. a	23. b	28. d
4. d	9. c	14. b	19. b	24. b	29. a
5. a	10. b	15. c	20. d	25. a	30. b